Mass Media and Contemporary Social Issues

MASS MEDIA AND CONTEMPORARY SOCIAL ISSUES

Naval Prabhakar
Narendra Basu

Commonwealth

Mass Media and Contemporary Social Issues

Edition : 2024

ISBN 81-311-0022-7

Published by :
COMMONWEALTH PUBLISHERS
4831/24, Prahlad Street,
Ansari Road, Darya Ganj,
New Delhi - 110002
Ph. : 23275511, 23257835
e-mail : e-mail : commonwealthbooks@gmail.com

Typesetting by :
Rishu Computers
Delhi

Printed at :
Divine Digital Press
Delhi

Preface

The mass media have an important role in modern society as the main channel of communication. The stronger and more purposeful the communication channels, the more developed the countries and *vice versa*. The population relies on the news media as the main source of information and the basis on which they form their opinions and voting decisions. Any selection of messages in the mass media will thus have a profound effect on the entire society.

The media help to upgrade the quality of our lives. They affect our aesthetic, cultural, civic, social, political and economic outlook. They are a very intricate part of the matrix of society. Their sustained discussion can contribute to purposeful thought and collective action among people.

The present volume is devoted to the discussion of the role of the media in presenting contemporary social issues. Specific instances of media coverage of issues related to human rights, women, environment, consumerism, etc., are duly discussed. The potential of media to improve our social situation is contrasted with the actual trends in addressing these issues. It also attempts to identify the areas in which media can bring about radical changes for the better future.

Naval Prabhakar
Narendra Basu

Contents

1 Introduction

The first records of written news stretch back more than two thousand years to the Han dynasty in China and to Julius Caesar's reign in ancient Rome. Daily handwritten news sheets, circulated by the government, presented news on trials, military campaigns, and political developments. After the invention of a printing press using movable type in the mid- 15th century, international commerce became the main impetus for newspapers in Europe. Newspapers with international commercial news and advertising appeared in Germany in 1609 and spread rapidly throughout Europe. (Because of tight government regulation of information, domestic political news became a feature in newspapers only in the middle of the 19th century.) The press also became an impetus for commerce.

Newspapers gave accounts of commercial voyages and the risks and opportunities of new trading routes. Advertising stimulated the demand for products. Frequent features of financial reports, insolvency proceedings, and trials of merchants and manufacturers helped merchants choose their business partners. All this information expanded trade links beyond tightly knit trading associations and communities, stimulating competition among traders and manufacturers from different nations.

Today, with higher literacy rates, lower printing costs, and new broadcast technologies (and the Internet), the media are even more important in informing traders, consumers, and investors. The vernacular media, particularly radio, carry information and encourage commerce in geographically isolated markets. In Indonesia, for example, local-language radio broadcasts of agricultural prices helped develop vegetable markets for poorly educated farmers.At the other end of the spectrum, the growing global and foreign media report on international economic issues, moving currency markets and international trade.

The media also provide information on political markets, exposing corrupt and unethical politicians and giving people a platform to voice diverse opinions on governance and reform. Because of their reach, the media can inform poor and marginalized people, giving them voice as well. Radio broadcasts reaching poor areas where illiteracy is high are particularly effective in this. And because of the media's ability to provide information otherwise unavailable, they can supplement traditional school education. In Nicaragua, for example, an innovative radio program to teach mathematics to primary school students improved test scores, especially for children in rural areas with less access to quality schools.

Publicizing information through the media has also made public services more responsive to the poor. In Brazil, for example, school lunches in one state cost eight times as much as those in another state. With media publicity, prices were equalized at the cheaper rate in two weeks. The media can also improve public health efforts, as demonstrated by successful AIDS education campaigns in Thailand and Uganda. Empirical studies show that women's access to the media is associated with better health and fertility outcomes, even after accounting for different income and education.

The media are also involved with civic education as well- a study in Botswana showed that media programs about the government, its procedures, and civil rights substantially increased people's knowledge about ways for them to participate in government processes.And the media can affect politics and culture, supporting institutional change and market development. Open information flows can promote institutional reform by affecting people's incentives and by sharing ideas and knowledge. New information can change people and culture-and create demand for new institutions.

Information on how other institutions work can stimulate public debate and facilitate collective action. And greater access to all media, including the foreign and the vernacular, can provide a voice for social groups to press for changes in institutions and norms of behavior. To achieve these outcomes-improving governance and supporting markets-the media need to be independent, accountable, and able to provide relevant information and reflect diverse social views. Too often, however, the media do not have these qualities. Concentrated ownership, restricted competition, financial dependence, and onerous regulations on press freedom distort the provision of information and can reduce independence.

Poor access to information and the low capacity of journalists also reduce the quality of information. Finally, lack of competition, as well as poverty and low levels of literacy, human capital, and technology, can limit the reach of the media. But the media also need checks and balances. And competition in the industry, as well as some kinds of regulation, keep the media in check.

The main factors that make the media effective in producing better social, economic, and political outcomes independence (including accountability), quality, and reach are described here. First, effective media are independent. Higher levels of perceived media freedom or independence are associated with lower levels of perceived corruption, regardless of differences in a country's level of income, and with better responses from public actors.Second, effective media provide highquality reporting, defined as the capacity to provide information demanded by diverse market agents in society.

Competition among media firms, open access to public and private information, and journalistic capacity are key elements affecting quality. And third, effective media have a broad reach in society. Literacy, access to communications technologies, and the removal of entry barriers all expand the media's reach. Complementary institutions can strengthen the role of the media. For example, while information provision can affect behavior through reputational penalties, it may not be sufficient to change outcomes. An effective judiciary and independent regulatory agencies can strengthen the media's effect on outcomes.

INDEPENDENCE

What determines independence? Ownership is a central factor because it is the owners who control information flows and thus influence economic, political, and social outcomes. That is why control of media enterprises is likely to be concentrated in the hands of a few individuals or politicians. Some analysts have argued for state ownership of the media, asserting that information is a public good.

Once supplied to some customers, it is costly to keep it away from others who have not paid for it. So the commercial media tend to provide less information than is desirable because they cannot extract a private return. In addition, the provision and dissemination of information are subject to strong increasing returns. The fixed costs of gathering information and establishing distribution facilities are significant, but once these costs are incurred, the marginal costs of making information available are relatively low. For these reasons, many countries have made a case for organizing the media industry as a government-owned monopoly.

Another argument for public ownership is consumer protection. In the extreme form, private ownership is seen to corrupt the media industry by serving a narrow interest group in society. More moderate is the view that state ownership of some parts of the media is justified because the public needs to be exposed to educational and cultural information, or public values, that privately owned firms might not provide. For example, one of the objectives of publicly owned television in many European countries is to ensure broadcasts of locally produced content in local languages.

Critics of these views counter that government control of the media could distort and manipulate information in the incumbent government's favor, undermining markets and precluding voters and consumers from making informed decisions. They believe this to be less likely with private media enterprises, which might also be more responsive to consumer demand for betterquality information.

Ownership structures

Private ownership is mostly in family hands rather than in

widely dispersed shareholdings. Some privately held media are also closely related to the state, through business, family, and personal associations. So, the influence of state control is even greater. State ownership also varies significantly by region. On average governments in African and Middle Eastern countries are more likely to own media outlets, but media outlets in North and South America are owned almost exclusively by families. Although most countries in the sample permit foreign ownership of the media, only 10 percent of the top five newspapers and 14 percent of the top five television stations are controlled by foreigners.

Why is state ownership much more prevalent in television than in the press? Perhaps because television has higher fixed costs and greater economies of scale. And perhaps because governments believe that commercial media organizations are unwilling to invest in markets with small audiences-such as services for minorities, remote and rural markets, or educational programs. But the evidence does not support this.

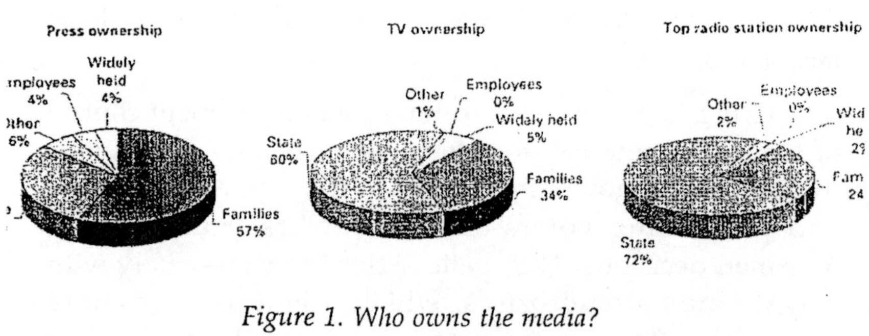

Figure 1. Who owns the media?

The percentage of state-owned firms is still high even when ownership is weighted by market share of the audience. If the state-owned media serve mainly minority markets, their market share should be low. Besides, governments could require privately owned broadcasters to serve rural markets and provide cultural or educational content by regulation rather than by ownership.

A second argument is that state ownership of television is higher because of limited availability of broadcasting frequencies-that it may be more efficient for the state to control television stations directly than to regulate the allocation of frequencies and monitor compliance. This argument has been disputed on the grounds that a simple system of property rights is enough to overcome problems of signal intervention.New cable and satellite broadband spectrum technologies make the argument even less relevant.

Monopolies

It mean worse outcomes. The evidence indicates that monopoly control over information or high levels of state ownership reduce the effectiveness of the media in providing checks and balances on public sector behavior. Analysis of the 97 countries in the same study established that media in countries with high levels of state ownership are much less free, measured by the media freedom indexes; they also transmit much less information to people in economic and political markets.

In addition, state ownership of the media is found to be negatively correlated with economic, political, and social outcomes. Generally speaking, this translates into more corruption, inferior economic governance, less-developed financial markets, fewer political rights for citizens, and poorer social outcomes in education and health. For all regions of the world, these associations between ownership and outcomes hold even after accounting for different levels of income, general state ownership in the economy, and a measure of political freedoms. This is important because poorer countries- and those with high state ownership in the economy and more autocratic governments-were more likely to have high state ownership of the media.

Privatization can help reduce monopolies. The negative consequences of state control of information through ownership highlighted by the experience in several countries underscores the importance of media ownership in pressing for better governance. In Mexico, for example, the privatization of broadcasting in 1989 substantially increased the coverage of government corruption scandals and other stories previously unreported by the state station. This greater coverage contributed to a 20 percent increase in the private station's market share, forcing the government-owned station to cover these issues as well.

Similarly, a new, privately owned television station in Ghana in 1997 reported more information on government activities and evaluated government performance more openly.The privatization of state-owned media in transition countries, for example-supported by broader market liberalization and knowledge transfers from foreign owners with experience in journalism-has generated dramatic increases in the coverage of economic and financial news as well.But private ownership can also restrict media freedom. For example, private owners associated with the state or political parties-or protecting their business interests-can control information flows.

In Ukraine, for example, privately owned television stations with links to the state provided more favorable coverage of the incumbent party during elections than did more independent privately owned television stations. In some Latin American countries, privatization led to increased market concentration and reduced competition among the private media. In short, monopolies or concentrated ownership of the media industry that provide control over information to any individuals or organizations, public or private, will reduce the effectiveness of the media in improving economic, political, and social outcomes.

Independent state media organizations

To reduce state control of media ownership, countries have established independent state media organizations-new institutional structures that provide checks and balances. The aim is to provide public interest programs that the private sector would not offer, without the drawbacks of political interference. For example, the British Broadcasting Corporation (BBC) is state owned, and its board of governors, appointed by government officials, is accountable to the government. But its charter establishes it as an independent corporation.

Explicitly guaranteed in the charter and accompanying agreement is freedom from government interference in the content and timing of its broadcasts and in the management of its internal affairs. And funding is provided almost entirely by government-regulated license fees, not directly from the government budget. Other countries have experimented with more extended arrangements to ensure autonomy from the state. Austrian state television, besides having the same safeguards for independence as the BBC, has various stakeholder groups represented on its board of directors, with only one-third of the appointees from the federal government.

Some developing countries, such as Ethiopia in the mid-1990s, have implemented similar models to grant autonomy to state-owned television. And Benin established an oversight committee of state and nonstate appointees to protect the government-owned newspaper from interference. Then, in stark contrast, there is Myanmar. The largest television station is controlled directly by the Ministry of Information and Culture, and the secondlargest by the military-with full powers to manage content and appoint and remove staff. Similarly, in Turkmenistan the state maintains direct control over the press, with the president officially the head of the major newspapers.

A problem with autonomous state media organizations is that their independence can be eroded. In 1981 the Zimbabwe government established the independent Mass Media Trust to manage Zimpapers, the only national newspaper chain. The trust emerged as an innovative solution, combining public ownership with politically independent management. Yet in June 1985 and again in September 2000 the government dismissed the entire board in retaliation for unfavorable media coverage, and it now regularly intervenes in content decisions.

Developing countries are not the only ones to have government interference in ostensibly independent state media. But in developing countries, with their lessdeveloped systems of checks and balances, maintaining independence can be more difficult. Experience shows that without the political commitment and supporting institutions to maintain autonomy, ensuring independent content is unlikely.

Regulations of media

Throughout the world, government regulations-ranging from constitutional freedom of expression provisions to tax and business laws-affect media enterprises. Many of them aim to balance freedom of speech and protection of the public interest. Three such regulations are reviewed here: licensing, content laws, and defamation and insult laws. Licensing. Licensing media enterprises can be a way to control content. For television some form of licensing broadcasters is needed to define property rights for the limited broadcasting frequencies. Yet many governments extend licensing systems beyond what is required for technical reasons, including imposing restrictions on the content of broadcasts.

Some restrictions are explicit, as with licenses that prohibit the broadcast of local news, as in Zimbabwe. Others are implicit, as when licenses might not be renewed unless broadcasting content is perceived as favorable to the government. Nor is there a technical reason for licensing newspapers, unlike the case for licensing television and radio broadcasting, so its primary purpose is to allow governments to influence information flows. In some countries newspapers have to renew their licenses annually. And editors of newspapers that publish views critical of government have been pressed to resign before licenses are renewed.

To avoid suspension under such conditions, the media censors itself. Removing newspaper licensing restrictions can thus do much to enhance competition and improve information coverage. In Korea the government replaced the newspaper licensing requirements with a more liberal set in 1987, simply requiring publishers to inform it of their plans to publish newspapers. As a result, the number of daily newspapers grew from 6 to 17 in Seoul alone, and dozens more were launched in other parts of the country. Newspapers also became more diverse, with opposition, progovernment, business, sports, and church papers competing with one another.

Licensing of journalists can also influence media content. Proponents argue that it serves the public interest by encouraging responsibility and standards in reporting. Opponents counter that licenses allow regulators to prevent the employment of journalists who might cover the government unfavorably. International courts have supported the latter argument. In 1985, in a landmark case concerning an uncertified journalist in Costa Rica, the Inter-American Court of Human Rights found that licensing journalists contravened the American Convention on Human Rights. Yet more than a third of Latin American countries regulate journalists through licensing or accreditation procedures.

Content laws

Censorship is another direct way for governmènts to distort the provision of information, often through legal requirements for prepublication or prebroadcast reviews by government agencies. Often the restrictions are defended on the grounds of protecting cultural interests. And it is possible to have content regulations that reflect cultural preferences while still allowing diverse opinions. In the Netherlands a 1998 act requires that public service programming be at least 25 percent news, at least 20 percent culture, and at least 5 percent education. Italy requires that 50 percent of broadcasting be of European origin.But these days the control of information published on the Internet is posing basic challenges for regulators of content. Defamation and insult laws.

Restrictive defamation laws can repress investigative journalism.They are necessary to protect the reputations of individuals and ensure the accuracy of reported news. But they also justify harassing journalists in many countries, leading to self-censorship.There are three key issues in striking a balance between protecting people from defamation and encouraging investigative journalism. The first is whether libel is considered a criminal rather than a civil offense. When libel is a criminal offense, journalists lean toward self-censorship. A second issue is whether truth is a defense in a defamation suit.

In Germany and the United States truth is a defense, and the plaintiff bears the burden of proof that allegations were untrue, giving journalists considerable freedom in reporting. In Turkey, by contrast, truth is not a defense for libel, unless the accused is a government official and the alleged libel relates to the performance of duties. If the defendant does not prove truth in such cases, the sentence is increased by half. That creates strong incentives for journalists to limit their investigations.A third issue is whether the law provides protection for libelous statements about matters of public interest. If it does, journalists can better investigate arbitrary government behavior and predatory business practices.

India and Korea are examples of countries where defamation can be defended on the basis of truth if the statements are in the public interest. Requirements to show that defamatory statements are knowingly or recklessly false, and made with malicious intent, also favor the freedom of journalists. Particularly restrictive are insult laws, protecting select groups such as royalty, politicians, and government officials from criticism. Usually, insult laws make it a criminal offense to injure the "honor and dignity" or reputation of these selected individuals and institutions, regardless of truth. A study of 87 countries found such laws to be surprisingly prevalent, particularly in developing nations.

In most industrial countries insult laws are rarely, if ever, invoked. Yet in many developing countries, they are the primary means of harassing journalists. In the Arab Republic of Egypt 99 journalists and writers were prosecuted under insult laws in the 12 months following their introduction in May 1995. Such laws, at their best, are an anachronism-and at their worst, a severe restriction on media independence. That is why some governments, such as those of Argentina and Ghana, have taken steps to abolish them. Financing and other economic pressures Economic pressures can also interfere with the independent provision of information. When government owns the printing presses or restricts the import and distribution of newsprint, it can influence content.

Preferential subsidies and advertising are another way to influence media content. In Cameroon the government refused to advertise in the privately owned press after some critical coverage. And in Uganda in July 1993 the government banned its departments from advertising in the one privately owned daily newspaper; since state advertising accounted for 70 percent of its advertising revenues, this had a significant negative impact. Such heavy state support provides incentives for favorable coverage of the incumbent government and reduces the watchdog role of the media.

To prevent biased reporting, the Mexican government recently stopped subsidizing the press. Some European governments, such as Germany's, prohibit by law direct subsidies of media organizations to prevent the state from jeopardizing independence. But several countries in Western Europe provide direct subsidies to media outlets. France subsidizes radio stations if their profit from advertising and sponsorship is less than 20 percent of revenue. Since the criteria for allocating these subsidies is not directly linked to media content, it is argued that such state support does not compromise media independence.Advertising revenues from concentrated private sources can also influence content.

In a recent survey of journalists, editors, and news executives in the United States, more than one-third responded that news is not reported if it might hurt advertising revenues and thus harm the financial position of media firms. Advertising from diverse sources is likely to reduce bias in content. In Russia the Press Development Institute, with support from the World Bank, trains newspaper managers to build independent sources of finance through advertising and paid subscriptions-and thus to reduce reliance on state support and improve editorial independence.

Quality

The media do more to support integrated and inclusive markets when they have the capacity to provide highquality information demanded by diverse market agents, reflecting a diversity of opinion. Three factors that affect the quality of the media are discussed here: competition among outlets, access to public and private information sources, and human capacities.

Competition

Competition among media outlets promotes the supply of alternative views to voters and consumers-and helps prevent one firm from distorting too heavily the information it supplies. It is argued that competition from state media stimulates private media to provide more educational and culturally diverse content. Competition between media outlets is closely related to ownership issues. One potential downside of publicprivate competition is that governments can give advantages to the media firms that they own. In practical terms, the issue of monopoly pertains solely to state ownership, since no country has private newspaper or television monopolies.

The global incidence of state monopolies of newspapers and television is surprisingly high. In countries with media monopolies, political, economic, and social outcomes are worse than in those where the media are competitive, in part because the former are less effective in improving institutional quality (governance). The data also show that dominance of state media, even if some private media exist, can affect the relationship between information flows and outcomes. For example, 75 percent state ownership of the media still leads to outcomes comparable to those when there is 100 percent state ownership.

For newspapers, state ownership, on average, is detrimental whether there is a state monopoly or not. But the only countries with significant state ownership in newspapers are those in which there may be other reasons for weak institutional quality as well. For television, monopolies appear to account for most of the associations between state ownership and poor outcomes. Competition among privately owned media firms is also critical for effective media. When there is little competition, information flows reflect only the views of a private elite or the government and private firms can collude in distorting information flows.

Rivalry among firms in the media industry ensures a broader range of social and political views and greater incentives for demand-driven reporting. With such information, voters, consumers, and investors are less likely to be exposed to abuse in economic and political markets, and minority views-including those of the poor-are more likely to be represented. These arguments have gained prominence because of increasing media market concentration over the last decade, especially in Europe, spurred by new technologies and national deregulation.Across countries the concentration of media firms is high.

Many countries try to encourage competition in the media by regulating market concentration. In most of Europe the state limits the share of audience and circulation that media outlets (and their owners) can control. In Germany broadcasters are limited to 30 percent of the national audience, and in the United Kingdom, to 15 percent. How these laws work in practice depends greatly on the details of the law. In Italy media firms are limited to 25 percent of the national communications market, but because of the difficulty in defining this cutoff, the law has never been applied.

Access to public information

Access to public information is essential for the media to investigate issues effectively and transmit news to the public. And because better information flows can improve resource allocation, they may be able to mitigate global financial volatility and crises; as a result, more attention now goes to building institutions that guarantee access to information. To understand and anticipate market movements, investors require timely and accurate information on company financial indicators and macroeconomic data.

Similarly, information on asset ownership, government contracts, and public agency expenditures helps the public monitor government officials. Information on price and product standards helps consumers select products. Records of health inspections, school performance, and environmental data help citizens make informed social choices. Data on politicians' voting records enable more informed choice of candidates. The media can transmit most of this information-if they have access to it.

A recent study in Southeast Asia revealed that few countries are close to providing open access to data of interest to the media and citizens.It looked at the availability of 40 public records, including economic, education, and health indicators, as well as information on government and court proceedings, financial disclosures of firms and officials, and government budgets and contracts. The Philippines ranked highest. At the other end of the spectrum was Myanmar, where even such basic macroeconomic data as GNP and inflation are not always available. Ill-defined procedures for access to information and inadequate information infrastructure were identified as common problems across countries. Legal frameworks to support access to information vary tremendously.

The United Kingdom has a tradition of protecting information, captured in law by the Official Secrets Act, which provides broad powers for government to classify and restrict access. Until 1989 even the type of biscuits served to the prime minister was an official secret. Many countries that adopted aspects of the British legal system have official secrets acts. Some, such as Fiji, have taken steps to introduce a more liberal approach to information access. Others, such as Kenya, Malaysia, and Singapore, retain their official secrets laws.

Other countries use laws to guarantee, rather than limit, access to information. In many cases governments incorporate freedom of information provisions into constitutions, into other government directives, or into media laws. Another solution growing in popularity is the freedom of information (FOI) law, imposing disclosure obligations on government departments, courts, regulatory agencies, the military, and private organizations that carry out statutory functions. FOI laws also enable access to certain information on request, such as personal information held by the government. Since FOI laws tend to be more detailed and operational then constitutional provisions, they can provide strong guarantees for the media of access to information.]

In Nepal, for example, even with the right to information enshrined in the constitution, access remains difficult because is no FOI law or other mechanism to support it. Beginning with Sweden in 1766, 44 industrial and developing countries have adopted FOI laws. Twothirds were passed in the last 10 years, including those in many transition countries, where information access had been severely restricted.Many more countries, such as Fiji, India, and Nepal, are considering FOI acts to improve information flows.

Experience shows that FOI laws can have limitations, for the freedom of information must be balanced with privacy and the legitimate need to retain informa- tion for national security. But some FOI legislation is constrained severely by broadly defined exemptions and loopholes that extend beyond these public interest concerns. For example, the FOI law proposed in the United Kingdom in 1999 enabled the government to withhold information if disclosure would lead to prosecution of the authority concerned. Clearly this would check the ability of journalists to investigate corruption charges. The code on access to information in Hong Kong, China, is considered ineffective because it permits departments to withhold information in 16 categories.

Another limitation of FOI laws is that their success in guaranteeing access to information depends on the capacity of the government to collect, process, store, and manage information. The ongoing costs can be significant estimated at $286 million annually in the United States. And without an adequate information infrastructure, the cost, time, and complexity of obtaining information may be prohibitive. This lack of capacity has proved to be a barrier to FOI laws, especially in developing countries. An added element of capacity is the ability to produce timely statistics.

Information on such statistics as public finances and the balance of payments needs to be reliable and timely if it is to improve the functioning of markets. As Thailand shows, the laws may also take time to implement because of lack of understanding. But building capacity in communications management can help to overcome the obstacles. In Romania efforts to increase government capacity to manage and communicate information significantly improved the media's ability to report on economic reforms and secure public support for them.Even with FOI acts, journalists may lack the training to cover such issues as privatization, economic reforms, and environmental issues. Several countries are addressing this by training reporters in business journalism and investigative journalism.

A World Bank evaluation in Uganda and Tanzania found that such training raised the quality of newspaper reporting on corruption issues.Broadening the media's reach Access to the media, and being able to provide a diversity of views through the media, holds enormous potential for supporting integrated and inclusive markets. But the reach of newspapers, television, and radio varies tremendously, with wealth a clear determinant of media penetration. On average, residents of industrial countries are more than 25 times more likely to receive a daily newspaper than residents in African countries, as measured by newspaper circulation (figure 2). But in many African countries, according to the World Association of Newspapers, the average newspaper copy is read by as many as a dozen people.

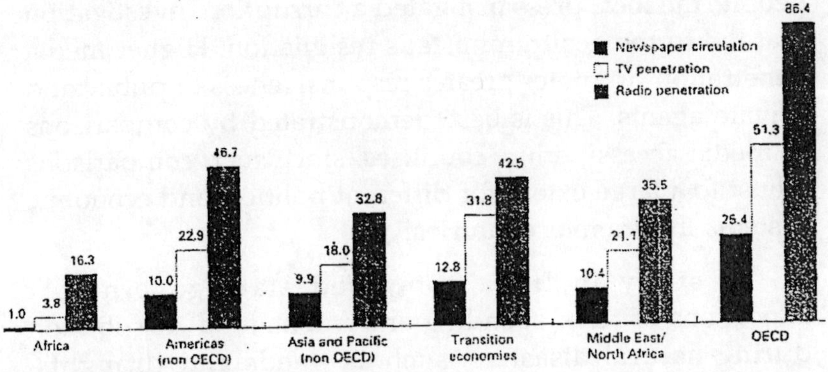

Figure 2. Media penetration rates by region and by OECD compared with non-OECD countries

Literacy also plays a role, but even after accounting for it, large disparities in newspaper circulation remain. Both GNP per capita and literacy are lower in Ecuador than in the former Yugoslav Republic of Macedonia, but newspaper circulation is more than three times greater in Ecuador.

Television viewers do not have to be literate, but they do need costly equipment, technology, and electricity. Radio broadcasting is cheaper, does not require electricity mains, and can be transmitted to remote areas to people who do not know how to read. Not surprisingly, radio receiver penetration is higher than other media penetration in all regions, and radio is the primary medium for reaching citizens in many developing countries. The difference between the reach of radio and the reach of other media is far greater in developing than in industrial countries.

Even in countries with low penetration rates, the media can affect behavior and improve outcomes. In Kenya, despite the low newspaper penetration rate of 9 per 1,000 people, the local press instigated a corruption investigation that led to the health minister's resignation. Higher media penetration promotes greater responsiveness of public and private agents. This is best demonstrated by comparisons of media access within countries, since such comparisons adjust to a large extent for different political and economic systems in different countries.

A study in India compared state government allocations of relief spending and public food distribution during natural disasters, such as floods and droughts. Adjusting for the size of shocks, distribution of relief was greater in states with higher newspaper circulation. The greater local presence of media allowed citizens to develop a collective voice, and the effect was greater for newspapers in local languages than for those in English or Hindi.Access to foreign media can also create demand for institutional change. Foreign or global media enable access to information on issues not reported by local media- as evidenced by countless examples of citizens first receiving news of domestic political crises through the foreign media.

They also provide a yardstick for local media- and for the performance of governments.

Three main strategies have proved successful in increasing access to the media. The first is to remove barriers to entry for new media enterprises. This includes eliminating restrictive licensing and registration requirements, or introducing competition when there are monopolies-factors closely related to media independence (see above). Second, private participants and donors have been innovative in their efforts to expand the reach of the media, especially in poor and remote areas.

In Nigeria and the Democratic Republic of Congo, newspaper vendors charge one price for buying a newspaper, but customers can pay a fraction of this price to read the newspaper at the stand. And international donors have supported telecenters, which provide public access to a range of media and communications facilities in remote areas. Community and nonprofit efforts have been instrumental in increasing media penetration in poorer countries, as demonstrated by the distribution of newspapers in Nepal. Nonprofit foundations have significantly increased access to community radio in developing countries, through wind-up radios and satellite technology. These services have proved especially important in delivering leading-edge information on health, education, environment, and microenterprises. They have also provided a channel for residents of remote communities to voice their concerns and share information with other communities.

Third, a broader development policy framework can enhance access to the media. Increasing literacy rates expands the demand for newspapers. Establishing or strengthening journalist schools expands the supply of the media. Developing the technological infrastructure for the media-installing telephone and cable systems for the Internet to distribution of radio receivers-also increases access. In Korea, for example, government distribution of radio sets as a part of a literacy program significantly increased access to the media and stimulated rapid growth in community radio stations in the 1960s. And competition among media organizations can increase access by broadening supply.

Institutions to complement the media The media can be more effective if complementary institutions reinforce their independence and quality- and act on the information provided. But the independence to freely publish information must also be balanced with systems to ensure responsibility and accountability of the media. Some types of government regulation are needed. Self-regulation is another supporting institution for the effective functioning of the media.

Self-regulatory bodies are well established in some industrial countries, but they are only beginning to emerge in developing countries. Guyana, Tanzania, and Trinidad and Tobago are all building self-regulatory press councils, which establish codes for honesty, fairness, respect for privacy, and general standards of taste. The councils use these codes to guide their decisions on complaints. In many cases the press councils replace traditional court processes. In Australia the complainants are required to sign a declaration that they will not take their complaint to court if they are dissatisfied with the council's decision. What determines the success of councils? Ethical guidelines have to balance press freedom and responsibility.

The application of standards has to be consistent. And media firms have to comply with their decisions. Civil society organizations for media freedom and responsibility can reinforce the work of councils. Effective judicial systems and other mechanisms that penalize undesirable behavior can complement the media's role in improving governance. In the Philippines the media's exposure of toxic waste dumped by foreign military forces led to a congressional investigation, then to an official government investigation, and eventually to government enforcement of orders to discontinue the dumping.

By contrast, media coverage of corrupt activities in Ukraine did little to instigate further investigations or remove the allegedly corrupt officials from power.So even with the best of investigative journalism, the ability of the media to effect change is diminished severely if court systems or enforcement agencies are inadequate. Media also have more impact when political parties, democratic elections, and civil society organizations hold governments accountable. Greater media penetration encourages greater government responsiveness. The reach of newspapers, television, and radio is particularly important when citizens can make political choices based on information they receive. Governments are more responsive when they are held accountable to informed citizens.

2

Contemporary Social Issues

Media Sterotyping

Media stereotypes are inevitable, especially in the advertising, entertainment and news industries, which need as wide an audience as possible to quickly understand information. Stereotypes act like codes that give audiences a quick, common understanding of a person or group of people-usually relating to their class, ethnicity or race, gender, sexual orientation, social role or occupation.

But stereotypes can be problematic. They can:

— reduce a wide range of differences in people to simplistic categorizations

— transform assumptions about particular groups of people into "realities"

— be used to justify the position of those in power

— perpetuate social prejudice and inequality

More often than not, the groups being stereotyped have little to say about how they are represented.

Media Portrayals of Minorities

Anyone who examines the entertainment and news media

will notice that members of ethnic and visible minorities are inadequately represented in entertainment and news media, and that portrayals of minorities are often stereotypical and demeaning. This tendency is particularly problematic in a multicultural country like Canada, where 15 per cent of the population are immigrants and visible minorities comprise 25 to 51 per cent of the larger urban centres. Toronto is the first city in the Western world in which the majority of inhabitants are people of colour.

Members of ethnic and visible minorities are portrayed in news coverage and entertainment media in Canada and the U.S. It also explores the representation of minority groups behind the scenes, as journalists and media producers. When asked, in a 2002 poll, whether the government should preserve and enhance multiculturalism, 82 per cent of Canadians said yes. So why, asks Lionel Lumb, from Carleton University's School of Journalism, "are the millions of minorities that are so visible on our streets and in shopping malls, our offices and health care centres, so invisible on our television screens?" Seventy per cent of the dramas, sitcoms and series that Canadians watch are produced in the U.S. Images of minorities are lacking on those screens and they're lacking on Canadian screens as well.

Back in 1993, the American Screen Actors Guild (SAG) began to collect statistics on the number of ethnic and minority actors appearing in American television and films. The results were grim. Members of visible and ethnic minorities were significantly under-represented across the whole range of entertainment media. The face of North American entertainment was overwhelmingly white, mostly male and young. Critics and advocacy groups began to pressure the industry to produce shows and films that adequately reflect the racial and ethnic diversity.

In its 2000 report, SAG announced a seven per cent increase in industry jobs and record numbers of roles for performers of colour, with African Americans accounting for 15 per cent of all characters in television and film. However, the National Association for the Advancement of Colored People (NAACP) pointed out that of the four major networks' 26 new prime-time shows for the 2000 season, none featured people of colour in lead roles.

Canadian television-both public and private-is well known for creating programming for children and young people that reflects the multicultural society. But critics of adult programming echo concerns voiced in the U.S. A 1994 study by Magali Dupont and Fo Niemi found that minorities in Quebec-based dramas were cast in secondary roles, usually in poorly paid occupations and unstable domestic situations, and non-white men tended to be less heroic and virile than their white counterparts. A small study released in 2002 by researchers at B.C.'s Simon Fraser University shows similar patterns. In the nearly 70 hours of Canadian programming examined, visible minorities made up 12 per cent of 1,200 characters-not far below the actual percentage of visible minorities in the national population. But again, it's the way these minorities are represented that comes under fire.

"What we're seeing is a very superficial level of inclusion, says researcher Shane Halasz. These characters aren't too central to the story line," he points out; and the workplace "seems to be a convenient place to include a person of colour for cosmetic purposes-without being obliged to look at their culture or what happens in their homes." According to Canadian actor Dhirendra, the problem of treating minorities like props is rooted in the producers' discomfort, behind-the-scenes, with challenging the status quo. Nor, he adds, do writers like to write about things they don't understand.

Though television has established a learning curve with respect to fair minority portrayals, the video games industry seems not yet to have got the message. A 2001 study by the U.S. organization Children Now, entitled Fair Play—Violence, Gender and Race in Video Games examined some of the most popular games to assess the extent of stereotyping. It found that:

— most protagonists (86 per cent) were white males

— non-white males were portrayed in stereotypical ways-seven out of ten Asian characters as fighters, and eight out of ten African-Americans as sports competitors

— nearly nine out of ten African-American females were victims of violence (twice the rate of white females)

— 79 per cent of African-American males were shown as verbally and physically aggressive, compared to 57 per cent of white males

Entertainment media say a lot to their viewers about who counts in society. George Gerbner is concerned that portrayals of minority characters in entertainment media affect the ways children see themselves and others. Children Now's 1998 study *A Different World: Children's Perceptions of Race and Class in Media* supports that conclusion. Their research found that children associate white characters with various attributes: having lots of money, being well educated, being a leader, doing well in school, and being intelligent. Conversely, they associate minority characters with breaking the law, having a hard time financially, being lazy, and acting goofy.

Gerbner argues that if you are over-represented, you see many opportunities, many choices. The reverse is true if you're under-represented. The media can grant legitimacy by including people and showing them respect, he argues, and so fair and equal representation is an essential part of a healthy and tolerant multicultural society. In 2002, a UCLA study concluded that "minorities are even more underrepresented in key behind-the-scenes creative and decision-making positions than they are on the [television] screen." Many analysts are concerned that the dearth of minority executives, producers, directors and screenwriters is fuelling the tendency to ignore or misrepresent ethnic groups.

The NAACP's 2000 survey of Hollywood and Beverly Hills screen writers found that only 7 per cent of the 839 respondents were members of minority groups. Furthermore, says the NAACP, ethnic writers in the television industry are ghettoized-83 per cent of the black writers surveyed in 2000 wrote for shows starring primarily black people. It was almost unheard of for a black writer to "cross over" into shows with white stars-even though white writers often made the transition to black shows. As one network told black writer Jay Dyer, "This isn't a black show. I don't need a black writer."

The dearth of multicultural movie writers and producers can also directly affect how minorities are portrayed on the big screen. Actor Garret Wang reports that a casting director once told him he wasn't doing a correct Japanese accent until he began using a Cantonese-Chinese accent-"you know ... 'I give you two free egg roll if you bring laundry into my store.' And she said, 'That's it. That's the one.'"

Many advocates argue that it's time for significant change. In 1961, visible minorities accounted for 3 per cent of the population of Toronto. By 1991, the figure was 30 per cent and today, it is over 50 per cent. Canada's minorities have entered the mainstream, but Canada's broadcasting mainstream still flows along blindly in some sort of self-created canyon from which it can't see the Canadian reality... Diversity is not a drawback-it's a treasure for Canada and Canadians to celebrate. There could be so much more to television and radio programming, and it's time that broadcasters got the message that reflecting diversity is not a duty, it's a delight.

Ethnic Minorities in the News

A good journalism is about objective, independent and balanced reporting. But study after study confirms that members of ethnic and visible minorities are underrepresented and stereotyped in the news. In his landmark 1991 study of Canadian news media, Charles Ungerleider examined the gulf between objective reporting and the distorted image of ethnic and visible minorities so prevalent in most news coverage. Ungerleider argues that news reporting is essentially an exercise in story telling which means that a crucial part of news coverage consists of casting people as heroes, villains and victims.

By either ignoring minorities or casting them in the role of villain, journalists unconsciously tell us stories about who is important, who is trustworthy, and who is a troublemaker. As these stories are repeated in the news, they become the "accepted understandings among those to whom alternative interpretations are not evident."

Colour-Coded News

In fact, immigrants are less likely to break the law than Canadian-born citizens. A federal study of serious crimes in 1989 and 1991 found that foreign-born citizens were "very significantly under-represented" in the Canadian prison system. (They are also, according to Statistics Canada, more likely to have higher levels of education and social stability.) And yet immigrants continue to be over-represented in Canadian and American news stories about crime.

York University's Dr. Frances Henry surveyed articles in the three major Toronto papers for a four-month period in 1997. She found that 54 per cent of all articles in the Toronto Sun that contained the word "Jamaican" were about criminal activity. Forty-six per cent of stories on drug offences in all three papers referred to East Asian and Vietnamese "drug gangs." Some academics claim that this kind of reporting can have an impact on social policy. In their 2000 study Racist Discourse in Canada's English Print Media Frances Henry and Carol Tator conclude that the press creates a sense of "moral panic" in which "isolated incidents of violence are represented as an indication of a profound social crisis that imperils the nation."

Minority stereotyping is in no way limited to crime. The Canadian Nation of Immigrants Project reports that newspapers over-represent immigrants in stories about sports and entertainment, and under-represent them in politics and business coverage. On the other hand, most mainstream media position white males as authority figures, while marginalizing the expertise of members of minorities. Approximately 90 per cent of all experts featured in U.S. news stories are white. When minority experts are called upon, it's typically in response to minority community matters, drugs and crime.

Research indicates that white Canadians tend to think that news coverage of ethnic and visible minorities is adequate, and that not much is wrong. The picture seen through minority eyes is quite different. In 1995, the Canadian Newspaper Association commissioned a research study to explore the views of minority readers. They found that members of ethnic and visible minorities have "a positive view of Canada and their communities" and a "great sense of patriotism." However, a majority felt that Canadian newspapers treat visible minorities like foreigners, unfairly link race and religion to crime stories, and fail to provide balanced coverage of their communities.

Canadian journalist Haroon Siddiqui agrees:

> Issues of interest to [visible minorities]-indeed to most Canadians these days, such as immigration, integration, equality of access to jobs and services, race relations, multiculturalism, cross-cultural understanding, multiple identities-have a low priority with the media. When they do cover these contemporary topics, their narratives tend to be outdated-hostile or primitive, or both.

Hiring Practices

In 1993 the Canadian Daily Newspaper Association (CDNA) surveyed the ethnic and racial diversity of the newspaper industry. Questionnaires were sent out to 82 of the largest daily newspapers. The 41 papers that replied-representing 2620 reporters, copy editors, photographers, artists and supervisors-had only 67 members of ethnic or racial minority groups on staff. More than half of the papers said that increasing the number of non-white journalists was not an immediate priority and publishers placed "managing and covering diversity" nearly last on a list of concerns.

Seven years later, in 2000, a study by Florian Sauvageau and David Pritchard at Quebec's Laval University revealed that 97.3 per cent of Canadian journalists across all media are white. An earlier study by the Quebec-based Centre de recherche-action sur les relations raciales (CRARR) reported that none of the Quebec television stations (other than Radio-Canada, the French-language public broadcaster) had an employment equity program-despite the fact that these stations recognized that the makeup of their newsrooms did not reflect the population they served.

The most recent Canadian inquiry into minority representation comes from an informal survey conducted by Federico Barahono for the April 2001 issue of Thunderbird Magazine. The managing editors Barahono interviewed felt that the shortage of minority journalists is attributable not to any conscious effort to keep people of colour out, but to institutional barriers that are largely systematic and unconscious.

Ryerson professor John Miller agrees. "People hire people who they're comfortable with, who look and think like them," he says. A Canadian Race Relations report from 2000 attributes the lack of minority representation in newsrooms to:

— networking barriers

— referrals for hiring from white producers, writers and editors

— the lack of recognition for qualifications and experience gained from outside Canada

— the lack of employment and training for people of colour

American newsrooms have been similarly slow to make diversity a priority. Although the American Society of Newspaper Editors (ASNE) pledged in 1978 to make their staffs representative of the general population by the turn of the century, they have failed to do so. Only 11.6 per cent of U.S. newsroom staff in 2000 were members of ethnic or visible minorities, compared to 27.3 per cent of the population as a whole. ASNE's 2002 survey produced similar numbers-twenty-four years after ASNE first committed itself to diversity, 88 per cent of newsroom staff were still white.

According to the Center for Media and Public Affairs, 88 per cent of evening news stories televised on ABC, CBS, and NBC in 2001 were reported by whites. There were no African Americans in the year's top 25 reporters and a study by Professor Joe Foote reports there were no Hispanic or Asian news correspondents on the big three American networks.

In Canada, since the early '90s, governments, schools of journalism and professional associations have made a concerted effort to increase the number of journalists who are members of visible minorities. Radio-Canada instituted a program in 1990 and by 2000, members of all minority groups had increased to 4.8 per cent and Aboriginal people to 1.3 per cent of all employees-an improvement, but nowhere near the 15 per cent of the overall population these groups represent.

There have also been gains in the number of visible minorities who report and anchor news programs for the CBC and other national networks, though there has been no study to quantify these gains. A number of media organizations, like the Canadian Newspaper Association and the Canadian Association of Broadcasters, have committed themselves to promoting a more diverse workforce. And progress is being made.

However, as publisher Nicolas Hirst warns, it is not a simple problem to solve. When Hirst's newspaper, the Winnipeg Free Press, started a scholarship for students of colour and aboriginal students in the journalism program at Red River College, no one applied. Hirst was advised that minority students, "did not wish to enter into a competition where they were chosen because they were members of visible minorities." Creating a diverse workforce will require a continuing commitment from the industry to examine its own biases. There are no quick fixes. In Hirst's words, "I need to think.

Economics of Ethnic Stereotyping

Media producers often argue that the lack of diversity in programming is about money, not racism. Foreign markets and domestic advertisers, the story goes, pay more for entertainment products which feature white people in lead roles. The foreign market is a huge influence on the cultural content of films and television programming. Software and entertainment products are now America's biggest export, and exportable movies bring in more on the world market than they do domestically. This means that the foreign market, to a great extent, drives content.

Journalist Sharon Waxman reports that U.S. film executives and producers are very aware that "foreign distributors have almost no interest in movies that have African-American or other minority casts and themes." Since studios anxious to cash in on the foreign entertainment market believe that action films with white characters are what foreign box offices want, they are reluctant to include minorities in casting for domestic films and television.

Canadian journalist, Janine Jackson points out, the industry treats mainly white audiences and more diverse audiences differently, in terms of ratings and advertising dollars. For instance, WB's two most successful black series-The Steve Harvey Show and The Jamie Foxx Show-draw the same number of viewers as the predominantly white-audience show Felicity, and yet a 30-second commercial on Felicity costs twice as much. And even though The Steve Harvey Show attracts 500,000 viewers more per episode than the popular white series Dawson's Creek, a 30-second commercial on the Creek still brings in $63,000 more in advertising revenues.

A Federal Communications Commission report in 1999 attributed the disparity to a variety of factors, including "economic efficiencies derived from common ownership, assessments of listener income and spending patterns, or ethnic/racial stereotypes that influence the media buying process." It went on to say that in certain instances, the media buying process is guided by "ethnic/racial stereotyping, underestimations of disposable income, the desire to control product image, unfounded fears of pilferage, etc."

In Canada, the lack of minority representation in advertising was addressed in 1990, when the Canadian Advertising Foundation (now Advertising Standards Canada) set up the Race Relations Council on Advertising. With funding from the Department of Canadian Heritage, the Council commissioned a study to find out the actual and projected numbers of visible minorities in Canada. The Council polled 600 advertising executives and 2000 citizens across the country on the issue of diversity in advertising. It found:

— Canada's population of visible minorities was projected to hit 5.7 million, or 17.7 per cent of the population by 2001

— most Canadians expected and wanted to see visible minorities included in advertising

— public opinion was well ahead of executive thinking

As a result, the Council began a campaign in the advertising industry to raise awareness and sell the business case, and the situation improved steadily throughout the '90s. Today it's quite normal for TV viewers and readers of advertising to see a variety of races in ads for everything from cold medications and breakfast cereals to luxury cars.

Media Portrayals of Aboriginal People

Aboriginal people have been vigorously stereotyped in words and images for hundreds of years. Film, television and comic-book producers have perpetuated these stereotypes over several generations, and so old notions of what it is to be a Canadian Aboriginal or a Native American have lived on well past the emergence of a public consciousness that knows better. This section identifies some of the major media stereotypes of First Nations, Inuit and Native American peoples in film, television and the news. It explores the effects of such stereotyping, and of the use of Native symbols by professional sports teams, on both the perceptions of non-native young people, and the self-image of Aboriginal youth. And it takes a brief look at the successful efforts of Canadian Aboriginal people to create their own media networks and programming.

For over a hundred years, Westerns and documentaries have shaped the public's perception of Native people. The wise elder (Little Big Man); the drunk (Tom Sawyer); the Indian princess (Pocahontas); the loyal sidekick (Tonto)- these images have become engrained in the consciousness of every North American. Hollywood's versions of "how the West was won" relied totally on the presence of Native tribes, who were to be wiped out or reined in. "And, for the longest time," says Canadian Ojibway playwright Drew Hayden Taylor, "there wasn't a real 'Indian' to be seen on the movie sets: Native 'representation' was taken care of by Italians or Spaniards-anyone with dark enough skin to save on makeup."

As the portrayals of Native characters-either as primitive, violent and deceptive or else as passive and full of childlike obedience-extended to TV, novels and comics, they became familiar, comfortable signposts for much of Western civilization whenever it needed to acknowledge the Aboriginal presence. Since few people, especially in larger urban centres, actually came into contact with Indigenous populations, these portrayals, however inaccurate, had all the more impact. Though popular U.S. films rarely looked north of the border, these stereotypes etched themselves just as deeply into the Canadian psyche.

"We were well into the second half of the 20th century before it occurred to filmmakers that Native people were still around, and even leading interesting lives," says Taylor. "Groundbreaking films like Pow Wow Highway, Dance Me Outside and Smoke Signals provided fresh and contemporary-though still romanticized-portrayals of the Native community."

Film-maker Arthur Lamothe broke new ground in Québec from 1973 to 1983, with his 13 part documentary series La chronique du Nord-Est du Québec. The series, and Lamothe's subsequent work, puts First Nations people centre-stage and provides them with a venue to tell their own stories. In the 1980s and 1990s, the Canadian Broadcasting Corporation (CBC) made a real effort to improve the portrayals of Aboriginal people in its television dramas. Spirit Bay, The Beachcombers, North of 60 and The Rez used Native actors to portray their own people, living real lives and earning believable livelihoods in identifiable parts of the country. The Beachcombers and North of 60 drew substantial audiences among Natives and non-Natives alike.

Television in the United States has been slower to respond to criticism. Indigenous faces are still almost entirely absent from the small screen, except in the news or in documentaries. There have been a few efforts to change the situation, however. In the late 1990s, the American Indian Registry for the Performing Arts in Los Angeles published a directory of Native American performing arts professionals. And in 2001, after acknowledging that "Native Americans are virtually invisible on TV," CBS and NBC held talent showcases in major cities across North America to strengthen their databases of Aboriginal performers.

The new climate of "political correctness" has combined with genuine effort to counter some of the more overt forms of racism in films and television-but subtle vestiges of Native stereotyping still remain. Some of the most common stereotyping traps are various forms of romanticization; historical inaccuracies; stereotyping by omission; and simplistic characterizations.

Romanticization

Some images of Natives that have captured the imagination of the non-Aboriginal world for nearly a century are the Indian Princess, the Native Warrior and the Noble Savage.

The Indian Princess: The Indian Princess is the Native beauty who is sympathetic enough to the white man's quest to be lured away from her tribe to marry into his culture, and further his mission to civilize her people. "The Indian princess is strictly a European concept," writes Native American Joseph Riverwind. "The nations of this country never had a concept of royalty. We do not have kings, queens or princesses."

Gail Guthrie Valaskakis, director of research for Canada's Aboriginal Healing Foundation, agrees. In a 2000 exhibit called Indian Princesses and Cowgirls-Stereotypes from the Frontier, Valaskakis and Marilyn Burgess traced the use of the Indian Princess, from romanticized paintings intended to represent an "exotic, beautiful and dangerous New World" to gratuitous brand labels on fruit cans and cigar boxes. None of these women, says Valaskakis, remotely resemble the "powerful, competent, articulate" women she grew up with on her reserve in Wisconsin.

The Native Warrior: Surely one of the most widely used stereotypes in cinematographic history, the Native Warrior is fierce and formidable and a threat to civilized society. Bare-chested and brandishing a war lance, this warrior is the epitome of the savagery that must be courageously overcome by "progressive elements" pushing West. A more recent incarnation is the romanticized (and eroticized) figure of the strong silent brave flashing, as journalist Paul Gessell notes, "a lot of skin, [and] looking for some White woman to ravish."

These images appear in many forms and in surprising places. In his photo exhibit Scouting/For Indians, 1992-2000, Jeff Thomas, from the Six Nations Reserve in Ontario, captured images of the Warrior in forms ranging from historical statuary, and coats of arms carved on the walls of Ottawa banks and office buildings, to contemporary book covers. Thomas says he took these photographs to raise awareness of the often unconscious "demonization and eroticization" of Indians.

The Noble Savage: In an effort to redress past wrongs, there has been an increase in another time-honoured romantic stereotype -- the mythic Noble Savage. Elevated to a sphere of goodness unreachable by those in contaminated white society and usually possessing some spiritual connection to the land, the Noble Savage (who American academic Rennard Strickland calls "the first ecologist") communes in a cloud of mysticism and places no value on material possessions. Not even the popular Thunderheart avoids the romantic brush. "That movie says that every time you get half a dozen Native people in a room, you can get a prophecy or a vision," says Canadian Cayuga actor Gary Farmer.

Historical Inaccuracies

Farmer cites the successful Canadian film Black Robe, about a Jesuit missionary's quest to save the Huron's souls, as typical of the one-sided historical accounts that upset Aboriginal people. "Black Robe misses a key element," says Farmer. "Nobody explains the Iroquois Confederacy's five centuries of peace between the six nations. The Hurons saw the devastation from the alcohol brought by the newcomers as a decay that had to be rooted out. The Iroquois told the Hurons that everyone not affected should leave, and they would go in and clean the area out." Farmer contends that there's never been an understanding of why that was done-and so the story of a classic conflict between Indigenous and non-Indigenous peoples has never been told.

All vestiges of truth-and thereby of intercultural understanding-give way here before the onslaught of movieland's mythic creation. Film and TV producers have never let details get in the way of a good story. Nowhere is this more true than in depictions of Aboriginal life, where artistic license is liberally taken in portraying dress, customs, livelihoods and spiritual beliefs and ceremonies.

This reduction of cultural heritage and diversity (which most audiences do not even notice) is seen by critics as both a symptom of the problem (not taking Aboriginal people seriously) and an unconscious yet systematic way of perpetuating erroneous stereotypes. What occurs in many films, says social critic Ward Churchill, "is roughly parallel to having a Catholic priest wear a Rabbi's headgear and Protestant cleric's garb while conducting High Mass before a Satanist pentagram, simply because each of these disparate physical manifestations of spiritual culture is visually interesting in its own right."

Stereotyping by Omission

Most film depictions of Native people are set in a 50-year period in the mid-19th century. Where were Native North Americans before the coming of the white man, and where are they now? Apparently "Indians" did not survive the transition to modern society. The article "*Stereotyping Indians by Omission*" notes that Indians are "the only population to be portrayed far more often in historical context than as contemporary people." Considering the size of Chicago's Native population, for instance, the article asks, "why has not one Indian ever received emergency care on ER? And where are the nurses, a primary career choice for many Native women?"

The most flagrant omission in movies and television is the Aboriginal woman. When she is included, it is most often as a "sexual savage" (who cannot be tamed and must therefore be degraded and eventually conquered). In Canada, the National Film Board of Canada tried to counter this cultural amnesia in 1986 with a four-part drama series entitled Daughters of the Country—produced to "re-open the history books" and document the evolution of the Métis people through the lives of four strong women.

Simplistic Characterizations

Perhaps most destructive to the image of Aboriginal people is the lack of character and personality accorded them by the media. Aboriginal people are almost always cast in supporting roles or relegated to the background, and are rarely allowed to speak or display a real personality. And what character they do have tends to reveal itself only in terms of their interactions with white people. Rarely is an Aboriginal portrayed as having personal strengths and weaknesses, or shown acting on his or her own values and judgements.

Nor is the Native ever allowed to tell his or her own story. Most stories are conveyed through the lens of the European experience. A common device used by Hollywood to attach familiar values to Native acts has been to script a white character as narrator (Dances with Wolves, Thunderheart). While this purports to treat the American Indian sympathetically, the reality is that the Aboriginal is robbed of voice.

A number of academics contend Hollywood's depictions of Aboriginal people are based on much broader motives than simply winning audiences. In American Indians: Goodbye to Tonto, J.R. Howard says that in the American psyche, Native people have fulfilled their purpose: "Indian resistance having served to fuel the myths of conquest and glory, and the American divine right to conquest."

And there's a whole school of thought that believes that the stereotypes of Native people and the "Wild West" must still be maintained in today's society. "Somebody is benefiting by having Americans ignorant [about] what European Americans have done to them," writes Wendy Rose in her New Yorker article, "Who Gets to Tell Their Stories?" Ward Churchill argues that the myths and stereotypes built up around the Native American were no accident. He maintains that they served to explain in positive terms the decimation of Native tribes and their ways of life by "advanced" cultures in the name of progress, thereby making it necessary to erase the achievements and very humanity of the conquered people. "Dehumanization, obliteration or appropriation of identity, political subordination and material colonization are all elements of a common process of imperialism," he says. "The meaning of Hollywood's stereotyping of American Indians can be truly comprehended only against this backdrop."

Myths and Misperceptions in non-Aboriginal people

Many of the myths and misperceptions that persist among non-Aboriginal people are perpetuated by no communication, poor communication or one-sided communication. It often seems that the only coverage Native people receive in the news media centres on political and constitutional issues, forest fires, poverty and substance or sexual abuse. Occasionally, stories about cultural activities appear on some local stations-but these are usually given only passing mention. And when it comes to issues that affect all Canadians Aboriginal people are rarely, if ever, consulted.

Of course, the fundamental nature of news and news reporting is that the bad news gets all the attention. Tragedies, conflicts and crises get reported; success stories rarely do. But the end result is that a non-Native audience may well come to the conclusion that Aboriginal people are a troubled, plagued and contentious people. Rudy Platiel, who spent 27 years covering the Aboriginal beat for the Globe and Mail, notes that, "There are an awful lot of good things happening that are not going to get reported in the mainstream press unless somebody pushes to get them there."

The mainstream media owe it to their communities to reflect the cities, towns and rural areas by making their newsrooms as diverse as their communities. There are a number of causes for poor reporting on Aboriginal issues. Journalists have tight deadlines and are rarely given adequate time to thoroughly investigate issues; the gatekeepers of newsrooms and newspapers are seldomwell-versed in Aboriginal affairs; and there is a dearth of experienced Aboriginal journalists. Aboriginal people make up over three per cent of the Canadian population. But in a 1994 study by the Diversity Committee of the Canadian Newspaper Association, of the 41 mainstream papers surveyed (employing 2,620 reporters, copy editors, photographers and supervisors) only four people were Aboriginal.

These factors all contribute to the perpetuation of incomplete and, in some cases, biased information. Over the years, for example, much coverage has been given to the "tax-free" status of Canadian Aboriginals-leaving many Canadians to believe that all Native people share a lucrative tax-exempt status. What is less well known is that only those working on reserves are eligible, and the unemployment rate in these communities is high since opportunities for work are quite limited.

In a 2000 study by York University professors Frances Henry and Carol Tator, journalistic bias in Aboriginal-related reporting was documented in relation to the Jack Ramsay case. A former RCMP officer and Reform Party MP, Ramsay was accused and convicted of the attempted sexual assault in 1969 of a 13-year-old Aboriginal girl.

Henry and Tator's research revealed that media articles focused overwhelmingly on the girl's alcoholic and abusive parents, her impoverished childhood, and her own bouts with alcohol and drugs. By contrast, the review of Ramsay was more sympathetic. It focused on his career, his service to the community, and his supportive family. Henry and Tator contend that such biased coverage served to enlist support for Ramsay, and to minimize the charges against him.

The 1990 Oka crisis was another telling departure from journalistic objectivity. In the summer of 1990, Mohawks in the town of Oka formed a barricade to protest the expansion of a golf course onto Native lands and burial grounds. Over a period of 78 days, mainstream press coverage evoked images of fierce Native warriors and focused on the threat of present and future violence from angry, lawless young men. The media constructed what Gail Guthrie Valaskakis called "exaggerated monolithic representations of Aboriginal activists" that mobilized 4,000 soldiers and police. At the end of the stalemate, Valaskakis writes, when "the warriors" emerged from the blockaded building, it was seen that 27 were Aboriginal men, 16 were Aboriginal women, 6 were children, 1 was a non-White teenager and 10 were journalists-"all," says Valaskakis, "yoked together under one dominant image-the Mohawk Warrior."

The Oka standoff highlighted another problem with the reporting of Native issues. Non-Native journalists are often put in an untenable position: if they go into an Aboriginal story "cold," they can both encounter resistance, and get the story wrong; but if they do their preliminary research and work to gain community trust, they can be accused of being "biased" or "too close" to the story. Likewise, Aboriginal journalists may be limited professionally to covering "Native beats" and then criticized for their pro-Native bias.

Nor do Aboriginal communities themselves always cooperate in telling their story. "We can't use the quick-hit approach," says CBC journalist Loreen Pindera. "It takes an awful lot more time to re-establish trust with a community after they've been so frequently misrepresented by the media."

In the future, as media ownership becomes concentrated in the hands of fewer and fewer communications companies, it's possible that the news we receive from radio, television, newspaper and some Internet sources will become increasingly homogeneous. The native-owned Aboriginal Peoples Television Network gives Canadians the option of consulting a different news source for views and perspectives.

Media Portrayals of Men and Masculinity

For several decades now, media critics and feminists alike have been examining the role of the media in creating and reinforcing stereotypical representations of women and femininity. But only recently have they expanded the research to consider how the media also construct, inform and reinforce prevalent ideas about men and masculinity. This section addresses the representation of men and masculinity in the media. It covers topics such as media stereotypes, the prevalence of male characters in TV and film, and male authority in media news coverage; and it addresses the role that the media play in shaping attitudes about masculinity.

Families, friends, teachers, and community leaders all play a role in helping boys define what it means to be a man. Mainstream media representations also play a role in reinforcing ideas about what it means to be a "real" man in our society. In most media portrayals, male characters are rewarded for self-control and the control of others, aggression and violence, financial independence, and physical desirability.

In 1999, Children Now, a California-based organization that examines the impact of media on children and youth, released a report entitled Boys to Men: Media Messages About Masculinity. The report argues that the media's portrayal of men tends to reinforce men's social dominance. The report observes that:

— the majority of male characters in media are heterosexual
— male characters are more often associated with the public sphere of work, rather than the private sphere of the home, and issues and problems related to work are more significant than personal issues
— non-white male characters are more likely to experience personal problems and are more likely to use physical aggression or violence to solve those problems

These dominant trends in the media's portrayal of men reinforce and support social attitudes that link masculinity to power, dominance and control. The portrayal and acceptance of men by the media as socially powerful and physically violent serve to reinforce assumptions about how men and boys should act in society, how they should treat each other, as well as how they should treat women and children.

Various media analysts and researchers argue that media portrayals of male characters fall within a range of stereotypes. The report *Boys to Men: Media Messages About Masculinity,* identifies the most popular stereotypes of male characters as the Joker, the Jock, the Strong Silent Type, the

Big Shot and the Action Hero. The Joker is a very popular character with boys, perhaps because laughter is part of their own "mask of masculinity." A potential negative consequence of this stereotype is the assumption that boys and men should not be serious or emotional. However, researchers have also argued that humorous roles can be used to expand definitions of masculinity.

The Jock is always willing to "compromise his own long-term health; he must fight other men when necessary; he must avoid being soft; and he must be aggressive." By demonstrating his power and strength, the jock wins the approval of other men and the adoration of women. The Strong Silent Type focuses on "being in charge, acting decisively, containing emotion, and succeeding with women." This stereotype reinforces the assumption that men and boys should always be in control, and that talking about one's feelings is a sign of weakness.

The Big Shot is defined by his professional status. He is the "epitome of success, embodying the characteristics and acquiring the possessions that society deems valuable." This stereotype suggests that a real man must be economically powerful and socially successful. The Action Hero is "strong, but not necessarily silent. He is often angry. Above all, he is aggressive in the extreme and, increasingly over the past several decades, he engages in violent behavior."

Children's Perceptions of Male Stereotypes

In 1999, the research group Children Now asked boys between the ages of 10 and 17 about how their perceptions of the male characters they saw on television, in music videos and in movies. From the study, the group concluded that the media do not reflect the changing work and family experiences of most men today-and that this fact is not lost on the boys, who noticed the discrepancies between the media portrayals and the reality they knew. Some of the study's main observations:

— on television, most men and boys usually keep their attention focused mostly just on women and girls
— many males on TV are violent and angry
— men are generally leaders and problem-solvers
— males are funny, confident, successful and athletic
— it's rare to see men or boys crying or otherwise showing vulnerability
— male characters on TV could not be described as "sensitive"
— male characters are mostly shown in the workplace, and only rarely at home
— more than a third of the boys had never seen a man on TV doing domestic chores

The study also revealed that the boys were quite aware that these male characters on television differed from their own friends and fathers, and from themselves. They had also noticed that media portrayals of success do not necessarily reflect their own ideas of real-life success.

The work of French sociologist Pascal Duret sheds a different light on the subject. In his 1999 study Les jeunes et l'identité masculine, Duret attempted to analyze young peoples' perceptions of male "virility." Though responses varied according to sex and social class, most kids saw virility in terms of physical strength and a muscular body. Courage, and the ability to protect, were also considered to be virile traits.

When young people were asked to name models of virility from the movies, actors like Bruce Willis and Arnold Schwarzenegger were common choices. But it wasn't just the actors' physical appearances that made them virile in the eyes of the young people; it was also the context in which they appeared. What these actors had in common was violent scenes in their films, and Duret concluded that even though the young people may have been unaware of their bias, for them violence was an essential aspect of virility.

As well, social class had a major impact on perceptions of virility: young people from disadvantaged backgrounds viewed virile characteristics much more positively than youths from more advantageous backgrounds. Duret attributed this difference to the value poor people can give to the idea of the "self-made man," who can become what he (or she) wants by dint of hard work.

Although most contemporary research on the portrayal of masculinity in the media has focused on violence, research has also begun to examine the portrayal of masculinity in men's magazines such as Playboy, Maxim, GQ, and Esquire. These magazines, which focus on matters such as health, fashion, sex, relationships, and lifestyle, play a part in defining what it means to be a modern man. Some critics argue that these magazines represent an improvement in media portrayals of gender since they focus on topics previously thought to be solely the concern of women. But others argue that such magazines still rely on stereotypical portrayals of men and masculinity, featuring handsome, white, well-built and well-dressed men, interested only in acquiring the finer things in life.

Media commentators argue that these magazines continue to relegate women to the background and, in doing so, are examples of social backlash directed against specific gains made by women in the paid labour force, mass media industries and other professions. They say that it is no coincidence that as women are achieving greater social, political and professional equality, these magazines symbolically relegate them to subordinate positions as sex objects.

While magazines such as Playboy and Maxim are criticized for objectifying women's bodies, recent discussions about men's magazines are focusing on what these magazines say about men and masculinity. Academics argue that the recent popularity of these magazines is a reflection of men's uncertainty over the roles they are expected to assume in society, at work, and in their relationships.

In her 1983 discussion of Playboy, Barbara Ehrenreich notes when the magazine emerged in 1953, American men were beginning to feel constrained by the demands of marriage, work and fatherhood-and Playboy unapologetically celebrated the bachelor's lifestyle. She argues that Playboy painted an idealistic picture of the well-educated, confirmed bachelor who appreciates the finer things in life: wine, jazz, scotch, art, and women. Playboy's success was built on its celebration of male independence from the domestic responsibilities of marriage and fatherhood.

Sports Media

Sports media also contribute to the construction of masculinity in contemporary society. A study conducted by the Amateur Athletic Foundation of Los Angeles reports that 98 per cent of American boys between the ages of 8 and

17 consume sports media. Since professional sports are virtually dominated by men-from the athletes and coaches to the commentators and reporters-sports media have the potential to transmit powerful ideas about manliness and masculinity.

Recent studies on gender and sports media find that sports commentary reinforces perceptions of "violent masculinity." By praising athletes who continue to play while injured, and by using language of conflict and war to describe action, sports commentary reinforces violence and aggression as exciting and rewarding behaviour. Sports broadcasts focus heavily on violence in professional sports, often replaying and over-analyzing footage of graphic injuries, accidents and fights.

A 1999 Children Now study points out that conflict between players of opposing teams is often created or inflated to promote upcoming games. The studies conclude that this focus on personal rivalry, conflict, and fierce competition reinforces the social attitude that violence and aggression are normal and natural expressions of masculine identity.

Masculinity and Advertising

In its study of masculinity and sports media, the research group Children Now found that most commercials directed to male viewers tend to air during sports programming. Women rarely appear in these commercials, and when they do, they're generally portrayed in stereotypical ways. In fact, in his analysis of gender in advertising, author and University of North Texas professor Steve Craig argues that women tend to be presented as "rewards" for men who choose the right product. He describes such commercials as "narratives of playful escapades away from home and family." They operate, he says, at the level of fantasy-presenting idealized portrayals of men and women. When he focused specifically on beer commercials, Craig found that the men were invariably "virile, slim and white"-and the women always "eager for male companionship."

Author and academic Susan Bordo (University of Kentucky) has also analyzed gender in advertising, and agrees that men are usually portrayed as virile, muscular and powerful. Their powerful bodies dominate space in the ads. For women, the focus is on slenderness, dieting, and attaining a feminine ideal; women are always presented as not just thin, but also weak and vulnerable. These critics and others suggest that just as traditional advertising has for decades sexually objectified women and their bodies, today's marketing campaigns are objectifying men in the same way.

A 2002 study by the University of Wisconsin suggests that this new focus on fit and muscled male bodies is causing men the same anxiety and personal insecurity that women have felt for decades. "Representation of the world, like the world itself, is the work of men; they describe it from their own point of view, which they confuse with the absolute truth."

Non-white or working class men are also marginalized Men who are members of minority groups are typically called upon as experts only in response to minority community matters, drugs and crime. And, as Barbara Ehrenreich notes, news and current affairs programming portrays working class men as dumb, inarticulate and old-fashioned.

Although information media are often presented as informed and "objective," many commentators argue that white male dominance of these media helps perpetuate sexism, racism, and class privilege in society. It is also argued that such coverage presents white masculinity as the social and cultural norm.

Entertainment media reinforce the stereotypes of the rich white male and the working class buffoon. Richard Butsch argues that television programmes tend to exaggerate affluence, and portray working class men as immature, irresponsible, and requiring the supervision of their "betters."

Media Portrayals and Lesbians

Media educators Larry Gross and George Gerbner argue that the media participate in the "symbolic annihilation" of gays and lesbians by negatively stereotyping them (often consigning them to the margins of entertainment media, playing either "colourful" and "flamboyant" characters or dangerous psychopaths), by rarely portraying them realistically, or by not portraying them at all.

Gross and Gerbner argue that the commercial structure of the mass media limits the opportunity for representing diverse characters. Too often networks and film companies shy away from portraying gays and lesbians for fear of alienating or offending advertisers, investors, and audiences. This section addresses the portrayal of gays and lesbians in news, advertising and entertainment media. It also examines homophobia in the media, and provides examples of gay-positive media.

Any discussion of the portrayal of gays and lesbians on television must consider the commercial demands of the medium. In her article "Gay Activists and the Networks", Kathleen Montgomery discusses the process involved in creating a made-for-television movie that featured a gay character in a prominent role. Since the main objective of the movie was to reach as wide an audience as possible, various compromises were necessary:

— the story had to be told within the constraints of a popular television genre: the crime-drama

— the narrative had to focus on the heterosexual lead character and his interactions with gay characters

— the movie could not depict any scenes of affection between characters of the same sex

Montgomery concludes that "these requirements served as a filter through which the issue of homosexuality was processed, resulting in a televised picture of gay life designed to be acceptable to the gay community and still palatable to a mass audience."

But in recent years there has been some improvement in the representation of gays and lesbians on mainstream network television. The popularity of shows such as Will & Grace, La vie, la vie... or Queer Eye for the Straight Guy illustrates that networks are willing to feature gay characters, as long as the shows draw high ratings, and generate profits for advertisers. This profit-motivation means that networks are careful in their portrayals of gay and lesbian characters. While Will & Grace does feature two openly gay male characters, there is little or no discussion about gay relationships or romance. The two gay characters are friends, not lovers, and are rarely shown in romantic situations. The primary relationship for both gay men is with the heterosexual female characters.

In fact, this seems to be an emerging trend. In the past few years, Hollywood has developed a new genre: the gay/straight romance. Television shows such as Will & Grace and films such as My Best Friend's Wedding, The Object of My Affection, and The Next Best Thing all portray a gay man and straight woman as the "perfect couple." While some critics have suggested that this trend represents an attempt to include gay and lesbian characters, others state that such representations still marginalize and silence the experiences of gays and lesbians.

Though mainstream television and movies continue to "sanitize" the portrayal of gay and lesbian life, specialty and pay-TV channels have begun to show more cutting-edge, controversial and critically acclaimed series about gays and lesbians. In 1999, for instance, Britain's Channel 4 made history when it broadcast a miniseries focusing on the lives and loves of three gay men living in Manchester. The series, called Queer as Folk, was highly rated not only by the gay community but also by the mainstream press.

The series was not without controversy-some people complained that the subject matter was inappropriate and others were upset that one of the characters was only 15 years old. Still others worried that it portrayed gay men as over-sexed. But despite these criticisms, the series also enjoyed international success; it aired on ShowCase, Canada's specialty channel and it also inspired an American version, which airs on Showtime.

Many people see the success of Queer as Folk as evidence that "lesbigay" shows can still be enormously popular and profitable. However, advertisers and sponsors are cautious about affiliating themselves with such cutting-edge programming. When the American version of Queer as Folk was in production, fashion houses such as Versace, Prada, Polo Ralph Lauren and Abercrombie & Fitch refused to allow their brands to appear in the series. And although the show is set in Pittsburgh, the marketing director of the Pittsburgh Steelers wrote a letter to the producers demanding that all references to the team be removed.

"In a hundred years of movies, homosexuality has only rarely been depicted on the screen. When it did appear, it was there as something to laugh at-or something to pity-or even something to fear. These were fleeting images, but they were unforgettable, and they left a lasting legacy. Hollywood, that great maker of myths, taught straight people what to think about gay people ... and gay people what to think about themselves."

Recent controversies over Hollywood's negative depiction of homosexuality have focused on how such portrayals marginalize and silence gays and lesbians. Organizations such as the Gay and Lesbian Alliance Against Defamation (GLAAD) argue that films such as Basic Instinct and The Silence of the Lambs demonize gays and lesbians by portraying them as psychopaths. In his book *The Celluloid Closet*, Vito Russo analyzes the representation of gays and lesbians in Hollywood films from the 1890s to the 1980s, and demonstrates a history of homophobia. He argues that Hollywood's portrayal of lesbians and gay men has often been cruel and homophobic. Gay and lesbian characters have been defined by their sexual orientation, and lacked any complex character development.

During Hollywood's early years, from the 1890s to the 1930s, homosexuality was often presented as an object of ridicule and laughter. The character of the sissy was popular at this time, and Russo asserts that such a character was a source of amusement and reassurance for the audience. The sissy was not a threatening representation of homosexuality because he occupied a middle ground between masculinity and femininity. From the 1930s to the 1950s, religious and women's groups criticized Hollywood films for contributing to immorality. As a result, the industry introduced a self-censorship code that affected the portrayal of homosexuality. During these years, films could not feature overtly homosexual characters-so homosexuality was suggested through a character's mannerisms and behaviour.

This strict code was loosened in the 1960s and 1970s, which also saw the dawn of the women's movement and the gay rights movement. While gays and lesbians were becoming more visible and vocal in public life, their representation in films was becoming even more homophobic. At this time, gay characters were often represented as dangerous, violent, or murderous. Since the 1990s, Hollywood has improved its portrayal of gay and lesbian characters. The popularity of films such as The Birdcage, Philadelphia, To Wong Foo, Flawless and In & Out demonstrates that audiences can and do enjoy films with gay and lesbian characters. But despite these advances, critics say that the industry is still too cautious in its portrayals of gay themes, characters, and experiences.

Hollywood films are designed to appeal to as large an audience as possible; and producers fear that focusing on gay and lesbian themes risks offending a large portion of the audience, as well as potential investors. While considerable progress has been made with respect to the depiction of gays and lesbians in television and movies, critics argue that news media still systematically ignore and distort the lives and experiences of gays and lesbians.

In a 1998 study that analyzed 50 years of coverage of gay and lesbian issues in Time and Newsweek, Lisa Bennett found that news media reinforce prejudice and discrimination against gays and lesbians. She observes that gays and lesbians are often linked to deviant or criminal behaviour without evidence to support such claims; and that the media often reprint offensive and homophobic comments. Bennett concludes that such practices reinforce assumptions that gays and lesbians are inherently inferior.

Before the dawn of the gay rights movement in the 1970s, gays and lesbians did not figure prominently in mainstream news media. But with the emergence of HIV/AIDS as a public health issue in the 1980s, coverage became more intense, and more negative. During this time, media coverage often portrayed gay men as a serious risk to society.

Activists and academics such as Simon Watney, Douglas Crimp and Jan Zita Grover argue that news coverage of HIV/AIDS has consistently drawn on negative stereotypes about gays and lesbians. In their view, the coverage of HIV/AIDS in the 1980s reflected mainstream society's fear of and dislike for the gay community-and essentially blamed gay men for AIDS. The media coverage of HIV/AIDS improved in the 1990s, largely as a result of the efforts of activists fighting for gay and lesbian rights. But the mainstream media still tend to cover the gay community only when it is perceived to be in crisis. Many argue that, since gays and lesbians comprise approximately two to five per cent of the population, their interests and perspectives should be more readily addressed.

Organizations such as the Gay and Lesbian Alliance Against Defamation (GLAAD) maintain that print, news and entertainment media do not adequately address or reflect gay experiences and perspectives. Gays and lesbians tend to appear in the news or on television only when there is a specific issue that interests or directly affects the gay community. Participants at a 2000 Roundtable of Gays and Lesbians in Quebec came to the same conclusion, saying in their report that the lack of gay news items and the reduction of questions touching the gay and lesbian communities renders the presence of homosexuals in the news "occasional and marginal."

According to an article by Benoît Migneault in a 2001 issue of the National Library of Quebec's monthly publication *À rayons ouverts*, there has, in fact, been a great improvement in the coverage of gay issues in Quebec. La Presse, one of Montreal's most-read dailies, is now publishing more than 400 articles a year on gay themes-up from about fifteen a year in the eighties. Furthermore, Migneault feels the tone of the writing is now more objective and more sympathetic. Migneault says that media coverage of homosexuality contributed, in former years, to the build-up of prejudice against gays and lesbians, and that it is now working against these biases. And he feels that the gay community press itself has contributed to a changing attitude over the last 20 years.

Advertising and Gay Consumers

The media are making progress in its depiction of gays and lesbians. Perhaps the most striking example of this is the active courting of gay and lesbian consumers through gay-positive advertising and marketing campaigns.

In 1994, IKEA aired a commercial that depicted two gay men shopping for a dining room set, making the store the first company to actively target gay consumers. Since that time, many companies have started to target gay and lesbian consumers with gay-positive marketing campaigns. These campaigns are directed to a specific market: gay men and lesbians who live in cities, are single and have a large amount of disposable income. Advertising critic Michael Wilke questions whether this trend is actually an attempt to court gay consumers. He says that advertisers are capitalizing on the cultural cachet and perceived hipness of the gay lifestyle only as a way of selling their products-and are not specifically interested in attracting gay consumers.

Writer Michelle Moinier disagrees. In an article in Altema, a publication on consumer trends, Moinier maintains that certain products, though not actually conceived for the gay population, are nevertheless marketed that way, with messages and images clearly targeted at the lucrative gay market. Critics argue that the visibility of gays and lesbians in advertising is not an indication of the increased social acceptance of gays and lesbians, but simply an attempt by advertisers and network executives to access an untapped market.

They worry that after almost thirty years of political struggle, gay and lesbian rights have been reduced to increased consumer choice. An increase in positive representations of gays and lesbians in commercials, films, and television shows is an improvement, but such progress does not signal the achievement of social and political equality.

White Authority in the Media

"White people create the dominant images of the world, and don't quite see that they thus construct the world in their image." Discussions of media stereotyping have tended to focus on how traditionally marginalized groups such as women, gay men, lesbians, and ethnic minorities have been negatively affected by stereotypical portrayals. But increasingly, scholars are considering how stereotyping privileges certain groups. This section deals with whiteness and white privilege in the media; how white privilege is reinforced and supported by the media; and how the media marginalize the perspectives not only of visible minorities, but also of working-class women and men.

Biology alone does not determine racial identity. The concept of race is equally shaped by social norms and expectations, which are based on historical events and current practices. In North American society, being white is perceived as the norm. Often the fact that whiteness is also a race is not acknowledged. As a result, researchers have begun to examine whiteness and to define it in terms of social impact. Such research concentrates on "white privilege"-the differences in power between whites and non-whites, and the advantages white people automatically take for granted.

The advantages of being white include learning the history of one's own race in school, to seeing members of one's own ethnic group widely represented in the media, to being confident that job refusals are not based on one's race. Most of the decision-makers in North American news and entertainment media are white. Media ownership is mainly concentrated in the hands of white males; white journalists dominate the mainstream media; and white people hold most creative positions in the entertainment media as actors, writers and directors. All these factors contribute to the prevalence of whiteness in media, and help to reinforce white privilege as the norm.

Most mainstream media content also reinforces white privilege by featuring white characters and addressing white interests and experiences. When programming does feature non-white characters, they usually appear in supporting roles. News and information media also demonstrate the preponderance of white privilege:

— In the early 1990s, the media watchdog Fairness and Accuracy in Reporting (FAIR) surveyed the makeup of the guests on ABC's Nightline. It found that 80 per cent were professionals, 89 per cent were male, and 92 per cent were white.

— FAIR also found that on PBS's MacNeil/Lehrer NewsHour, 90 per cent of the guests were white, 87 per cent were male, and 67 per cent were current or former government officials.

— A 1996 survey conducted by Women, Men and Media found that subjects interviewed for the evening news were predominantly (75 per cent) professional white men. As well, 86 per cent of American network news was also reported by white men.

Social researchers and scholars point out that the mainstream media typically skew their portrayals of economic classes towards the white middle and upper classes, with all their privileges. They rarely represent the interests or perspectives of working-class women and men. Richard Butsch, in his article "*Ralph, Fred, Archie and Homer: Why Television Keeps Recreating the White Male Working-Class Buffoon*," notes that the entertainment media tend to exaggerate affluence, and under-represent working-class men and women. Working wives in television series tend to be middle class women in pursuit of careers. Depictions of working class wives are rare. Working-class men tend to be shown as immature, irresponsible, and requiring the supervision of their "betters."

In her article "The Silenced Majority," Barbara Ehrenreich writes that the media rarely represent the interests or experiences of working class women and men. In news and current affairs programming, the "experts" who discuss issues affecting the working classes are often white, professional, middle class men. She continues that members of the white working classes are portrayed as dumb, inarticulate and old-fashioned. Such stereotypes serve to silence the concerns and perspectives of working class women and men in the media.

Impact of Stereotyping on Young People

Generations of North American children have grown up watching "cowboys and Indians" films and TV shows and reading books such as The Adventures of Tom Sawyer and Little House on the Prairie. Popular films and novels reinforced the notion that Aboriginal people existed only in the past-forever chasing buffalo or being chased by the cavalry. These images showed them as forever destined to remain on the margins of "real" society. Such impressions and childhood beliefs, set at an early age, are often the hardest to shake.

While the old-style Westerns are long gone, today's media producers still continue their tradition. For instance, Disney's Peter Pan may be a new take on an old tale, but its stereotyping of Indians as cruel and malicious, with their articulation reduced to "ugh" and their dress to loincloths, is as strong as ever. The same can be said for Pocahontas even though that film was more politically correct. How can a child negotiate the distance between portrayals like these, and "real" First Nations people?

Canadian Cayuga actor Gary Farmer is most concerned with the effect of such portrayals on young Aboriginal people themselves. "Consider the impression left when they see themselves portrayed this way time and time again. It's hard for them to have a positive image of themselves." Even Disney's arguably positive portrayal of Pocahontas, Farmer says, "will have kids walking away with the stereotype of the 'sexual savage.'" It's worth noting that Pocahontas' appearance falls well within white mainstream media norms. In fact, her facial features were a composite of several non-Aboriginal models, one of whom was British fashion star Kate Moss.

Anyone who understands or studies the social development of children and young people knows that attitudes, values and self-esteem are well developed by the mid-teen years, or even earlier. What young people see and hear in the media helps them to figure out how the world works and who and what is valued in our society. If the media's take on Aboriginal people is interpreted at face value, then kids are growing up with a skewed vision of what it means to be part of a First Peoples society. If they get their impressions from the news, they'll likely view Aboriginal people as a negative force. And if their impressions come from films and TV programs, they'll learn to think of Aboriginal people as inferior (passive, aggressive or drunk) or simply as non-entities, obliterated by omission.

When young Aboriginal people read the newspaper or turn on the TV, how often do they see their own life experiences reflected? Almost never, says Children Now, the U.S. research organization that analyzed the presence of Native American children on TV in 1999, and conducted focus groups with children from 20 tribes. Furthermore, they contend, those children have learned to associate positive attributes with white television characters, and negative attributes with non-white characters.

"The media have a lot of power to endorse stereotypes," says Susan Swan, an Ojibway from the Lake Manitoba First Nation. "We go into First Nations communities to talk to youth about gangs. When asked, the kids estimate that about 95 per cent of Aboriginal youth is involved in gangs. The actual number is three per cent. Why do they think these numbers are so high? It's because this is what they get from television and newspapers."

The popular media are "cool" in the eyes of most kids. If the existence and value of a group of people is not affirmed by inclusion in media information and entertainment, the message is clear-they're not important. In Aboriginal communities, this can contribute to, as one community sociologist calls it, "learned helplessness, alienation, and a sense of having no control." In Canada, new sensitivities and support for cultural diversity have brought some positive changes. Aboriginal children are periodically featured or interviewed in children's after-school television; the National Film Board has made films for years that document real Aboriginal lives; the CBC has had many seasons of successful dramas that focus on Aboriginal communities; and Aboriginal entertainers have been "going mainstream" for two decades. (See Aboriginal Voices in the Arts and Media, below.) These measures, along with the establishment of Aboriginal television and radio networks, all contribute to a more balanced view and more diverse voices.

Practically speaking, though, these voices still represent only a small proportion of the popular media that kids consume today. The evening news, the "Indian" images in sports-culture hype, the products of the Disney empire, and the misrepresentation (and non-representation) of Aboriginal people in most mainstream media-all continue to influence kids' views of Aboriginal cultures and peoples. In 2000, two young Canadians, Ojibway journalist Laura J. Milliken and Saulteaux entertainer Jennifer Podemski, conspired to buck this trend. They produced The Seventh Generation, a television series presenting the lives of empowered and successful Native people-doctors, scientists, journalists and performers. "We want Aboriginal youth to see these stories so they will strive for their goals, make decisions educationally and career-wise," said Milliken, "but above all else, just feel secure about who they are and that they are part of this generation."

Importance of Media Education

Media education can help young people put current images and messages about Aboriginal people into perspective by helping them understand how the media work, why stereotyping exists, how decisions are made, and why "it matters who makes it." Media education is not about learning the right answers; it's about consuming media images with an active, critical mind and asking the right questions.

The following are the kinds of inquiries that can help to raise awareness about the portrayal of Aboriginal people in movies, television entertainment and current affairs programming. Media education is that nothing is objective-each and every media production is created with a viewpoint and for a purpose. The "reality" depicted in film or television productions is the result of many choices and each of these choices is based on the experience, knowledge and bias of the producers involved. To date, very few films and TV shows featuring Aboriginal people have been written or produced by Aboriginal people-and it shows.

The ownership of a TV station or newspaper, the makeup of its management team and its political leanings will all have an impact on who is interviewed on a current affairs program, which "experts" are chosen for sound bites on an issue, and whose perspectives are ignored completely. When Aboriginal voices are heard, it's almost always on Aboriginal issues and rarely on general topics affecting society as a whole.

A groundbreaking land treaty may get much less coverage than a group of Aboriginal people setting up a blockade. Blockades and the potential for violence have visual appeal for television; men and women negotiating around a table don't. Likewise for sensational stories on murders, prostitution and drug abuse; they keep the ratings up, and high ratings mean good advertising revenues. Newscasts have to move along quickly and stereotyping is a kind of shorthand that people can comprehend without explanation. Understanding how the news works isn't going to change the news, but it does help kids understand that "newsworthy" stories are not necessarily the most important stories. Comparing the news coverage of APTN (Aboriginal Peoples Television Network) with that of a national television network provides a strong lesson in media voices and behind-the-scenes decision-making.

Are Aboriginal people shown as real human beings in films and TV programs or do they seem wooden and two-dimensional? Media producers, especially those in Hollywood, have used Native people to tell white people's stories for generations. Rarely are Native characters given complex personalities or autonomous roles. Rarely do they rely on their own values and judgements, or act upon their own motivations. Although efforts have been made to undo this tradition, old stereotypes die hard.

Anyone with knowledge of the various Aboriginal cultures will pick out outrageous and often amusing inaccuracies-tipis where longhouses were used, horses where foot-and-canoe travel was the norm, feather headdresses on the Pacific coast. Distinctions in dress, language, abodes and beliefs of the many Aboriginal cultures are often ignored in favour of a shorthand that "speaks" to the audience. This may be due to laziness, ignorance or the desire to use visual props that will be recognized by audiences and visually arresting onscreen.

A convenient convention of the old Westerns was to have Native people speaking in broken English, their thoughts and emotions restricted to their limited knowledge of English (and, it was usually implied, to their limited intellect). This tendency toward simplification has extended in some degree to modern-day characterizations of Aboriginal people. If set in the past, the script should at least show Aboriginal characters speaking fluently in their own languages. There are over 350 different North American Aboriginal languages-a fact unacknowledged by the film industry.

With few exceptions, Hollywood seems to have thought so. Native tribes flourished for thousands of years before the coming of Europeans and today there are over a million Canadian Aboriginal people and nearly two million Native Americans-some on reserves and others in rural and urban communities.

3

Media and Human Rights

Until a decade ago, the word 'media' was synonymous with the word 'the press', which in turn was synonymous with newspapers. However, the Iraqi invasion of Kuwait in 1991, which led to the first Gulf War between America and Iraq, gave birth to the cable television network, and became a springboard for the Cable News Network (CNN) founded by Ted Turner of the Media Corporation. This was followed with the advent of the Internet, which has virtually revolutionized the scope and the reach of the media across the globe.

In India, the Press played a crucial role during the freedom struggle. The role played by great statesmen like Bal Gangadhar Tilak, Mahatama Gandhi and Pandit Jawaharlal Nehru is unparalleled, thanks to the zeal with which they devoted to their respective newspapers - Kesari, Harijan and National Herald. They succeeded despite the repeated efforts made by the British regime to curb their writings by charging and then sentencing them in one sedition case after another.

The imposition of an eighteen-month emergency in the mid-eighties curtailed freedom of expression with censorship measures adopted by the then Union government. However, it was this emergency which led to the birth of various news magazines like India Today, Sunday, Onlooker, etc. and which in turn gave a stiff competition to the daily newspapers. They profited by printing analytical reports, based on first hand information gathered by their correspondents in the field. Previously, many of the newspapers used to depend on the wire services like PTI, UNI, Samachar, etc. for culling the news due to the financial constraints and had limited access to the information. It would not be an exaggeration to say that the emergency turned out to be a blessing in disguise for the printed media in the country, as it definitely helped them to reshape the definition of 'investigative journalism' in the post emergency era.

The Press Council Act - 1978

In 1978, the then Government introduced 'The Press Council Act - 1978' to 'preserve the freedom of the press and also for maintaining and improving the standards of newspapers and news agencies in India'. This Act has to some extent helped the Press to be more transparent and also simultaneously be accountable. What is a little astonishing is the fact that even after the infusion of electronic media, i.e. cable channels and internet, the government has not made any effort to enlarge the scope of the Act, so as to include these two new modes of communications within its ambit. It would not be out of place to mention here that the Press Council has no punitive powers and therefore sometimes it is not taken seriously, as the strictures passed by it have little bearing on the editor, reporter, printer and publisher of the newspaper. One feels it is an exercise in futility.

Maiden human rights violation reporting

In early eighties, a revelation made by Sunday magazine published by Anand Bazar Patrika from Kolkata with a front page story of the blinding of prisoners in Bhagalpur Jail had virtually rocked the entire nation when copies were waved in parliament. This was the first major case of human rights violations ever to have been reported in the media, and which threw light on the alarming state of affairs in the jail. Thereafter in mid eighties, Sheela Barse's investigative story on the condition of exploitation and abuse of female inmates of Arthur Road Jail in Mumbai, also in Sunday, resulted in an enquiry into the condition of prisons all over Maharashtra.

The printed media has played a significant role during the last twenty-five years or so in reporting the violation of human rights. However, of late the printed media has been receiving stiff competition from television with the advent of news channels such as Star News, Zee TV and Aaj Tak were thrown to air. This healthy competition between print and electronic media has compelled them to carve out a new kind of readership and/or viewership in other areas such as fashion, cuisine, health care, real estate, environment, sports etc. While defending the latest trends, the media say, "we cater for the demands of our readers and viewers".

Modernization of Media

But one fears that in the entire modernization and revolution process of the Indian media, human rights might take a back seat. This fear is further compounded due to the constant changes in the global economic pattern, which began with the introduction of the WTO six years ago. The recently concluded US-led war on Iraq is also going to change the financial and economic equations around the globe, in which 'human survival' might assume more importance than 'respect for the human rights'. Although the concept of 'human rights' came into existence way back in 1948 with the UN's Universal Declaration to that effect, in India the National Human Rights Commission Came into existence forty-five years later, in 1993, with 'The Protection of Human Rights Act - 1993'. The State Human Rights Commission has came into existence barely two years ago and is still in the embryonic stage.

One might wonder why the enactment of a nationwide law was delayed for 45 years? Well, no such necessity was felt as many of the Articles of the Universal Declaration of Human Rights have already found place in the Fundamental Rights enshrined in our Constitution. The Indian Constitution is one of the classical documents of its kind and has been drafted in such a systematic and simplified manner that is easy to understand, even for a layman. This speaks the volumes for the vision and energy of Dr. Babasaheb Ambedkar whose efforts in the making of the Indian Constitution were quite gigantic. However, when it comes to the reporting of the human rights-related incidents, the newspapers devote very little space to them, unless the incidents it self is a very newsworthy and has national importance. Newspapers seldom make a serious effort to follow up such stories, which they report with a greater zeal in the beginning.

Basic legal knowledge

It is regrettable to note that in none of the educational institutes, colleges or universities in which journalism courses are conducted do topics like the Indian Constitution or human rights find any place. The apathy of these institutes towards these issues is to be deplored. A journalism student, aiming to become a reporter or a correspondent with a newspaper or a cable TV news network must know precisely that it is 'Freedom of Expression' under Article 19 of the Constitution of India which empowers him to express his views without any fear or favour according to his conscience.

Although the concept of fundamental rights under our constitution and human rights are quite synonymous, the reporting on the violation of human rights is a little difficult. A bare minimum knowledge of criminal justice system is essential to a reporter, if he or she wishes to report on human rights. At present, very few newspapers have reporters who are exclusively covering the legal beat. Frequently, the crime reporter who interacts with the police department is asked to cover the court reporting as well. Here again, there is a catch. Very few, indeed no, crime reporters are law graduates. Law graduates can earn more money by entering the legal profession.

It is a common belief that the violation of human rights takes place only at police stations or in prison. This is true to some extent. But there are other areas too, like railways, environment, health care, education, development, employment, etc., where the violation of human rights do take place but it is seldom reported.

Building Public Opinion

The violation of human rights, no matter in which sphere of life they occur, essentially takes place because 'human values' are not recognized in the first place. The importance of the human rights needs to be taught from the primary level in schools, when children are the right age to absorb them. Police are often accused of violating human rights, but sadly, no effort is made by the home department to include the subject in the curriculum of police training academies. Here lies an opportunity to train policemen about the importance of respecting and observing human rights and the consequences of the breaching them.

The media can play a pivotal role by way of building up public opinion, and also by impressing on the government the need to incorporate the subject of human rights, both in schools and also in police training academies, and also in the training institutes for municipal councils, corporations and other revenue departments. It is the duty of the government to provide its citizens with unpolluted air. But, if the local authority is going to give building construction permission in a 'green zone' or for the construction of a chemical plant in the area nearby to residential locality, then it would definitely be a violation of human rights. The de-reservation of plots for housing projects in metropolis is a huge scam, taking place with utter disregard to the human rights, but it is seldom reported in the media.

It is a common experience, at least in the big cities like Mumbai and Pune, that matters relating to de-reservation of plots by the builders, or the violation of environmental norms by the companies are rarely reported, as the reporting about their misdemeanors might deprive the newspapers of potential advertisements. The print media these days is undergoing lots of changes, thanks to the challenges thrown up by the electronic media. Time was when the editor was 'The Boss' of the newspaper and it was he who used to call the shots with the management. Now a newspaper is treated like any other manufacturing product, with the marketing (also known as 'Response') department at the helm of affairs. The editor is being reduced to a 'hired labourer', working purely on a contract basis.

Such a sea change in the attitude of the management of some of the newspapers means that they are unlikely to antagonize the government by reporting stories relating to the violation of human rights, lest these stories rob them of the advertisements issued by the Directorate of Audio and Visual Publicity (DAVP).

Freedom of Opinion and Expression

The freedom of opinion and expression - including the "freedom to receive and impart information and ideas for any media and regardless of frontiers" - is one of the basic civil and political rights, which is accordingly laid down in all respective human rights instruments. It has its roots in the struggle for personal freedoms in the 18th and 19th century, when it was enshrined in the US and European constitutions. The British philosopher John Stuart Mill called the liberty of the press "one of the securities against corrupt and tyrannic government". It is also a constitutive right for a democratic system in which everyone, not only the citizens of a state, have the human right to say what they think and to criticize the government.

In January 1941, President Roosevelt announced the freedom of speech and expression as one of the four freedoms on which to base a future world order after the Second World War. The access to and the free flow of information across frontiers is a major element of an open and pluralistic society. The "CNN factor" of bringing any conflict right into the living room has changed the role of the media. Because of the importance of public opinion, the media has become a more important part of the warfare as could be seen in the case of Kosovo. "Info wars" and "infotainment" stand for the trend that information is subordinated to other objectives.

EARLY AND MODERN CHALLENGES

The freedom of information, expression and the media was of particular importance during the Cold War, when people in the socialist countries of Eastern Europe did not have access to foreign or independent newspapers and magazines. Later on, the Government of China tried to limit the use of satellite dishes in order to prevent its people from following Western channels and today certain countries are limiting the access to the internet in order to prevent their citizens from reaching websites they consider undesirable.

The media can have a dual role as beneficiaries and violators of the freedom of expression. Their role can be of informing about global problems, strengthening global solidarity, but it can also be one of instrument of propaganda of the state or of particular economic and other interests. According to the UNESCO Commission on Culture and Development, modern communication technologies have made control of information flows more difficult, creating new opportunities, but also new threats, especially if the media become a target either of attack or of political control. The diversity and quality of programs may be reduced as a result of commercialization, eager to gain always wider audiences or to compete for a higher share of readers and viewers by concentrating on sex and crime-stories.

A major threat to the freedom of the media has been the concentration of the media, which exist both on the local and the global level. Therefore, in many countries and the European Union there are laws against media concentration in order to preserve media pluralism. Further and more elaborated new challenges of the freedom of information and of the media are brought about by technological developments like the spreading of satellite communication and the increasing access to the internet. Quite often, states try to restrict access to the new media because of oppositional views or contents they fear to be against their national policies, i.e. on religious or moral grounds.

Due to the borderless nature of the internet, answers are to be found mainly at the international level. In its Convention on Cyber Crime, the OECD already condemned child pornography and tried to enhance domestic criminal liability as well as international cooperation for prosecution; work on an additional protocol dealing with racist and xenophobic propaganda is in progress. The Convention has not yet entered into force. The United Nations Summit on the Information Society in Geneva in 2003 and in Tunis in 2005 deals with yet another extremely important issue: inclusion and exclusion in an age of communication, also called the "digital age". Its major aim is to develop an action plan on how to close the digital and knowledge gap between the "haves" and "have-nots" of access to information and communication technologies.

Since the so-called digital divide between the North and the South (but also within the North, where rural and less prosperous areas lag behind considerably) keeps on widening dramatically, it is indeed high time to find a global line of action. The freedom of expression is essentially affected by the denial of access to the information infrastructure, because the growing importance of the internet makes it almost impossible to retrieve and spread ideas anywhere else that easily. In any case it has to be pointed out that there can be no freedom without responsibility and that unlimited freedoms may lead to violation of other human rights, like the right to privacy. But restrictions need to be justified by the government with legitimate reasons, which can be scrutinized by public opinion and, as the last resort, judicial institutions.

Freedom of Expression: An absolute Civil Right

The freedom of expression is a framework right containing several elements, like the freedom of information and the freedom of the press and the media in general. It is based on the freedom of opinion and intrinsically linked to it. Its manifestations range from the individual expression of opinions to the institutional freedom of the media. Freedom of opinion is an absolute civil right, whereas freedom of expression is a political right, which can be subjected to certain restrictions. Freedom of expression is a dual right in the sense of the freedom to impart, i.e. express opinions and ideas of all kind, and the freedom to seek and receive information and ideas, both in any form - orally, in writing or in print, in the form of art, or through any other media, including new technologies. Frontiers must not be used to interfere with the right.

Consequently, the freedom of expression is an integral part of the "right to communicate". A declaration on this right is currently drafted, but since it is a compilation of already existing human rights (such as, besides freedom of expression, the right to freedom of thought, conscience and religion, the right to participation in cultural life and the right to privacy) rather than a new right in itself, the concept is not entirely clear yet. Certain elements of the right to expression are also connected with other human rights, i.e.:

— The Right to Freedom of Thought, Conscience and Religion (Art. 18 ICCPR) Religious Freedoms Module.

— The right of authors to benefit from the protection of the moral and material interests resulting from any scientific, literary or artistic production, i.e. the copyright (Art. 15(2) ICESCR).

— In relation to the human right to education (Art. 13 ICESCR), the freedom of expression results in the academic freedoms and the autonomy of institutions of higher learning to protect those freedoms.

A major qualification of the freedom of expression is contained in Art. 20 ICCPR prohibiting war propaganda and any advocacy of national, racial or religious hatred that constitutes incitement to discrimination, hostility or violence. The state is under an obligation to enforce those prohibitions by national legislation.

Violations of the Right, Threats and Risks

In practice, we witness wide spread violations of this basic human right through restrictions of the freedom of expression and of the media in many countries of the world as can be seen from the yearly reports of Amnesty International or Human Rights Watch. According to Reporters Without Borders, 31 journalists were killed and 489 imprisoned in executing their duties in 2001. The organization, therefore, proposed special legal instruments, such as the "Charter for the Safety of Journalists Working in War Zones or Dangerous Areas". The "war against terrorism" after September 11th , 2001 has brought new threats for the freedom of information by various governments. For example, the association of writers, PEN, urged a review of the US PATRIOT Act in this respect. However, the freedom of expression and of the media may also be misused to instigate hate and conflict as has been documented by the International Helsinki Federation in its publication on "Hate speech in the Balkans".

There is the threat of censorship, which may occur in the form of state censorship or censorship through economic or other means. It can mean that articles can be published only after approval by an authority as has been the practice in most socialist countries of Eastern Europe before the end of the Cold War in 1989. It can also mean that economic interests prevent the publication of certain opinions, for example if the military industry prevents articles with a critical attitude towards war.

Censorship may also occur through self-censorship, when political or other interests are already taken into account by the journalist or media director. Finally, the decision on the newsworthiness, what is "fit to print" may exclude information not considered opportune, minority views or what does not sell well. Decisions what to publish will often be disputable. Codes of good practice can give orientation. Otherwise, the purpose of media pluralism is to assure that different views can be read, heard and seen.

Restrictions of the Right

According to Art. 29 of the Universal Declaration of Human Rights the exercise of rights and freedoms of everyone is subject to limitations as are determined by law, in particular „for the purpose of securing due recognition and respect for the rights and freedoms of others ...". Art. 19(3) ICCPR reminds that the rights enumerated carry with them special duties and responsibilities. This shows that the freedom of expression and the media is a very sensitive right, which has to be handled with proper care. The duties and responsibilities are not indicated in the Covenant, but usually to be found in codes of professional ethics or state legislation, which, however, must not restrict the content of the human right. Typical duties and responsibilities relate to the duty of objective information, i.e. to seek for the truth or at least allow for different opinions, etc.

Some responsibilities coincide with reasons for restrictions of the freedom of expression, whereas there are no legitimate restrictions for the freedom of opinion. According to Art. 19(3), three types of restrictions are possible, provided they are done through legislation and considered necessary:

— for the respect of the rights and reputation of others

— for the protection of national security or of public order (ordre public)

— for the protection of public health or morals

According to legal interpretation rules, limitations of rights have to be interpreted restrictively, i.e. the main right should not be undermined and the restriction should not be larger as necessary to protect the rights of others and of the basic public goods mentioned.

In Art. 10 of the European Convention on Human Rights, the list of possible restrictions is even longer although more precise. It states that the exercise of the freedom of expression may be subject to "conditions, restrictions or penalties as are prescribed by law and are necessary in a democratic society". Such restrictions may be justified by:

— "interests of national security, territorial integrity or public safety,

— for the prevention of disorder or crime, for the protection of health or morals,

— for the protection of the reputation or rights of others,

— for preventing the disclosure of information received in confidence,

— for maintaining the authority and impartiality of the judiciary."

No other right has such a long list of reasons for exceptions. However, two major preconditions have to be met in order to legitimize the restriction of the right. The exception has to be:

— prescribed by law and

— necessary in a democratic society.

"Prescribed by law" means that the restriction has to be an act of parliament and not an executive order by the government. Of particular importance is the qualification: "necessary in a democratic society". This links the freedom of expression and the media to the concept of an open and pluralist society which is governed by democratic means. The European Court of Human Rights has been very strict on these requirements as can be seen from the so-called Lingens case. In 1986, the European Court of Human Rights in Strasbourg decided that a politician has to accept a higher degree of criticism than an ordinary person and cannot silence a journalist with reference to the need to protect his reputation. Accordingly, the laws on libel, which allow persecuting journalists who criticize persons in public positions, have to be balanced with the freedom of the press.

Monitoring and Implementation

There is a large variety of instruments and procedures to implement the human right of freedom of expression and its component rights. First is the obligation of states to incorporate the freedoms in their domestic law and provide legal remedies in cases of alleged violation. Accordingly, the right can be found in most constitutions as part of the catalogue of fundamental rights and freedoms. The minimum standards derive from international obligations on the universal and, where existing, the regional level.

The various media and communication laws and regulations are very important, too. They further specify the right and its restrictions in daily practice in conformity with international obligations and national constitutional law. They may set up national monitoring bodies - such as press or media councils - to regulate in particular the media, which are often composed of experts and/or representatives of civil society. In order to regulate the media sector, to ensure quality standards and to stimulate competition, the state may issue licenses, which have to be made available on a non-discriminatory basis.

Monitoring compliance by the state is the task of several control or monitoring mechanisms. For example, under the UN Covenant on Civil and Political Rights (ICCPR), states have the obligation to submit state reports in regular intervals (every 5 years) on the implementation of their obligations, which are considered by the UN Committee on Civil and Political Rights. It gave an interpretation of Article 19 in its General Comment No. 10 of 1983. The Committee may also receive communications, i.e. complaints by individuals, if the respective state has ratified the First Optional Protocol to the ICCPR of 1966 (104 out of 149 states by end of 2002).

Regional monitoring mechanisms like the Inter-American and the African systems provide for individual communications to Commissions, which can issue conclusions and recommendations. In the case of the European and the Inter-American system, the Court may give decisions binding on states and also grant compensation. In addition, there is a "monitoring procedure of the Committee of Ministers", which, inter alia, also covers the freedom of expression and information in member states. All conventions also foresee the possibility of "state complaints", which are hardly ever used.

Besides the conventional procedures, there are also so-called charter-based procedures like the Special Rapporteur on the Promotion and Protection of the Freedom of Opinion and Expression, who reports to the UN Commission on Human Rights on the situation of the freedom of expression world wide and provides observations, recommendations and a commentary on elements of the human right. For the 55 members of the Organization of Security and Cooperation in Europe (OSCE), a Representative for the Freedom of the Media has been appointed in 1997. His mandate is to follow the developments in the media sector of the participating states in order to promote free, independent and pluralistic media, which are crucial to a free and open society and accountable system of government, based on the international obligations and the OSCE standards adopted in a series of follow up conferences and expert meetings since the Helsinki Final Act of 1975.

Professional Associations and other NGOs

Professional associations like the International Federation of Journalists, the International Press Institute (IPI), International P.E.N. or the International Publishers Associations (IPA) do have comprehensive information on the state of the freedom of the media in different countries or regions of the world and support their members against restrictions. They draw attention to situations where those freedoms are neglected, denounce restrictions, launch campaigns or urgent action appeals and prepare reports on particular problems like media concentration, state secrets and transparency according to Freedom of Information regulations, or corruption. In doing so, they are supported by NGOs specialized in the protection of the freedom of the press and the media like Article 19 or Reporters without Borders as well as general human rights NGOs like Amnesty International or the International Council on Human Rights Policy.

Furthermore, they cooperate with intergovernmental organizations and their special institutions like the UN Special Rapporteur on Freedom of Expression and the OSCE Representative for the Freedom of the Media. Institutional monitoring bodies or professional associations and NGOs almost always also aim at the prevention of violations of the human rights in question, excessive libel laws and practices, which may silence critical journalists.

Perspectives of Intercultural Issues

Cultural differences lead to pluralism in the implementation of the right. Compared to the USA, Europe and other states take a different attitude in the case of hate speech which attacks the dignity of a group. Europe does not tolerate the advocacy of national, racial or religious hatred, in particular Anti-Semitism, Nazi propaganda or the denial of the Holocaust, and other forms of right-wing extremism, whereas this is at least partly covered by the freedom of expression (First Amendment) in the United States constitution. The sometimes subtle distinctions can be seen from the ECHR case Jersild v Denmark, when the Court found that the punishment of a journalist, who had broadcasted an interview with young racists making racist statements, had been a violation of the freedom of information in Art. 10 ECHR, whereas those who had made the statements were not protected by Art. 10.

According to the "margin of appreciation-doctrine" of the European Court of Human Rights, also between European states there is room for differences. This is of particular relevance for the protection of moral with regard to speech, literature or broadcasting considered as pornographic. The question of decency or protection of minors, as well as other harmful content, is left to the state, which often uses independent bodies to guide the media in this respect. Different standards do also exist regarding public criticism of politicians or religious institutions. For example, what is artistic freedom for some may be considered as blasphemy by others. Consequently, the freedom of expression and of the media is a very sensitive right which has to respect certain limits but also has to be protected against the tendency of the state and influential persons to silence their critics.

In Asian countries severe restrictions of the freedom of expression and of the media have been long justified on the ground of maintaining the stability of the country which was threatened by the "irresponsible reporting" of the press instigating political conflict. However, as an ASEM seminar held in 2000, dealing with this topic in a Euro-Asian dialogue, found, governments tend to overreact and so curtail the freedom of the media more than necessary. Common problems like media concentration or the lack of independence of journalists were found much larger than regional differences. In cases of dispute, it is the responsibility of the independent judiciary to draw the fine line between freedom of expression and the media, and legitimate restrictions for the sake of the stability of a democratic state and the moral integrity of a person, which has become subject to unjustified allegations in the media.

For example, in Banja Luka in Bosnia and Herzegovina few years after the end of the civil war, a newspaper published lists of persons alleged to have committed war crimes. This was legitimately interdicted by the authorities because of the danger that these persons, who had not (yet) officially been indicted, could become subject to personal revenge. In the case of Constitutional Rights Project, Civil Liberties Organisation and Media Rights Agenda v. Nigeria, the African Commission on Human and Peoples' Rights had to deal with the proscription of newspapers by way of an executive decree by the military government of Nigeria, which was directed against the opposition. The Commission found:

> "Decrees like these pose a serious threat to the public of the right to receive information not in accordance with what the government would like the public to know. The right to receive information is important: Art. 9 (of the African Charter on Human and Peoples' Rights) does not seem to permit derogation, no matter what the subject of the information or opinions and no matter the political situation of a country. Therefore, the Commission finds that the proscription of the newspapers is a violation of Art. 9 (1).

With regard to measures against journalists after a coup in The Gambia the African Commission found:

> "The intimidation and arrest or detention of journalists for articles published and questions asked deprives not only the journalists of their right to freely express and disseminate their opinion, but also the public, of the right to information. This action is clearly a breach of the provision of Art. 9 of the Charter."

Media and Democratic Society

Media pluralism is an indispensable element of a pluralistic democracy. The importance of the rule of the media as a so-called "fourth power", besides the legislative, executive and judiciary powers requires also particular care and responsibility from journalists and media owners not to violate human rights of others by exercising their freedoms. The freedom of a particular society can easily be determined by the freedom of the press and the media. The first step authoritarian governments or dictatorships are usually taking is to curtail or abolish the freedom of expression and of the media.

For the reconstruction and rehabilitation of democratic societies after war and conflict, a pluralistic media system, which works on the basis of respect and tolerance of other opinions and refrains from instigation to hatred and violence, is of utmost importance. This requires an appropriate legal frame-work, which assures the independence of the public media and pluralism among the private ones, and monitors the activities of the media with regard to the standards of objectivity, fairness and decency.

Media and Minorities

Minorities often face problems in the access to the media and in having media in their own language. In Europe, specific binding standards based on Art. 19 ICCPR and Art. 10 ECHR exist, i.e. in Art. 9 of the European Framework Convention for the Protection of National Minorities of the Council of Europe of 1995. Accordingly, persons belonging to national minorities do also have the freedom of opinion and expression. Their freedom to seek, receive or impart information or ideas in minority languages regardless of frontiers must be respected by public authorities. Governments have to ensure that persons belonging to national minorities are not discriminated in their access to the media, which should rather be facilitated. They must not be prevented from creating their own print media and, within the law, also their own electronic media.

Further standards do exist in the framework of OSCE. The situation, however, is often more problematic regarding the so-called new minorities stemming from migration. In contrast to the national or "old" minorities, they usually do not have any legally granted rights ensuring their access to the media. This is especially worrying when taking into account the rather xenophobic way in which they are sometimes portrayed in conventional media, while their possibilities for counter-statements are limited. The European Charter for Regional and Minority Languages of the Council of Europe of 1992, in Art. 11 commits States Parties to make adequate provision that broadcasters offer programs in the regional or minority languages or to ensure, encourage and/or facilitate the creation of at least one radio station and one television channel in the regional or minority languages.

Freedom of economic development

Freedom of the media and economic development is as much linked as are freedom from fear and freedom from want. The interdependence and indivisibility of all human rights requiring a holistic approach to human rights in general can also be seen in the importance of the freedom of expression and the freedom of the media for economic development, poverty elevation and meeting basic social and economic rights of the people. Without the reporting by the media shortcomings in access to or redistribution of resources and corruption may remain unnoticed.

War Propaganda

According to Art. 20 (1) ICCPR any propa-ganda for war

shall be prohibited by law. Accordingly, the media were found to carry part of the responsibility for the wars in former Yugoslavia by propagating the war or instigating hatred and ethnic cleansing. The transmissions of Radio Mille Collines have been found to have had a major role in the violence in Rwanda in 1994, during which more than one million people were killed. "Do not kill those inyenzi (cock-roaches) with a bullet - cut them to pieces with a machete" was one of the broadcasted statements, calling Hutus to slaughter Tutsis and Hutus who were sympathetic to the Tutsi cause. The radio station itself was founded in 1993 by family members of Hutu President Habyarimana, whose death was one of the main reasons for the outbreak of the genocide.

Media and Human Rights Education

"Within journalism there is a serious lack of knowledge of what human rights are. Many journalists - like many politicians and others working in civil society - are not familiar with the Universal Declaration of Human Rights and the international human rights treaties and mechanisms. Often they do not understand the difference between human rights law and the laws of war. As a result, human rights are often erroneously regarded as relevant only to reporting of conflict."

The *International Publishers Association* (IPA), which represents 78 institutions in 65 countries, in its comments on the UN Decade on Human Rights Education, highlighted the importance of awareness-raising activities concerning freedom of expression and freedom to publish.

Media and Information Technology

According to the UN Human Development Report 2001, the

internet has grown exponentially during the last years, from 16 million users in 1995 to more than 400 millions in 2000. In 2005, more than 1 billion people will use the internet. This rising of the World Wide Web has had a significant impact on the media, offering a variety of new options to both journalists and publishers. Even smaller media enterprises have a chance to reach the global public now. State control and censorship can more easily be circumvented.

Media in Developing Countries

During the last thirty years, the print run of daily newspapers in developing countries has more than doubled; in 1996, 69 out of 1000 people had their own copy - compared to only 29 in 1970. Compared to developed countries, where the share of people reading a daily newspaper has slightly decreased from 292 out of 1000 in 1970 to 226 in 1996, this figure is still not entirely satisfying, but it remains remarkable. The increased accessibility creates a new and more efficient "market of ideas" on which a much broader variety of opinions and views is available. Information can be published and retrieved more easily, thus providing a stable basis for democratic structures and good governance.

4

Media Intervention

For most journalists, reporting on conflict is not a special situation governed by a unique set of rules. The situation is, in fact, quite the reverse: reporting on political, economic and other collisions of interests within a society is very much a part of the journalist's everyday routine. Conflicts are, after all, part of daily life in a democracy. Subsequently, the absence of reports in the media on conflicts would suggest that democracy itself has been lost. Ethnopolitical conflicts differ from other forms of political conflict in several crucial ways. The fundamental distinction is that the conflicting parties often resort to violence because they see this as the only means of resolving their grievances with other ethnic communities.

In recent years, Europe has experienced a significant number of ethnopolitical conflicts, especially following the disintegration of authoritarian regimes in Central and Eastern Europe. Evidently, however, nationalism by no means seems to be restricted to eastern or southeastern Europe. In western Europe as well, the media plays a significant part in whipping up nationalist feelings of xenophobia, racism or ethnic chauvinism. As immigration into Europe increases over the next few years, these ethnopolitical conflicts are likely to gain in significance.

Nationalistic tensions, coupled with the creation and expansion of supranational institutions such as the European Union (EU), which are designed to serve as a counterweight and means to reduce or even eliminate nationalism, will continue to play a central role in European politics and thereby also in the media.

Most research into nationalism takes as its starting point the notion that centralised communications, social mobility and increased levels of economic contact can help surmount cultural differences between factions of the population and thus foster a more homogenous culture. However, there are also indications that increased communication can in fact produce the opposite effect, at least in areas where several equally developed cultures exist side by side. This occurs because improved communications and transport reinforce a sense of being different in those who belong to minority groups. It is not surprising then that ethnic tensions and separatist demands are on the increase throughout the world.

In ethnically diverse communities, the media often serves to reinforce existing differences and thus accelerate a disintegrating effect on the homogeneity of the population. The key issue is, then, under which conditions, as Anthony Giddens suggests, do "negative spirals of communication" (mutual negative perceptions which degenerate into hate, feeding more hate) between ethnic communities develop and ultimately degenerate into violence?" Moreover, "Under which conditions can the media actively promote empathy, peace and political stability between differing community factions?"

Consensus Democracy and Constructive Journalism

Throughout human history, there have been several

commonly employed methods of resolving ethnic tensions and conflicts. Among these are

a) genocide,

b) enforced population exchange,

c) partition of the state (secession/self-determination) or

d) integration/ assimilation.

Ethnic strife is generally regulated through four principal methods:

a) hegemonistic control,

b) third-party mediation,

c) cantonisation or federalisation and

d) establishing models of power-sharing or consensus democracy ('concordance democracy').

In reality, as intra-state conflicts are played out, these approaches tend to appear simultaneously and in varying combinations. Genocide and enforced population exchange are disapproved of from a moral perspective and are rejected by the international community. Secession too is generally considered unacceptable. The federalist model usually proves to be fragile if the population of the country in question is ethnically heterogeneous. Even the proponents of a federalist Europe have become noticeably quieter in the face of resurgent nationalism.

The political Zeitgeist instead favours consensus democracy (power sharing between political subjects) as a means of transforming ethnic conflict. It should be remembered that what we are witnessing is an experiment. Never before has a lasting solution to fundamental ethnopolitical conflict been brought about through consensus (consociation) democracy. Throughout the history of the formation of the nations in Western Europe, force has always been what defined political realities. Moreover, even established modern democracies such as Britain, France or Spain have failed notably in their efforts to end nationalist conflicts in places such as Northern Ireland, Corsica and the Basque Region.

The architects of the consensus democracy model for the resolution of ethnopolitical conflicts begin from the assumption that the usual democratic safeguards are insufficient to prevent the abuse of power in multicultural or ethnically divided societies. The principle of majority rule always harbours the danger that minorities will be overruled or disadvantaged. For this reason, political institutions have been proposed to ensure that all sections of society have their requisite share of power. The guiding principle is the proper balancing of interests on all levels of the political system. The prerequisite for such a balance between ethnic groups in the state must be a corresponding compromise between the political elites that head the different ethnic groups. This must include a renunciation of violence such as the forced assimilation or persecution of weaker ethnic groups, as well as attempts at secession. The concept of consensus democracy in an ethnically heterogeneous state thus rests on the following four elements:

1. a grand coalition between the political elites of the various sections of the population;
2. a proportional representation system, with corresponding precautionary measures to ensure equal rights in important areas such as education, control of public expenditure, employment policy and public service broadcasting;

3. a right of veto for all those sharing power, enshrined in the constitution;
4. the guaranteed internal autonomy (self-determination) of all ethnic segments constituting the state.

Such a model of consensus democracy is admittedly idealistic, as it presupposes, on the part of the nationalistic centres of power, a conscious renunciation of the type of politics which seeks unilateral advantage. Therefore, consensus democracy must be viewed not so much as a state that can be realistically achieved in full, but rather as a goal or aspiration. One can concede, however, that even a mere process of conflict transformation which is based on such a model already incorporates a significant element of peaceful conflict transformation, to the extent that unilateral objectives and their achievement by pressure or force are ruled out from the outset.

In an ideal world, the media should at least attempt to orient its reporting style towards the creation of peace, instead of intensifying prejudices that in turn heighten conflict. Such ideal journalism is a critical part of the consensus democracy concept, and represents the proper role of the media in conflict prevention and resolution. Despite this, the media is often perceived as giving priority to negative aspects in its reporting of conflicts, with a suspicion that they do this consciously because it 'sells better'. Demands are often made upon the media to adopt a more constructive role in conflict prevention and experienced journalists are frequently accused of being innately sceptical. Nevertheless, it is too simplistic to expect the media as an entity to feel collectively obliged to actively promote the peace and development of civil societies.

Time and again, international state and non-state organisations, as well as other institutions, have issued statements expressing the view that the media could have an important role to play in constructively reporting about conflicts and combating the propaganda of hate. For example, in the closing declaration of the European Conference on Conflict Prevention, the EU was called upon to examine how they might support the reporting efforts of independent local media in societies prone to conflict. In addition, special education was proposed for local and European journalists working in conflict regions. Journalists would be urged to convince the general public and politicians in power of the need to invest in conflict prevention. It was further suggested that this could begin with emphasis being drawn to the considerable humanitarian and material costs of conflict management.

The International Federation of Journalists (IFJ) remains convinced that the media can not only help to defuse conflicts, but also that it is uniquely positioned to encourage coexistence and co-operation between people of different origins. In the course of a debate about the reporting of ethnic conflicts in Africa, this organisation also drafted detailed and practical recommendations for more balanced and objective media reporting on such events.

Neither is there any lack of sophisticated suggestions from other important players on the international stage as to the precise nature of positive or constructive journalism. Besides the classic five 'w's, (why, what, who, where, and when) which should be covered in news items, for instance, demands from the United States of America (USA) also call for an 's' (solutions) as well as a 'c' (common ground). There are high expectations placed upon the journalist's role. These include the proposition that journalists reporting on conflicts should be trained in the techniques of resolving conflict, and should always aim at acquiring an impeccable reputation as promoters of peace. They are asked to enlighten the public, and tell the stories of the victims of conflict, rather than reinforcing the point of view of the perpetrators of violence.

It has even been suggested that the media may well be the most powerful means available for the resolution of future conflicts or even for the prevention of wars. Furthermore, journalists are well supplied with well-intended proposals to help them realise these expectations. Johan Galtung for instance suggests that journalists should:

— illuminate the story in detail from all sides;

— be careful to draw from diverse sources;

— restrict overuse of elites as sources, but should make use of different experts;

— avoid glorifying the technology of war;

— also use dramatic imagery to portray the horrors of war;

— offer sensible and well-written reports about ordinary people;

— supply more background reports;

— be aware that news makers (spin doctors) are out to manipulate them;

— avoid treating their work itself as a story;

— give ample coverage to and promote peace initiatives.

Reviewing these recommendations for good journalism in crisis situations, it is easy to fall into the false assumption that all that is needed is to report clearly, without prejudice, and ask probing questions in such a way as to enlighten readers/listeners/viewers about the 'real problems'. It is further implied that their audiences will only then begin to understand the 'real costs' and reassess their views accordingly. In a similar vein, many commentators simply believe that the new and better information technologies, such as the Internet, will almost automatically generate more peaceful means of overcoming conflict.

The Internet includes many kinds of people, it is also much more subdivided by interest and identity groups that may or may not communicate with one another. It seems best at linking those who already have some interest in communication and not as effective at reaching the unconverted. But before we engage in a debate on how Internet and other new technologies might alter the ways in which conflicts and wars are perceived and opposed worldwide, we should first pose the question as to why humbler and simpler ideas have so far been unsuccessful. Any realistic evaluation of the degree to which the media can contribute to conflict prevention and resolution must be founded on an analysis of the general political, economic and social framework for media development in the country in question; only then can we hope to properly examine the specific opportunities for the individual members of that media.

Role of media

We can best assess the role of the media in the prevention and resolution of conflict and in the safeguarding of peace if we see that role as essentially a component and expression of overall social conditions. Any framework describing the most important influences on the media should therefore highlight four fundamental areas:

— *political context*: the rule of law versus despotic authority;

— *economic conditions*: the media as an autonomous economic organisation or one subject to governmental control (media as part of the state apparatus);

— *quality of journalism*: critical and analytic reporting or mere functioning as 'stenographers of power' using the 'language of hate';

— *public attitudes*: enlightened democratic traditions or authoritarian value systems.

Under this model the media is seen as a vector, the direction of which is determined by the influence of each of the four individual elements. A weakness in one factor can only be partially compensated for by the strength of another. In short, no element can exert its full weight if the others are lacking or flawed. This analytical framework allows for the exploration of the inter-relationships of the four elements under various scenarios. If, for example, journalistic training is seen as the best starting point to inculcate higher standards of reporting in the long term, it must be realised that any efforts in this direction will unfortunately remain unsuccessful, while authoritarian forms of rule do not allow for media autonomy or as long as economic necessity stymies any increase in media consumption.

On the other hand, media which has succumbed to the language of hate will find that their impact will be limited by the extent to which they are addressing an educated public raised in an enlightened, democratic tradition. Certainly, the evidence of established western democracies in times of economic prosperity supports this assumption. Moreover, in any state governed by the rule of law, media outputs that incite either ethnic hatred or illegal political action is usually dealt with in the courts. There is, however, also some evidence that the long-term effects of the language of hate can be highly deleterious even in established democratic societies, and that legal counter-measures undertaken to combat it can themselves cause controversy.

Different legal and political traditions also play a significant role here: whereas US courts will, in general, hesitate to impose limitations on the freedom of expression, most western European judges are notably apprehensive about Nazi propaganda or other similar remnants of an evil past. Certainly, the propaganda of hate, even in marginal media, is capable of achieving a profound effect on the public if, under conditions of economic crisis, the fears and aggressive inclinations of the target audience are on the rise. In such situations, authoritarian political elites can come dangerously close to the levers of power, thus undermining the legitimate rule of law.

The analytical framework presented here points out at least three particular situations which can emerge whenever the media is forced to operate under conditions of increasingly violent tension and conflict. These can arise before, during and after such situations, although, in real life, these transitions are fluid. If reports about tension and conflict are issued in a genuinely free and independent manner and presented in a fair and balanced way, they can indeed help to overcome conflict in that they will serve to educate the public, allowing their readers and listeners to form independent opinions. On the other hand, biased and manipulative reports can all too easily accelerate and intensify the crisis.

If the media is to be expected to function as a part of the consensus democracy approach to intra-state conflicts, other essential conditions and preconditions must also be fulfilled. These include: a clear commitment on the part of the political elites to resolve the conflict by peaceful means;

a willingness to respect the rule of law; economic stability; high levels of education and a democratic awareness on the part of the target audience. Again, any strengthening of one of these fundamental elements will only bring about the desired result if progress has been achieved in the other areas as well. The establishment of economically stable and a politically balanced media presupposes both an effective rule of law and a functioning market economy. Media that is well organised and functions democratically has a vested interest in ensuring that the public gains an insight into the workings of government and economic players. Only then, can it develop best practices and play a positive role in conflict transformation.

External efforts to transform conflicts

'Freedom of the media' versus 'control of the media'

There are certain conditions that contribute to the prevention of conflict. These can be summarised as: the rule of law, a tradition of tolerant and democratic political culture, and (financial) independence of the media. If in the course of conflict, it becomes clear that national justice is being perverted, international law provides some further measures that can be taken into consideration by international political committees. Nevertheless, there is not much evidence of effective measures undertaken to counter national authorities who fail to follow the media guidelines set out in internationally recognised documents such as those of the Council of Europe or of the Organisation for Security and Cooperation in Europe (OSCE), even though issues of this kind appear regularly on the agendas of international committees.

International agreements and authorities that can exercise political control serve as an important point for orientation. Thus ideal conditions, as set out in international agreements, can be invoked by democratic bodies in areas affected by conflict, as well as by the democratic media itself. Since the end of the Cold War, membership in the Council of Europe and observance of OSCE regulations have taken on a particular importance for former communist countries where there is believed to be a threat of intra-state conflict. For these countries, the incorporation of the political, legal and other principles of the Council of Europe is seen as an important prerequisite for subsequent entry into the EU, which is the most important means of integration into the European continent.

The post-communist elites in these countries thus derive much legitimacy from their various promises to take their countries into the EU as a 'zone of permanent peace'. Effectively, they can always be taken at their word by comparing, particularly in times of crisis, the actual situation in their countries with the rules and standards implied by the international legal and political obligations their countries have agreed to. A number of cases involving alleged infringement of press freedom in western European states have already been tried before the European Court of Human Rights. Most observers expect an increasing number of cases linked to intra-state conflicts to arise in other parts of Europe.

However, it can take many years for infringements to be properly addressed in the international courts. The international community, insofar as it seeks to emphasise its declared belief in the need for the timely prevention of conflict, must be constantly on the alert for problems affecting the media in crisis-ridden areas. The respect for freedom of speech and freedom of the press must become a primary component of international politics and not dealt with as something of secondary importance. A move in this direction was made at the end of 1997 with the appointment of Freimut Duve, a member of the German Social Democrat Party, as the first media ombudsman at the OSCE.

In 1993, in direct response to the experiences of the civil war in Yugoslavia, the Council of Europe organised a seminar in Strasbourg dealing with issues faced by the media in situations of conflict and tension. The Deputy Chairman of the European Court of Human Rights, Rudolf Bernhardt, took this opportunity to analyse existing legal safeguards for media autonomy in the context of the state in crisis situations, Article 10 of the Convention on Human Rights, in particular, protects freedom of speech and the press. It allows that "in the interests of national security, territorial integrity and public safety..." and other overriding interests, restrictions on this freedom are certainly possible. In fact, Article 15 states explicitly that in emergencies which "threaten the life of the nation", extensive restrictions to the freedoms guaranteed in Article 10 are permissible, as long as they are provided for under international law.

Bernhardt accentuated this crucial problem when he asked: "Where is the borderline to be drawn between media freedom and the permissible restrictions, especially in situations of conflict and tension?" And his answer was: "The extent of permissible intervention in the activities of the mass media is difficult to circumscribe". Thus, this senior judge held that advanced censorship is not permissible under any circumstances and that none of the available measures may be used without a legal basis. He added three further conditions that must be fulfilled before any restriction of media autonomy could be considered justified:

— Restrictions and interventions that are imposed by public authorities must serve the purposes laid down in Article 10 of the Convention on Human Rights, such as "protection of national security, territorial integrity or public order."

— All restrictive measures must meet the test of being 'necessary' in a democratic society. The appropriate national authorities shall decide whether they are necessary, but their conduct must be reasonable. Furthermore, all national conduct shall come under international scrutiny, and must therefore be verifiable by the European Court of Human Rights.

— No measures taken by the authorities, even in situations of tension and conflict, may be outside the control of independent courts.

Bernhardt pointed out in particular that Article 15, which relates to the empowerment of the authorities in public emergencies and states of war, permits even more extreme restrictions than Article 10 that is intended for use in normal times. He writes, resignedly, "It is extremely difficult, and even impossible, to demonstrate clearly and convincingly the powers of public authorities as well as the limits of any measures taken in such emergency situations". His conclusion follows the same vein: "Any measures taken in such exceptional situations which are not designed to restore order, peace and democracy fall outside the proper function of public authority".

On the occasion of International Press Freedom Day, the Council of Europe's Committee of Ministers issued a declaration and recommendations concerning the protection of journalists in situations of tension and conflict. These recommendations emphasised the importance of the role of journalists and the media in alerting the general public to infringements of national and international law and to human suffering in situations of conflict. In this way, they can help to prevent further infringements of human rights and human suffering. Principles for the physical protection of journalists and the guarantee of their rights and working conditions were also described in this document.

The recommendation was essentially an extension of Articles 10 and 15 of the Convention on Human Rights, augmented by a few practical tips stressing the need for adequate insurance cover for journalists reporting in war zones. National authorities were urged to make the work of journalists easier by removing restrictions on the use of telecommunications equipment and relaxing entry requirements. The recommendation also drew attention to the hotlines manned by the International Red Cross in Geneva and by other international organisations, to which journalists can turn for help whenever they feel their safety is threatened.

Activities of NGOs

It is only relatively recently that NGOs have come to the fore in the fight to protect freedom of speech and the rights of journalists. Within the political framework established during the Cold War, governmental organisations such as the OSCE or UNESCO always functioned as the arena (among others) in which issues of journalistic freedom were discussed. Since the end of the Cold War, however, a growing number of NGOs have become increasingly involved in this process as well. Among the best known of the organisations specialising in the field of media are: the International Federation of Journalists in Brussels, Reporters sans Frontières in Paris, the Committee to Protect Journalists in New York, the Glasnost Defence Foundation in Moscow, the International Press Institute in Vienna, Article 19 in London, the International Freedom of Expression Exchange in Toronto and many other NGO's and human rights groups.

All of these organisations collect and publish information about censorship and other forms of infringements on the freedom of expression and autonomy of journalists. Also acting as international pressure groups, they further demand that public authorities move to rectify such violations. Governments are, in general, sensitive to such exposure, as it tends to have a significant impact on their standing in the international community. Thus, criticism from international civil society, as personified by the NGO community, can sometimes produce highly adverse effects on uncivil governments, often making further external financial support conditional on demonstrated improvements to the country's human rights record, a record that must include respect for press freedom.

However, the debate surrounding legal and political protective measures designed to safeguard the freedom of the press and the safety of journalists in crisis situations has led most analysts to the disappointing conclusion that journalists and the media have only very limited direct means available in order to contribute significantly to the ending of conflict. As paradoxical as it may seem, the amount of media autonomy that can usually be achieved in violent situations is limited.

Nearly every intra-state conflict will attract the intervention of external powers. Whether it is through the will of major external powers acting alone or as a result of concerted action undertaken by the international community, the authorities of the country in question can almost always be induced to make concessions in the area of media autonomy in return for political, military and other forms of support. This was evident, for instance, in all parties' relative tolerance of pointed critical media attention in the course of the Yugoslav civil war. What remains unclear, however, is just how durable such media organisations can be, especially after international attention to their crisis region has dissipated.

Coercive information intervention

In the summer of 1997, the peace process in Bosnia had essentially ground to a halt. Diplomatic initiatives and threats of military action appeared to be having little effect on the situation, particularly on the actions of the extreme nationalist faction of the Bosnian Serb leadership. In fact, quite the opposite had occurred: the international peacekeeping troops were increasingly referred to as occupation forces in the television channels controlled by Serb nationalists. Thus images of NATO tanks were shown, interspersed with archive footage of Nazi occupation troops taken during the Second World War. Tension mounted.

Along with other Western politicians, the then German Foreign Minister Klaus Kinkel proposed that the international peacekeeping force should 'jam' such broadcasts in an effort to combat "one-sided, anti-Western, demonising reporting". Carl Levin, the Democratic Senator from the US state of Michigan pointed out the US military should make use of its capability to transmit radio and television programmes directly to the Bosnian-Serb population, using the EC-130E Commando Solo Aircraft, in order to suppress and drown out undesired propaganda. The US had already effectively employed similar methods in Grenada, Iraq and Haiti.

International peacekeeping troops in Bosnia moved to occupy important broadcasting centres, in a concerted effort to get some of the worst 'offenders' off the air. The wide reach of modern electronic media and the accelerated development of information technology have lent credence to the idea that it may indeed be possible to develop highly complex news systems. These systems would be aimed at eliminating or at least transforming conflict through a combination of political and military means. Such 'information intervention' was discussed at length in several issues of the influential US journal Foreign Affairs in 1997.

Since the major powers are evidently becoming ever less willing to fight on a massive military scale the infringement of human rights, the author proposes the creation of an independent UN Information Intervention Unit, specifically geared for intra-state conflicts. The proposal envisages three principle duties for such a unit: the monitoring of information provided in crisis-torn regions; the broadcasting of peace promotion material - peace broadcasting, - and in extreme cases, the jamming of radio and television broadcasts in order to halt the flow of hate and war propaganda.

Earlier, two former high-ranking members of President Clinton's administration had voiced the opinion in the same US-journal that information campaigns "to spread the truth" early on in the Rwanda conflict might well have alleviated the tragedy. They also asserted that US air strikes in the summer of 1995 on communications equipment of the Bosnian Serb army could have produced the additional advantage of impeding Bosnian Serb propaganda. Their arguments rested on consideration of the many opportunities for effective intervention available to the United States by virtue of its technological advantage in the fields of data processing and communications, as well as in satellite monitoring and the direct broadcasting of programmes. It was felt that these methods, combined with military force, could well help the US to resolve successfully regional ethnic conflicts and effectively to expand its role as a world power by the successful resolution of regional ethnic conflicts.

Certainly, hate propaganda can be suppressed in part, but it is highly doubtful that the 'delicate plant of democracy' can be transplanted by force. Even the long-term effect of proactive measures such as the beaming-in of broadcasts from external transmitters is open to question. As media communication is always an expression of national culture, external broadcasts of programmes in the language of the recipient country can never achieve the authenticity and credibility of home-grown media material.

While it is true that in situations in which armed conflicts have broken out and the internal authorities have imposed open or covert censorship on the media, information from whatever source gains in importance, this is usually only the case for a relatively short period. Besides this, as the history of external broadcasting shows only too clearly, even neutral information prepared abroad is viewed by most of its recipients as merely an expression of the political strategy of the country from which it comes.

In principle, the optimal conditions for rapid and irreversible change come about only in the aftermath of larger crises and violent conflicts, as was the case after the unconditional surrender of Germany after the Second World War, or with the demise of most of the former socialist countries of Europe after the collapse of the Soviet Union. Under such conditions, the great majority of the population becomes receptive to change and there is little opposition on the part of those formerly in power. But ethnopolitical intra-state conflicts, of the kind that have increasingly shaken Europe and the world in recent years, seldom end with a clear resolution - as the peace agreements in Bosnia and Chechnya have demonstrated all too clearly. It is far more likely that the crisis itself will create a lasting and determining influence on all aspects of life.

The media will thus remain a perpetual victim of conflict, as the authorities maintain political and economic control over them and intensify conflict as they aggravate societal prejudices through biased and manipulative reporting. The aim must be the safeguarding of peace by changing post-war society in such a way that future conflicts can be effectively resolved without resorting to violence. It seems clear that only concerted actions and initiatives on all fronts, involving politics, economy, media, society and, above all, education, can hope to have a lasting effect. Such actions are, unfortunately, rare.

It is, however, unfair to say that the West stood by passively while nationalist media reinforced conflicts in crisis areas. Many millions of Euros and US dollars have been invested in equipment, training and other forms of media aid. In addition, Western willingness to provide outside support for securing long-term peace is all too often overshadowed by other, for the most part geo-strategic and power political, considerations.

5

Environment and the Mass Media

CIVIC AND ENVIRONMENTAL JOURNALISM

Civic journalism, also known as public or community journalism, became one of the most heated controversies in the news business during the 1990s. It developed during the decade as a response to the perceived decline in the public interest in civic culture and public life. As scholar Lewis Friedland notes, "this erosion of confidence in our civic culture corrodes the very rationale for journalism in a democratic society. If there is no public to serve, and if journalism serves no public function, then it becomes reduced to one other media institution among others."

Civic journalism stipulates that journalists, instead of simply documenting and recording events, should actively seek to strengthen civic culture. Civic journalism is an approach to the daily business of the craft that calls on journalists to (1) address people as citizens, potential participants in public affairs, rather than victims or spectators; (2) help the political community act upon, rather than just learn about, its problems; (3) improve the climate of public discussion, rather than simply watch it deteriorate; and (4) help make public life go well, so that it earns its claim on our attention.

Newspapers across the country have experimented to varying degrees with "civic teams " of reporters and editors who actively engage community members to assess attitudes and address pressing concerns. Articles written in this manner focus on subjects like crime, youth, community development and revitalization, politics, and the environment.

Environment-focused writing has actually developed into a subset of the civic journalism movement. Building on the precedent of strong activist writers like John Muir and Annie Dillard, environmental journalism is, as journalist Michael Frome states: writing with a purpose, designed to present the public with sound, accurate data as the basis of informed participation in the process of decision making on environmental issues ...It is more than a way of reporting and writing, but a way of living, of looking at the world, and at oneself. It starts with a concept of social service, gives voice to struggle and demand, and comes across with honesty, credibility, and purpose. "

Important recent environmental journalism has focused on stories like drinking water contamination on Long Island, beach-building projects in Florida, a military reservation clean-up in Massachusetts, fertilizer-borne hazardous wastes in Washington, and mountaintop removal coal mining in Appalachia. The civic and environmental journalism movements have faced heavy criticism both inside and outside the news media. Critics argue that the movements cross the line between reporting and advocacy and undermine journalism 's already ebbing credibility in society.

Environmental Communication Campaign

The media, that collection of opportunities for communicating with the masses, carries tremendous power. In the United States, we have seen television episodes plant seeds of change in a nation's conscience when Maude chose to have an abortion or when Fonzie, a street-smart teenager, got a library card. The American public began to debate the merits of legal abortions and nearly one half million youths rushed to public libraries to get their cards. We have also seen televised political debates sway public opinion after leading contenders falter. And we have seen powerful advertisements sell cars, toothpaste, and peanut butter. It is no wonder that environmental communicators seek to harness this powerful force aimed at informing and changing public opinion.

In some cultures, people are bombarded with over 3, 000 advertising messages per day. Furthermore, environmental behaviour is often a series of complex actions and opportunities. Publicly broadcast communications reach the masses, but since the public usually holds a wide variety of beliefs and knowledge about any one environmental topic, it is difficult to reach the right group with relevant information.

Strategies of Communication Campagin

Communications campaigns are varied, multifaceted, highly planned, and strategically assembled media symphonies designed to increase awareness, inform, or change behaviour in target audiences. There are many forms of public media:

Paid and Public Service Advertisements: For instance, Green COM developed a series of six 30-second television and five radio spots on water conservation for Egyptian farmers. The spots were launched with a well-attended news conference where Ministry of Public Works and Water Resources staff expressed their pleasure with the campaign. At the same time, field engineers in the Ministry were given packets of information to support their discussions with farmers, and a press kit was distributed to reporters. Hats, posters, and a calendar for school children helped create a festive atmosphere that kept the serious subject of water conservation alive.

Making news: Many environmental organizations make effective use of "media events " to encourage news reporters to cover their stories. Greenpeace, for example, has climbed smokestacks to hang signs that draw attention to air pollution. Tired of bureaucratic delays, another group wrapped the Toronto City Hall with red tape and had reporters on hand when the first employees came to work. Less confrontational events might include a press conference, a special lecture, a government hearing, the first showing of an important documentary, or a major announcement of a scientific finding. By themselves, these events can begin to increase awareness. Launched in conjunction with brochures, programs, and other activities, they can be part of a campaign.

Entertainment and Celebrities: The entertainment industry offers highly effective opportunities. GreenCOM worked with a local television producer in the Philippines to adapt a series of daytime drama episodes where popular characters discussed issues. Many advocacy groups, from animal rights to ocean protection, use prominent actors as spokespersons for their causes in newspaper articles, paid advertising, entertainment, and public service announcements.

A communications campaign may involve a variety of these strategies, or only one. The design of a campaign depends upon the financial resources available to create, field test, and implement the campaign, the goal of the campaign, and to a certain extent, the existing awareness and controversy associated with the issue. Some of the many possibilities for communication channels are listed in Table 1).

Table 1. Sample Communication Channels

Media events	Media releases	Interview shows
Editorials	TV shows	Topical theater
Advertisements	Posters, signs, and banners	Radio soap operas
Flyers and brochures	Comic Books	Pencils
Public service announcements	Manuals	Hats

When a decision has been made to use a media campaign to advance an environmental cause, it may seem natural for those closest to the situation to define the main message of the campaign. "One less car, " or "Don 't litter " may come to mind. This is a temptation that must be overcome. Premature efforts to identify the message may lead to missing the needs of the audience. Experts on the issue often know little about the audience. It is crucial to know the audience -to know what they already know about the issue, what they associate it with, how they feel about it -in order to design an effective message.

In Egypt for example, officials of the Ministry of Public Works and Water Resource told GreenCOM that they know what messages would get farmers to conserve water. But in a pretest of only 40 people, 39 did not even understand the ministry's message -let alone find it persuasive. As with an educational effort or a training program, the development of a communications campaign should follow a basic process that involves carefully developing a realistic goal, assessing the audience, developing a strategy that uses appropriate media, and, finally, crafting a message that pretests successfully with the audience. All of these elements: the goal, the audience, the media, the strategy, and the message, interact with each other to create a successful campaign.

After the campaign is launched, it can be evaluated in several ways: by recording the exposure (number of ads in number of magazines with a circulation of so many people); by surveying people asking them to recall the message; and by observing changes in behaviour or the environment that could be attributed, in part, to the campaign. Communications campaign having four stages. In the first stage formative research helps define the goals and the target audiences, as well as the "media diets " of the audiences. In the second stage, the audiences ' the campaign strategy is developed, messages are developed and pretested. Third, the campaign is implemented. Finally, the results are evaluated and used to further refine the strategy.

Stage 1: Goal, Audience and Medium

In the first stage, formative research helps define which behaviours the campaign will attempt to change to achieve its broad goals. To select the most effective behaviours it is necessary to explore what people already know, believe, and care about. You must understand the difference between those who already perform the desired behaviour ("doers ")and those who do not ("non-doers "). Finally, formative research for a communications campaign should explore the media "diet " of our audience. . Are they literate? Do they listen to radio? If so, which station(s) and at what time(s)? Do they read any publications regularly? Do they have access to TV, Internet, or other media and do they use it regularly? This information, along with your budget, will help define the strategy and choice of media.

With the goal in mind and information about the "media diet " of the audience in hand, strategic decisions can be made about selecting markets, media, sequence, frequency, and times. These factors form the essence of the campaign. Critical information about funding and how to obtain access to a variety of media opportunities will be needed at this time. Is the effort blessed with a charismatic spokesperson? Is free radio time available? How many newspapers cover the target region and is it possible to advertise in them? Does the audience travel along a particular route frequently, making road signs an option? How often should the message be repeated to achieve your goal? Is it necessary for the campaign to generate more resources to enable you to achieve the goal?

Stage 2: Message

Finally, the main message of the campaign can be crafted, along with the design of all the media products -comic books, posters, story booklets, radio spots, billboards, etc. A team of creative people should work with the content experts and rely upon the results of the formative research for guidance. The process often requires several revisions before everyone on the team is pleased with the type of illustrations, the flow of the storyline, the wording, the gender implications of the message, and the ultimate action.

The experts are, of course, not the audience, so every element of the campaign should be pretested with the intended audience. This can be done through focus groups, interviews, classrooms, meetings, and other existing networks. But pretesting must be done. There are many examples of media products that were distributed broadly before the organizers realized they were not communicating the desired message. For example, Chevrolet neglected to pretest the name of its compact car in Latin America, only to learn after public embarrassment that Nova, or "no va " means "no go " in Spanish. . Translation errors are frequent, even for major advertising firms. Make sure local people, not just experts, are in the pretest audience. Pretesting is one of the most important ways to prevent spending money and effort in the wrong direction.

Stage 3: Implementing the Campaign

Implementing a campaign is never easy, but if stages one and two have been done well, implementation should go smoothly.

Stage 4: Monitoring and Evaluation

Evaluation should begin during implementation and be used to make mid-course corrections.

Theoretical Models of Campaign Strategies

For centuries, educators have assumed that if they provide students with information, that information will lead to new attitudes. They have also assumed that these new attitudes will then lead to new behaviour (see Figure 1). However, 20th century research shows, what many parents already knew -that the linkages between information and attitudes and, even more importantly, between attitudes and behaviour are not strong. This age-old educator's model is not really very effective at changing behaviours. The biggest gap in human nature is between what we know and what we do!

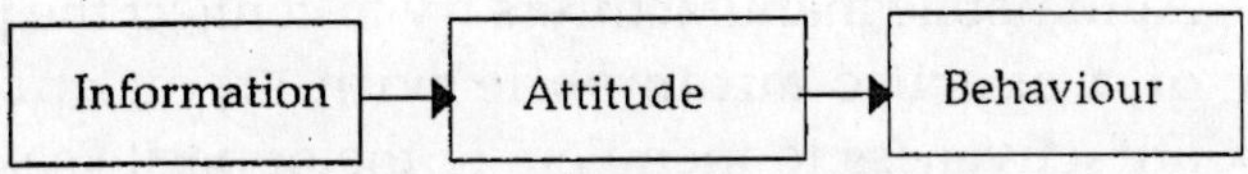

Figure 1. Educator's Model

When the advertising industry was born in the early 1900s, if found the educator 's model useless in selling products, especially in getting consumers to select their product over similar products. They created a different, effective model that spawned a multi-billion dollar industry (see Figure 2).

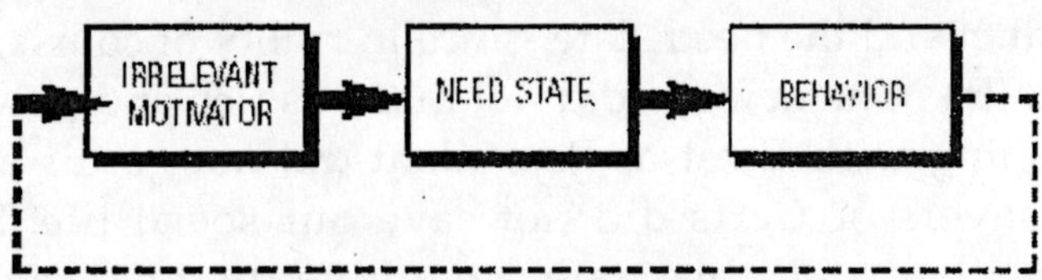

Figure 2. Advertiser's Model

The advertiser 's model clearly works. However it contains an element that can be unappealing to environmental communicators. Ads usually start with an "attention grabber " that we may think of as an "irrelevant motivator. " (The advertising industry does not use this term.)An irrelevant motivator is something that motivates the consumer to buy the product, but it is not related to the product. This motivator is connected to a "need state " of the potential customer. Some universal human need states are for status, sexual attractiveness, or being a good parent. The advertiser suggests that buying this product (changing your behaviour) will fill this need. The examples below demonstrate this model:

— Automobile manufacturers try to connect the purchase of a specific automobile with status, power, or attractiveness to members of the opposite sex.

— Toothpaste manufacturers and/breath mint makers suggest that the person of our dreams will suddenly show interest in us if we use their product.

— Cigarette producers try to convince us that their brand will make us "cool, " manly, and worldly.

As powerful as these appeals to human needs states are, a single exposure to an advertisement rarely has much impact on the consumer. Even after they buy the product, consumers may begin to question the link between the product and the need state -since in reality of course, there is no link. The new car did not make us rich and powerful. Brushing with Crest or Pepsodent did not get us a date. Lifesavers or Certs did not save our social life. Social researchers call this state "cognitive dissonance. " The consumer is performing a behaviour (buying Crest)for a reason that he/she intellectually knows to be untrue (It will help me get a date). This is an uncomfortable state that most humans will seek to resolve so that their actions are in line with their beliefs and knowledge.

One way to resolve the situation is to keep listening to the original message for reassurance that you are doing the right thing. Thus advertisers typically repeat their message endlessly not only to attract new customers, but also to reassure current customers. This repetition creates a direct relationship in our minds between the product and the fulfillment of our needs. In fact most advertising is aimed at customers who have already made the decision to buy the product and is intended to reinforce that decision.

An Environmental Communications Model

Dr. Peter Sandman, a noted environmental communicator, developed a third model in the 1970s that combines the educational and advertising models (see Figure 3). Sandman 's model follows the advertiser 's model except that almost all environmental messages can use a relevant motivator that addresses a need state to get people to perform an initial small behaviour. Performing this behaviour still induces some cognitive dissonance, as it does in the advertising model. For example , those of us who have circulated petitions know that it is better to ask people to sign quickly and then listen to the good reasons for supporting the cause. Once someone signs his or her name to a statement, he/she starts to question "Should I have done this? How will my name be used? Who is really behind this?

Did I read it carefully enough? " Another example: children often nag their parents into doing something -such as recycling -that they learned about at school. At first the parent responds to please the child, but later will ask "Why am I really doing this? Is it really worthwhile? "

Here the Sandman model departs from the advertiser 's model. Environmental communicators have something that most advertisers don 't -good reasons to continue the behaviour that can replace the initial irrelevant reasons. Rather than endlessly repeating the motivational message, environmental communicators can now switch to the real

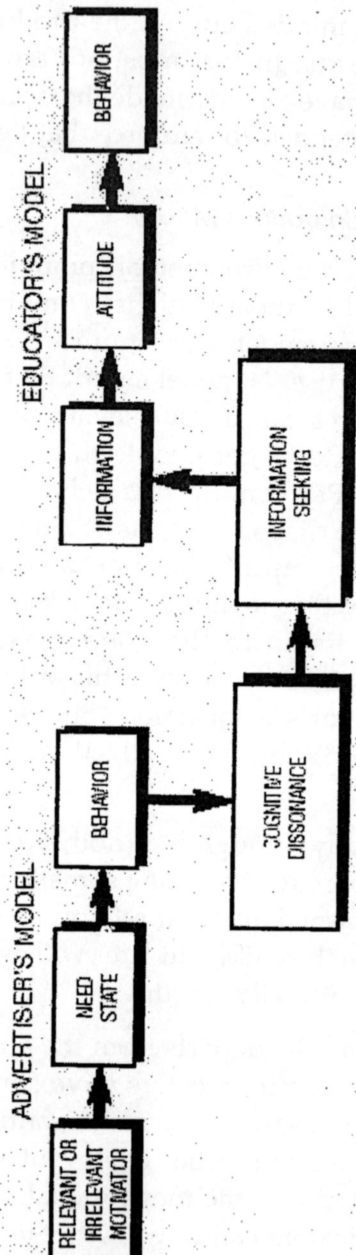

Figure 3. Sandman's Model

reasons for the behaviour by providing information. Why not just provide the information in the first place? Because the audience wasn 't interested in it then. Now they are. They are interested in finding information that will support their new behaviour.

In fact, they are seeking it in order to resolve the uncomfortable cognitive dissonance they feel at performing a behaviour for a not-very-good reason. Sandman cites research done at the Ann Arbor, Michigan recycling station (in the days before curb-side recycling) to explain how this works. Recyclers had to separate their trash and then drop the recyclables off at a recycling station in town -a considerable investment of time. At the station, Recyclers were interviewed about what made them come and how much they knew about recycling. New Rescuers didn 't know much and were there for basically irrelevant reasons (e. g. , their child nagged them to do it, they wanted neighbours to think well of them in this progressive community, they wanted to meet people like themselves).

Long-term Recyclers however, could tell interviewers how many trees were saved by a month 's worth of newspapers and how much energy was conserved by recycling glass bottles. They had replaced the irrelevant motivators with relevant reasons to continue the behaviour. The Recyclers who did not make this transition to finding good reasons, stopped recycling. The original motivator was not enough to sustain the behaviour of recycling. Thus information, delivered at the correct time and in a targeted manner, is crucial to maintaining environmentally friendly behaviours.

The best place for Recyclers to get this information would be at the recycling station itself. This research suggests that creating and maintaining recycling behaviour requires two messages to two audiences. The first message contains an irrelevant motivator (or partially relevant) and is aimed at the Ann Arbor population. It might be something like "You meet the nicest people at the Ann Arbor Recycling Station " or show a child reminding a parent, "But Mom, You could recycle that!" The goal of the message is to get people to the recycling station once. The second message is designed to reinforce the behaviour of people who have made the trip to the recycling station. It contains the reasons why they are doing a good thing and builds on the behavioral commitment.

A national recycling campaign in the United States used Sandman 's model. First, it encouraged people to call a toll-free number. The initial advertisements ended with the tagline, "If you are not recycling, you are throwing it all away, " and an image of a crumpled Earth tossed into a waste bin. The message appeals to Americans ' positive attitudes toward the environment and their ethic about not wasting things. The 200, 000 people who called received additional information about why recycling was important, where they could take recyclable materials, how to package them, and how to a start recycling program by finding local markets. The campaign didn 't spend its own resources putting this detailed information out to people who weren't paying attention. The first ad got their attention (based on an emotional motivator) and convinced them to take a simple action. As a result of that action they were given factual information that would support a longer-term behaviour change.

Positive attitudes support long-term behaviour (see Figure 1). Information alone is not enough to support behaviour, but information can lead to a change in attitude that can lead to behaviour -just as educators have told us it would. But, without a motivator and an initial action to create cognitive dissonance and start the information seeking process, there is nothing to trigger the uptake of the information. By combining the models of advertisers and educators, environmental communicators can have a bigger impact.

CHALLENGES OF ENVIRONMENTAL ENFORCEMENT

The communication media as it is known worldwide has undergone something close to a revolution in Africa, and indeed in Nigeria. The present state of journalism, especially print journalism which began about a century ago, shows that standards have improved from what it used to be, particularly in the areas of infrastructure, equipment, and personnel. However, perhaps because of the general poverty of the continent, an unconducive working environment still pervades the industry. Operatives lack tools and equipment as well as job security and opportunities for training. They are, however, expected to produce several editions of national newspapers in a country with a diverse population in location, language, taste, and interest and with a very erratic communication system. Besides, the print media exhibits a retinue of private investors whose interest vary from profit motive to the gains of political propaganda.

The government which had held the sole rights to the broadcast media only recently granted licences to the private sector under the private broadcasting scheme through the National Broadcasting Commission (NBC). The private broadcast stations, however, have yet to commence operation. However, the prevailing highhandedness of government is the most worrisome fear hanging over the media in Nigeria. The official control of the media, through various restrictive press-curbing legislations, some as ridiculous as stating punishments for publications which may embarrass government officials, put journalists in a position where they are extremely self-censored. There are others called security Acts which allow detention without trials. Public officers and organizations also engender repressiveness and intolerance.

Hence, ministers or heads of government parastatals and, of course, operatives in the private sector seek coalitions with sycophants. You therefore find a cowed journalism unable to question authority. Under these precarious circumstances the Nigerian media has striven to establish itself as one of the most free and vibrant in Africa. The public has also come to recognize the important role and power of the media in the sustenance of civil society, especially for its recent role in promoting democratic norms. Certainly the fate of the media is changing for the better, towards greater liberalization of media policies and empowerment of communicators.

Unlike the dominance of ill-trained job seekers who, in times past, chose the profession as a last resort, journalism is now marked by specialization and clear-cut division of labour, with a profusion of university trained staff. More journalists are now assigned to special beats, perhaps in response to the increasing competition for the market: advertisement and sales share. Currently, the Nigerian mass media has developed such specialized beats as Health, Science, Business and Economy, Tourism, Transport and Aviation, Education, Appointments and Vacancy, Women, Children, and Property.

The Guardian, has catalyzed the development of these specialized units. Its Property Desk, which started as a focus on the real estate industry, soon took over in more detail issues of the environment, architecture, building contracts, materials, housing, and physical planning in 1991. The discovery in June 1988 of a toxic waste dump in the port town of Koko stimulated greater attention and focus on environmental issues within the specialized science beats in both the broadcast and print media. A few periodic magazines also took their root in the toxic waste episode. Preparations for the 1992 United Nations Conference on Environment and Development (UNCED) further fueled the momentum generated. The specific challenges of the media in environmental enforcement are best highlighted by two case studies of national experiences.

Constraints of Media Enforcement

From the foregoing, several factors can be identified as constraints on media in enforcement and compliance monitoring. These are:

— Tendency for authorities, leaders of communities, and or journalist to connive with polluting bodies and therefore conceal information.

— Private sector influence over the media through law suits and advertisement control.

— Repression of the media by legislation and various forms of censorship, which limits or excludes the possibility of uncovering controversial issues.

— Absence of the right status for journalists to endear themselves to sources of information, and restrictive policies of government and industry on press interviews.

— Lack of proper training for specialized journalists in the language of the environment (technicalities and terms), leading to errors which further alienate the few available sources from disclosing information.

— Traditional attitudes and culture of researchers and scientists, which restrict them from granting press interviews for fear of their research findings being misquoted or misrepresented.

— The media's tendency to satisfy its commercial interest at the expense of social and scientific interest.

— Over-sensationalisation of certain issues leading to distortion.

— Inaccuracy in reporting by way of estimation, accessments, or statements which distort facts and lead to loss of credibility.

— The problem of editing to optimize space, and the urgency to meet deadlines which sometimes reduces the media houses' ability to sustain public interest and spur the community to action. This also arises from the media's oversimplification of complex and important issues.

— The absence of a national language which can coalesce the over 490 languages and dialects and ensure the transference of indigenous values and value systems. However, the various strengths of the media still present it as the first platform in the movement from public disclosure to public accountability. These strengths include:

— Its ability to reach more persons at less cost and to reach out to diverse persons and interest groups at a time.

— Due to its diversity of coverage, even persons who would normally not patronize environmental information are exposed to it in their search for other kinds of information.

— Where properly written and illustrated, media information is easier to read and comprehend when compared with scientific and technical documents.

— The speed at which the media reaches its audience and its ability to overcome barriers of culture and language, especially through pictorial illustrations which also give it strength over other communication medium.

— Its ability to create an "enforcement presence" and an atmosphere of deterrence due to polluters, especially industries, fear of the stigma of bad publicity.

Environmental Journalism: Case Studies of China, Taiwan and Hong Kong

The Beas River Jockey Club, nestled in the bucolic green hills of the New Territories, is just a stone's throw from the border with Mainland China. Dewy bouga-invillea blossoms glistened in the April sun when some twenty environmental reporters from Mainland China, Taiwan, and Hong Kong gathered here for a two-day conference. For Fang Sanwen, who just returned from a month-long reporting trip on the 3,000-kilometer path of sandstorms from Inner Mongolia to Beijing, the lush green world around him was almost unreal. His story on the villages deprived of water, crops, and hope by the encroaching desert spreads across three full pages of the Guangzhou-based South Weekly.

Environmental journalism has flourished in China over the past decade. Hundreds of reporters produced thousands of news stories and television documentaries covering subjects from the looming shortage of water resources to the endangered species in the wilderness. In Hong Kong and Taiwan, environmental reporting also has come a long way. Working closely with non-governmental organizations (NGOs), environmental reporters have helped forge not only an environmental consciousness, but also a political activism that pressures the Hong Kong and Taiwanese governments for change. Together, they share a professional commitment to reporting environmental degradation and raising public awareness of the endangered ecological resources. But different political systems, various stages of economic development, and editorial priorities have created a wide divide among Mainland Chinese, Taiwanese, and Hong Kong environmental reporters.

Mainland China: Environmental Propaganda

The abundant crop of environmental stories in China has not come about spontaneously. After the Chinese government became a signatory of the Agenda 21 and the Rio Declaration on Environment and Development at the 1992 Earth Summit (United Nations Conference on Environment and Development), China's National People's Congress (NPC) launched a massive publicity campaign to raise environmental awareness. The Environmental Resources Protection Committee of the NPC set up a special taskforce for organizing and implementing environmental news coverage. For each of the following eight years, the taskforce drafted plans, assigned topics, planned reporting trips, and made time-tables for the release of the feature stories.

In short, the taskforce created a top-down structure, working with exemplary efficiency in mobilizing the news media to raise the environmental consciousness in China.

This political approval actually has given journalists greater freedom and opportunities to write on environmental topics. Over the past eight years, some 13,000 reporters from all news media organizations in China have produced an astounding 104,000 pieces of work, according to a study by the International Media Studies program at Tsinghua University. Environmental reporters from Mainland China at the conference stated they enjoy more freedom in pursuing their stories than other beat reporters. With the blessing from Beijing, they are able to obtain cooperation from local authorities in doing their investigative work on certain issues.

China has come a long way in recognizing the legitimacy of environmental concerns. Hu Kanping, editor of China Green Times, the second largest environmental newspaper in China with a circulation of 100,000, recalls when his paper was launched in 1985, the unclear mandate was to "clean the environment and cleanse the spiritual pollution." At that time, the officials had very vague ideas of what the environment meant and what needed protection. With the deepening of China's economic reforms, many officials travelling abroad have found that industrialized countries openly acknowledge the existence of environmental problems. In fact, the more developed the economy, the more environmentally conscious people become, which removes much of the stigma from facing up to the environmental problems.

Environmental subjects also turn out to be very popular with readers, listeners, and viewers, which in turn draw talented and enterprising young journalists into the field. Sun Yanjun, a young broadcaster at Tianjin People's Radio, has breathed life into otherwise boring programming by creating imaginative segments that promote greater appreciation of nature and awareness of environmental problems, such as "Environmental Guardian," "Walk about Global Village," "Green Alarm Bell," and "Green Jeopardy Games."

Fang Sanwen said his publication South Weekly (a popular weekly with a national readership of 200,000) was particularly suited for long features on environmental investigative work. With the support of his editor, Fang, another reporter, and a photographer rode an old jeep along the trail of sandstorms from the Alashan League in Inner Mongolia to the hills on the outskirts of Beijing. "We tried to tell the story behind the oft-repeated statistics: The number of sandstorms rose from five in the 1950s to 23 in the 1990s. The year 2000 alone saw 12 sandstorms, and in the first three months of this year, six have already been reported." Fang continued to explain that "behind the environmental degradation and economic losses is a whole series of problems affecting the society.

The deterioration of meat, wool, and hide quality will force the pastoralists and ranchers to abandon their traditional livelihood and migrate to the cities. This impact on their culture is hard to imagine." The resulting report took the form of a diary, along with sidebars explaining scientific facts and policy debates. Zhang Kejia runs her green page at the China Youth Daily every Wednesday. Her green page acts as a forum for the public to debate on environmental issues. She also has broadened the participation through Web site discussions.

Wang Yongchen, an award-winning veteran broadcaster at China Central Radio in Beijing, commented that environmental reporters are fired by a sense that they feel they can make a difference. The environmental journalists in Mainland China are not just the medium through which most people come to understand environmental issues, these journalists also make things happen and correct what goes wrong. Wang Yongchen captured this spirit in her statement that "in the absence of enforcement of environmental protection, we journalists become guardians to the environment." Once while reporting on the ecological strains brought by population pressure and industrialization along the Yangtze River, Wang described in her radio program how the cruise ships threw plastic food containers into the waterway turning the 5,500-kilometer river into a giant public sewer. Within days of the broadcast, local officials were galvanized to action in the face of public outcry and the littering stopped. The result was a slightly cleaner river.

Similar positive actions resulting from Mainland reporters' exposés to protect the environment and save the endangered species abound. Television reports on the golden snub-nosed monkey and the Tibetan antelope all led to government intervention to protect the animals' habitats. Those are happy stories that received wide international publicity, but such reporting makes up only a small part of the environmental reporting in China. Most of the stories deal with water resources, forestry, and agriculture. Generally, stories praising the efforts by governmental agencies and enterprises to clean up the environment outnumber criticisms.

Mainland reporters also avoid politically sensitive topics. Not surprisingly the Three Gorges Dam is off-limits. "We support the government on major issues and direct our criticisms on minor issues," stated a Mainland reporter at the conference. Editors are unlikely to back their reporters in confronting officials. Moreover, for contentious stories it is difficult for reporters to get cooperation from local sources. In one of the conference sessions, an NGO representative showed pictures of a gigantic log on a flat bed truck with signs advertising logging opportunities in Tibet.

Notably, although China's State Council has promulgated decrees banning logging nationwide, the Mainland Chinese reporters stated candidly that they would not report this story because it takes place in the Tibetan Autonomous Region where the enforcement of the bans is much less rigorous than in other parts of China. The rights and interests of ethnic minorities are so complex in China that environmental reporters do not feel that they are up to the task to take on these national issues.

Relationship Between Environmental Journalists and Green NGOs in China

Chinese environmental journalists and activists are both "green." While they operate in different professional spheres they share feelings of social responsibility to fight against environmental degradation by unifying a variety of social forces. This common concern for the environment has created a solid basis for cooperation between journalists and environmental activists in China. However, because environmental journalists and green nongovernmental organizations (NGOs) ultimately play different roles in society, their methods, channels, goals, and range of influence differ. Therefore, Chinese environmental journalists and activists work both independently and together. Their similarities and differences can be expressed in the analogy that they are a harmonizing string quartet rather than ballet dancers moving with identical steps.

Reciprocity is the bond that ties environmental journalists and NGOs. A journalist and editor for an environmental newspaper, have been exploring successful ways to enhance social impacts of the news media by cooperating with both domestic and international NGOs for many years. For example, with the help of the International Fund for Animal Welfare, we at the China Green Times sent free subscriptions of environmental newspapers to biology and geography middle school teachers and teaching teams in Beijing. The Japanese NGO OISCA and my newspaper staff planted trees to create the Sino-Japanese Youth Green Memorial Forest.

Some on the newspaper staff also have worked together with the Beijing-based NGO Friends of Nature to develop the "Return the Birds to the Blue Sky" campaign, which opposes the caging of wild birds. The China Green Times also partnered with the China Wildlife Protection Association to create National Student Green Reporting Teams, which provide middle and elementary school students with opportunities to learn about journalism and wild animals. Through these activities, the China Green Times journalists not only attracted more readers throughout China, but also were able to identify new and relevant environmental problems to target in future reporting.

The increased recognition and new areas of reporting improved our newspaper's reputation. Notably, the green NGOs, with whom we worked closely, also benefited in that they obtained their goals using fewer resources and energy. Despite the different strategies, appropriate cooperation between environmental journalists and green NGOs empowers both in their efforts to raise environmental awareness among the public. Environmental news media organizations and NGO cooperation unifies their unique strengths. These two professional groups can support each other through exchanging information and human resources, as well as sharing insights on public opinion and environmental ideology.

In today's China, environmental NGOs are both the main organizing body and driving force in the civic environmental movement. The growing number of diverse NGOs are acting as the explorers and promoters of environmental ethics and values, as well as playing the role of information clearinghouses and idea generators for environmental issues. Therefore, green NGOs are irreplaceable sources of information and support for the environmental news media. Besides obtaining valuable news clues and analytical articles from environmental NGO activists, our editors and journalists often consult with them on questions of environmental politics and culture, as well as issues of green consumption, green products, green labelling, and green architecture.

All news media organizations in China (including those with an environmental focus) function to some extent as the voice of the government. Dramatically different from its counterparts in western countries, the Chinese news media is often depicted as the ears, eyes, and tongue of the government, with the news partially coloured and censored to fit the official line. However, in light of the intertwined relationship between the news media and government, environmental journalists may help build a bridge to link green NGOs with the government and other sectors of the society. Such linkages can help green NGOs develop their reputation, and facilitate their activities. One particularly striking "Chinese characteristic" of China's environmental sector is that there are many "ambidextrous" environmental advocators-in other words many "greenies" are both environmental journalists and NGO activists.

Most of the members in Chinese NGOs are volunteers devoting their free time. Clearly, the journalists who choose to actively participate in NGO activities are motivated to serve the public and not to make personal gain. Moreover, a mature journalist active as a volunteer in an NGO will not give up his or her independent judgment in reporting. In fact, it is not uncommon that journalists raise sharp criticism towards the NGOs to which they belong. Journalists are more often common members as opposed to leaders in the NGOs.

Today, environmental journalism is in its nascent stage in comparison to the broader news media in China. Similarly, green NGOs are a relatively new kind of social organization. Chinese environmental journalists and activists support each other, both struggling as their organizations steadily grow. While they stand on different soil, they are bathed in the same sunlight.

Taiwan: No Holds Barred, Seeking Hot-Button Issues

Taiwanese reporters take pride in their role of building the environmental consciousness as well as forging the democratic movement on the island. The political pressure and censorship in Mainland China cause reporters from Taiwan to cluck their tongues. In today's Taiwan, political pressure towards the news media would make reporters even more rebellious towards the Taiwanese government. Working with local environmental NGOs, Taiwanese journalists have mobilized the public to pressure the government to enact laws to protect endangered species, to enforce logging bans, and to push for environmental justice affecting economically disadvantaged groups.

Lin Ju Sen, a senior reporter at the United Daily News, distributed his article clippings collected over ten years to showcase the range of his environmental reporting. For two years, he followed the trafficking of rhinoceros horns-used as an ingredient for traditional Chinese medicine-and filed stories with datelines from many countries. He also reported on the returning of orangutans, which were smuggled into Taiwan as pets, to their home in Southeast Asian jungles. Chiu Yu-tzu, a reporter with the English language Taipei Times stated that environmental reporters have carte blanche in choosing their stories in Taiwan. She commented that "there are no taboos and no politically sensitive topics for us." She has written many conservation stories, ranging from black-faced spoonbills to Formosan rock macaques to preserving Chinese cypress forests in Chilan Mountain in central Taiwan.

Taiwanese reporters commented that in the past the news media cast the Nationalist (KMT) government officials as the "bad guys" on environmental issues while the opposition Democratic Progressive Party (DPP) used to play the role of environmental champions. As the DPP moved into power in the year 2000, the environmental movement has lost a clear-cut focus of the heroes versus villains. The building of the fourth nuclear reactor on the island was a hotly debated subject during the 2000 presidential campaign, which swept the DPP's candidate Chen Shui-bian to power. But much of the debate was overshadowed by corruption charges against the ruling Nationalist Party and ironically, the environmental reporting on the nuclear power plant took a back seat.

Facing a Half-Transformed Society

As the Taiwanese political system has increasingly democratized, the public in Taiwan has witnessed a growing diversity in news media organizations. The increase in privately run cable networks and the explosion in the use of the Internet have fundamentally changed the previous practice of the news media being the propaganda tool of the government. The growth in the number of media corporations and Web-based news outlets has broadened the kinds of news coverage in Taiwan , which has allowed a greater diversity of voices to be heard and opened up reporting on previously ignored issues. This expansion in freedom for the news media has enabled many journalists to seek out the previously unheard or weaker voices in the society, which explains why today there is considerably more coverage of environmental campaigns and activities in Taiwanese newspapers than ever before. Before the ending of martial law in 1987, the government limited news media reporting on protests against nuclear power plants and polluting factories.

Over the past two decades as Taiwan's political system has opened up, many newspapers have begun to report and print editorials voicing the concerns of environmentalists and the stories of pollution victims. While the news media organizations in Taiwan have begun to pay more attention to environmental issues, such reporting is not perfect. In an attempt balance the coverage and make up for the long-term neglect of environmental organizations, more journalists now try to report on environmental problems and activism. Despite their willingness to research and report on environmental issues, Taiwanese journalists today still are constrained in their environmental reporting. Today's obstacles stem not from political bans, rather from economic motivation of the news media industry.

Ultimately, news media organizations wish to publish only those opinions acceptable to the newspaper's financial backers and the mainstream political line. In short, the organizations and advertisers that back a news media company ultimately set the tone of the news reported. Not surprisingly, many of the demands that environmental groups make vis-à-vis the business community and the government in Taiwan often conflict with the profit motivation of the news media industry. In light of this pressure to tow the newspaper's line, journalists may not fully report the real opinions or main concerns of environmental NGOs. In addition, environmental reporting is sometimes incomplete because journalists may lack the scientific expertise to understand the environmental issues being debated. Taiwanese journalists reporting on the environment also need to be careful about being biased in their reporting or too shallow in their coverage.

Standing at the dividing line between pollution and a clean environment, with the cross of professional ethics on their back, Taiwanese environmental journalists face a semi-transformed society. Freed from the clasp of authoritarian control, the news media in Taiwan is now confronted with the temptations and challenges of a free market. Clearly, with the new pressures from the corporate (rather than the governmental) powers it is a constant challenge to ensure accurate representation-and interpretation-of environmental news in Taiwan.

Hong Kong: Environment as Local Health and Lifestyle Issues

For years, air pollution has been a staple subject for Hong Kong environmental reporters. The urban canyon of tall buildings traps emissions from vehicles and creates smog that poses health risks. Hong Kong environmental reporters have found it difficult to sustain reader interest in this chronic pollution problem. However, an event last year greatly energized environmental reporting. In October 2000, a coalition of green groups successfully challenged a HK$7 billion (U.S.$900 million) plan to build a rail spur in the New Territories that would cut through a wetland habitat for rare birds. The debate on protecting the wetlands, energetic anti-rail demonstrations, and the final defeat of the proposed project gave environmental reporters an exciting story to report. Some of the campaign stories even appeared on the front page of the newspapers.

Hong Kong environmental reporters also have covered controversies over the building of a refuse treatment plant on Peng Chau Island and the creation of a Disney theme park on Lantau Island, both of these projects will adversely impact the coral reef. Ironically, after the NGOs scored the wetland victory, many Hong Kong legislators have become more cautious on environmental issues. Because Hong Kong's economic growth is slowing and unemployment rising, legislators tend to avoid words and actions that could be perceived as anti-development by their constituents commented Olga Wong, a reporter at the Ming Pao newspaper. Rising public attention on the potential health impacts from consuming genetically modified foods challenges environmental reporters to educate themselves in order to present a balanced picture to their readers, Wong says. She also noted that environmental news often is tucked in the community section of the newspapers. Many Hong Kong journalists find it difficult to elicit editor interest in environmental topics that do not have an immediate impact on Hong Kong, such as Mongolian sandstorms.

Technical Knowledge and Access to Information

All the reporters attending the Green NGO and Environmental Journalist Forum in Hong Kong agreed that they need more training in the technical areas of environmental science, as well as an expanded knowledgebase in the global context of environmental problems. They also emphasized that learning from the personal experiences of veteran reporters and having thoughtful discussions on cultural and philosophical issues could help them do a better job. The overwhelming amount of available scientific information, much of which is presented as hypotheses, poses special challenges for reporters to communicate to the readers. Another issue that challenges reporters while writing their stories is the new twist to the perennial theme of development competing with conservation. Specifically, the option to use newer technology to solve environmental problems created by older technology.

Therefore, environmental reporters need to rethink their former dichotomous approaches to writing about the environment and explore the potential of new clean technology. For a variety of reasons, some environmental problems have been all but ignored in Mainland China, Taiwan, and Hong Kong. For example, in Taiwan and Hong Kong, the new dangers of high-tech indoor pollution have not been adequately addressed. As those economies are now heavily dependent on the electronic industries for growth, there is a reluctance to explore the health hazards from new sources of pollutants. In Mainland China sensitive questions of hazardous waste disposal and processing are rarely reported, for this issue is likely to highlight the tension between the rich coastal provinces and the poor inland provinces.

In a workshop session, Dr. Sai S. Chan (professor of medicine on leave from Oregon Health Science University) urged reporters to dig beneath the surface on environmental stories and not stop at the episodic level of reporting. Specifically, reporters should pay more attention to the range of possible solutions and how citizens can help the government to design laws to protect the environment. Dr. Chan gave a brief tour of intriguing topics in current international research on environmental health. For example, "gender discrimination" in the environment is a concept that refers to women's greater vulnerability to environmental hazards because of their hormonal cycles. Research has shown that the sharp rise of female cancer rates in the last decade is directly linked to pollutants in the environment. "We protect the environment to protect ourselves," Dr. Chan argued.

During the two days of the Green NGO and Environmental Journalist Forum, environmental reporters made large strides in understanding each other and the different political and economic systems that shape their views. All the reporters, to some extent, feel the commercial pressure on responsible coverage of environmental issues. For example, reporters in Taiwan and Hong Kong, where newspapers are commercial enterprises, are keenly aware that environmental stories can hardly compete with sensational crime and sex stories in attracting readers and advertisers. Unless stories become political, public interest in environmental issues is difficult to sustain. Even Mainland Chinese environmental reporters wonder aloud if their publications would survive on their own without government subsidies.

Many journalists at the forum also mentioned that environmental reporters also need better writing and editing skills to tell a good story. In telling their stories however, the journalists agreed they must strike a balance between promoting awareness and remaining unbiased. All came to a consensus that it is in this area that reporters from Mainland China, Taiwan, and Hong Kong can learn from each other. "We all use the Chinese language, but until now we have had less contact with each other than with other international environmental groups," one participant stated. The frank discussions at the Green NGO and Environmental Journalist Forum promised to be the beginning of a stimulating exchange and friendship for those environmental reporters.

6

Media and Emerging Youth Culture

The development of information and communication media generating a digital cultured teens, emerging as tomorrow's youth. Teen sex is a major public health problem. The physical, emotional, and social consequences of teen sexual activity include high rates of teen pregnancy, and sexually transmitted diseases including AIDS. Each year 25% of sexually active teenagers contract a sexually transmitted disease (STD), and the younger a female is when she first has sex, the more likely it is that she will have "involuntary or forced" sex. Many health professionals believe that mass media content depicting casual sex with no consequences has resulted in a host of negative behaviours among teens who may be persuaded that teen sexual activity is both acceptable and wide spread. Pediatric healthcare providers are being encouraged to assess patients' media use because of its potential association with unhealthy behaviours.

Although parents and educators try to promote abstinence or condom use, teens are increasingly exposed to media sexual content that does not provide information about health risks and personal responsibility. Both negative and positive advertising messages have been shown to influence young people, according to a pediatric medical association that calls on the mass media to promote responsible sex, and healthy behaviours. In addition to modelling unhealthy sexual behaviours, entertainment may negatively influence other aspects of teens' physical and psychological well-being. Research suggests that media portrayals of unrealistic body images negatively impact teens' self-esteem.

Teens, especially young females, become discontent with their bodies and may develop unhealthy eating behaviours in an attempt to achieve media-ideal body types. Although family and social relationships also have an influence, teens learn about society and sexual relationships from visual media images portraying body types, clothing, and other cultural norms. Sexual content in mass media has a profound real-life effect according to researchers who point to the co-evolution of media messages and sexual culture in American society. Mass media can either reinforce norms or offer insights into alternative ways of thinking. Entertainment content depicting sexual norms, stereotypes, double-standards, and sexual roles may have a profound influence on teens' perceptions about sex, body image, and social norms.

Teens often seek social and sexual information from mass media sources rather than their parents or other adults. These teens may be attracted to programs with sexual content. In a study of prime-time television shows popular among young viewers, sexual references accounted for as much as 50% of character interactions. These programs typically depicted sex as a "recreational" pursuit rather than something pertaining to relationships or reproduction, and the sexual content reinforced gender stereotypes of men as aggressors, and women as sexual objects who are valued for their physical appearances.

According to some studies, research implies that: teens who watch sexual content on television are more likely to engage in sex; teens who watch a lot of television tend to have negative attitudes about being a virgin; and teens who see sexual content as being more real are more impacted by the sexual content. Age and gender may also influence how teens select media, according to one study that found older teens were more likely to tune in to sexual content, and that females were more likely to learn about sex and relationships from sexual content in the media.

Music Television (MTV) is another example of electronic media programming that barrages teens with sexual messages. From the beginning, MTV transformed music into television programming by using fast-paced visuals to grab the attention of a very specific youthful audience -a new generation that had been raised with television and had different ways of processing information. In order to make the aural and visual elements fit together, music video producers and directors, rather than entertainers and writers, control visual images that may have nothing to do with the musicians' or artists' original concepts. MTV became a programmer's dream of nonstop commercial television that changed the way people hear popular music and how they see the meanings that are embedded in the music content.

Teens report that they watch MTV because it helps them to understand the songs better, and to understand what the music is about. However, the content that the teens are tuning into is more than 75% sexual, with stereotypical portrayals of males and females. MTV uses sexual images of women through "short, sharp, shots of intense visual pleasure" to encourage viewers to watch closely and stay focused so that they do not miss anything. Camera angles and other production techniques in MTV videos depict women in violent scenes and women giving ambiguous yes/no signals. Visual images in videos are sexual even when the lyrics are not, according to researchers who say that "sex sells, in music videos and elsewhere".

Some media effects researchers believe MTV sexual content influences how viewers perceive sex and sexual behaviours in society. Music videos that depict gender stereotypes and recreational sex without consequences influence teens' identity formation by modelling the world through these images. A startling view of how entertainment content may influence sexual attitudes comes from a review of the 1984 US Attorney General's Commission on Pornography. According to two researchers, whose studies were "cited throughout the two-volume work," the large government study condemned pornography, but failed to reveal that violent content, rather than explicit sexual content, was shown to have a greater impact on adult males' attitudes toward rape and sexual aggression.

In controlled studies, males who were shown pornographic sex without violence had more negative attitudes toward rape than males who were shown violence without sex. These findings directly relate to teens, and others, who typically watch television and non-X-rated movies. The prevalence of violence - even without sex - in mass media entertainment, according to the researchers, can contribute to more sexually aggressive attitudes among viewers. Despite myriad concerns over entertainment's influence on teens, some researchers argue that there is insufficient evidence of a causal relationship. They assert that studies demonstrating a correlation between sexual content in entertainment and teen sexual behaviours do not prove whether sexually active teens watch more sex or whether watching more sex encourages teens to be sexually active. These researchers take a broader perspective of media influence on teen sexual culture, going beyond content and effects, to see how individual characteristics of ethnicity, gender, developmental stage, and socio-economic class influence teens' media use and the incorporation of media ideas into teens' daily lives. These researchers situate media influence on teen sexuality in the context of family, friends, school and other social situations that provide information and influence teens' sexual perceptions.

For example, early sexual experience is associated with lack of parental involvement, and beliefs that other teens are sexually active, while mitigating factors include parental involvement and teen participation in social activities that do not provide sexual opportunities. This interactive association is further influenced by individual predictive factors such as onset of physical maturity. According to these researchers, teens select and use media messages either to socially reproduce media images by following the status quo, or to socially resist media images by finding and following examples of alternative behavior. While many parents, educators, activists, and health professionals are working on solutions based on the perception that media sexual content influences teen audiences, researchers who view media influence in this complicated, contextualized perspective call for long-term media use studies to determine the actual influence of media on teen sexual culture. Academic researchers provide multiple perspectives, theories, and data that contribute to this media influence debate, sometimes facilitating progress, and sometimes the opposite.

Multiple Academic Disciplines

Multiple academic disciplines including cultural studies, mass communications, communications science, psychology, linguistics, and English contribute to media influence research. These disciplines draw on various educational philosophies and myriad other political and social ideologies that inform research on message effects, content analysis, semiotics, audience analysis, and audience practice.

According to Blackman and Walkerdine, "uses and gratifications" research, that views audiences as homogeneous masses and ignores individuals' differences such as gender, has yielded to new research methods that focus on active audiences that select and interact with media. The active audiences, in these studies, do not simply absorb media content but instead negotiate meaning. These critics suggest that media and cultural studies are based on psychology and that the "active audience' is very much a reaction against the idea that the media have the power to manipulate the 'masses". They cite the influence of psychoanalysis on Screen theory which resulted in an objectified, vulnerable audience.

According to Blackman and Walkerdine, cultural theorists were dissatisfied because even though students could identify message intent, that awareness did not prevent those students from admiring and enjoying the messages. They point out that psychoanalysis was also incorporated in the feminist movement which focused on consciousness raising, though it was still mass mind oriented. Blackman and Walkerdine conclude their history of the evolution of audience research by praising the postmodern, post-structuralist concepts of Lacan,

Baudrillard, Lyotard, and others who influenced media study away from the mass audience focus.

Blackman and Walkerdine are extremely critical and limited in their approach to the media influence debate. They are representative of researchers who appear to reject the notion that the mass media play a very significant role in shaping the knowledge, beliefs, and attitudes of audiences and society. By arguing against studying the audience as subject they negate a large amount of research that could contribute to real-world solutions outside of the realm of academic research and politically-motivated disciplinary wars.

A more positive perspective of the evolution of audience research is provided by two cultural studies researchers, Cruz and Lewis, who see its interconnection with political and social activities as "cross-disciplinary convergences among the social sciences and humanities" that allow scholars to get beyond the boundaries of their academic disciplines. "[T]he scramble for interdisciplinarity is symptomatic of a crisis in the politics of knowledge after poststructuralism," according to Cruz and Lewis, who cite the common influence of postmodernism on English, cultural studies, and other fields. Cruz and Lewis are optimistic about research progress. They explain that reception theory, informed by Marxism, saw audiences as an influencable mass until structuralism and semiotics modified this thinking with a focus on symbolic systems that provided a way of analyzing language, signs, symbols and social contexts within a system.

Cruz and Lewis praise Saussure, Levi-Strauss, and others who developed semiotic theory to view the way culture functions similarly to language. According to Cruz and Lewis, semiotics, structuralism, and poststructuralism opened up the meaning-making activities of audiences, and postmodernism influenced audience studies by looking at the everyday lives of individuals as well as social and institutional structures. They explain that poststructuralism, semiology, and pscho-analytic theories were applied to media study in Screen and Screen Education, while "uses and gratifications" research began looking at audiences as selective individuals who were in control of their own consumption.

Feminist theory introduced individual experience and social influences that led to further study of the way culture and social forces interact, while literary theory and textual interpretation shifted meaning-making to readers and to audiences. These similarities in the evolution of theory, Cruz and Lewis note, highlight important connections between literary theory and cultural theory . Cruz and Lewis, unlike Blackman and Walkerdine, open the possibilities of interdisciplinary sharing by seeing common trends in research and respecting the strengths and limitations of competing theories and ideologies. According to Cruz and Lewis, the political right has two perspectives: choice enforced by audience dollars, or media influenced erosion of morals in society. The political left also has two perspectives: the media as a potent influence on culture and society, or empowerment of audiences made up of different individuals. Cruz and Lewis understand that ideological differences in cross-disciplinary perspectives enrich research and provide insights into the media influence debate.

Cultural studies researchers, such as Cruz and Lewis, contribute to the media influence debate by looking at politics, ideology, and psychology to evaluate the interactions of media and culture. Some cultural studies researchers are concerned with the social construction of culture through the normalization of behaviours characterized in media. Average students, for example, watch 5,000 hours of television before they ever get to school, so they may not recognize media bias about race, economics, gender, politics, and morals. According to some researchers, cultural studies methods have evolved from reception research and audience ethnography to social construction.

Cultural studies research has moved from audience "uses and gratifications" and "mass culture" to perspectives of the interactions among audiences, media, and culture. Feminist and post-structuralist theory influenced cultural studies perspectives of socially situated audiences within the power and dominance issues related to media messages, according to these researchers, so that "scholars no longer presume that the preferred readings of television producers are monolithically transcribed to the psyches of viewers who are indistinguishable from one another". This perspective of cultural studies research uses audience engagement and interaction as media practice to evaluate beyond message, or message reception, and look more deeply at the individual and the individual's empowerment of choosing how to interact with the medium of television.

Some researchers in the field of psychology argue that the mass media have a strong influence on audiences. From psychological processes perspectives, "the media are instrumental in developing the constructs that are available in memory, and in determining which of those constructs are chronically accessible". According to some psychology researchers, this concept of construct accessibility helps to explain the media process because ideas work on "associations in memory" and media messages influence the basic constructs that impact how viewers see their social world and society. These researchers explain that construct accessibility might cause viewers who have seen a negative portrayal of police in recent entertainment to have a negative image of a recent real-life police incident.

Researchers explain that the concept of message context is the reason why advertisers do not place commercials next to news stories that might cause unfavourable associations with the advertised products or companies. According to these researchers, viewers react negatively when they sense they are being manipulated, but audiences usually do not notice the controlling influence of messages that are placed adjacent to content. Media programmers are thus able to manipulate what is "accessible in memory" by controlling message contexts. Some researchers in psychology suggest that personality types should be included in media study so that researchers can better understand the influences involved between personality and media choice.

For example, extroverts self-report that television does not substitute for other social contacts, while neurotic people see television as a way of passing time and having companionship. New technologies also may be used differently as extroverts may find computer interactions limiting of social contact, while neurotics may seek out social safety where they have control over the Internet. Perspectives of viewer personality may impact other psychology research that looks at the cultivation paradigm. Cultivation researchers find, for example, that soap opera viewers (as compared to non-viewers) believe that society has higher rates of abortion, divorce, and extramarital affairs. Researchers also find that adolescent soap viewers are less likely to be concerned about pregnancies, STDs, and practicing safe sex. These researchers explain that since content analysis shows a high incidence of portrayals of unmarried sex on soap operas, there is reason to consider the cultivation hypothesis.

Communications research perspectives of audiences, according to one researcher, can typically be grouped in one of three categories: structural (measures media influence on audiences), behavioural (analyses choices of decision-making audiences), and cultural (focuses on media used in cultural contexts). Communications researchers using social judgment theory look at how the media are able to influence culture by getting people to buy into images to see themselves and others in particular ways. People "design or constrain [their] futures" based on their acceptance of meanings that are below the surface in media "archetypes, symbols, and images". Other communication scholars focus on message content evaluation, according to one researcher who states that while social psychologists are primarily concerned with social knowledge, and linguists with symbolic structures, communication scientists are concerned with the ways in which symbols affect social knowledge and vice versa.

Despite disciplinary separations, some researchers find that various other disciplines have enriched communication science with multiple political, social, and cultural perspectives. Rhetorical criticism, according to one scholar, provides methods to incorporate "identification and alienation" into communication theory. Another scholar suggests that communications research is enhanced by interdisciplinary perspectives including rhetoric and linguistics. Linguistic research perspectives see language as a signifying system that is constitutive of all knowledge so that thinking is constrained by language. For example, a language that uses only two words - black and white - for all colours, provides different possibilities of thinking and communicating than a language that has many words to describe colours.

Linguistic research in semiotics looks at how visual signs, rather than language and the spoken word alone, influence the way people construct thoughts. Semiotics looks at rapid-pace, multimedia images that viewers pick up on and make meaning of, oftentimes without thinking or questioning. Some linguistic researchers see semiology as a way of looking at how meaning is negotiated when message content interacts with viewer identity and socialization factors. For these researchers, semiology finds ambiguity to be inherent in all communication because there is always the potential for multiple interpretations or polysemy.

Linguistic researchers note that in the "extravagantly coded" messages of television, in which even a close-up shot can signify a meaning, research that focuses on shared meanings loses sight of potential ambiguity. These linguists point out that ambiguous programs can be just as "manipulative" as an unambiguous programs. If a television program, for example, is able to allow different audiences different interpretations of ambiguous messages, the ambiguity within the broadcast content makes the program more influential because "it demonstrates its potency in a variety of cultural contexts". Comparative media theory also views the success of polysemy in mass media messages that do not have to be received in unison by an audience in order to be effective. Audiences are not empowered just because they have different interpretations of messages, according to one theorist who states that seeing the audience as interactive and choice-making ignores the way audiences are being kept from responding in a democratic way.

Many academics, regardless of their political ideologies, are concerned with responding to media influences that limit free speech and free thought. These academic researchers offer insights into the issue of media influence, not only on American teen sexual culture, but also on cultures around the globe. Academic research perspectives of media influence are grounded in the history of mass communications technology and the struggle to control its influence on society.

Influence of Technology in Mass Communications

Communication technology has had an enormous impact on society by changing the distribution of information and assimilation of knowledge. Communication technology has facilitated the evolution of "entertainment" that has reinforced or challenged societal norms since bards entertained audiences by reciting epic poems and oral histories . From the time of ancient Greece, linear print technology (alphabets) has altered oral practices and dramatically expanded the capabilities of language by preserving written records of thoughts and ideas. Many centuries after writing was invented, the technology of the printing press enabled the first mass distribution of books, pamphlets, and newspapers that allowed single authors to inform and entertain large audiences.

United States of America, facilitated by print technology, argued for democratic freedoms from government tyranny and fuelled the fight for American independence. In the newly established democracy, "freedom of the press" protections guaranteed that print media sources would continue providing information and influence. These protections were invoked, later in American history, when debates raged over the power and influence of new mass communications technologies.

By the turn of the 20 th century, electronic technology was at the centre of American political and social power struggles over entertainment's ability to propagandize masses of people in society. From the time movie technology first appeared in 1894, censorship proponents sought to limit criminal and sexual content while other groups proposed using the new medium to teach social ideology. As early as the 1920's, movies were blamed for increasing youth sexuality. Movies were seen as reality-makers that clashed with values taught in school and contradicted societal norms. Studies during that time revealed that high school and college students were learning (and practicing) sexual techniques they had seen in the movies. Although censorship in the 1930s curbed sexual content in film, off-screen Hollywood sexual culture continued to influence American youth culture.

The mass medium of movies was seen as a vehicle to propagandize audiences with entertainment messages. In 1943, Elmer Davis, who was then America's Director of the Office of War Information, stated: "The easiest way to inject a propaganda idea into most people's minds is to let it go in through the medium of an entertainment picture when they do not realize that they are being propagandized". The mass audience reach of movies made them a battleground for numerous entities who wanted to promote a host of political and social agendas. Commercial interests soon became a major participant in the battle to wield mass media power in both entertainment and news. Despite economic and political influences, radio broadcasters attempted to create a perception of neutral and non-biased news reporting, and Americans began to rely on commercial radio as their primary source of news and information. After commercial interests won control over radio in the 1920s, broadcasting began to create a national culture for shared consumerism.

Although 1930s and '40s mass media images emphasized political rights and freedoms of speech, by the 1950s television stations did not want to air any content that would create controversy and affect advertising dollars. In 1951, in order to avoid government censorship, the television industry's National Association of Broadcasters (NAB) adopted a code of self-censorship that created a proper moral image for television. However, advertisers soon became the greatest source of television censorship as advertising agencies for companies such as Procter & Gamble sought programming content that presented positive business images.

By the 1960s, communications scholar Marshall McLuhan envisioned a shift away from the linear organization of print media to the orality of television that he believed would revive oral communication as the basis for knowledge and knowing. Television's high visual and audio impact, according to McLuhan, established new ways of meaning-making that reconnected viewers to the roots of oral communication. McLuhan anticipated electronic technology's potential to influence every facet of personal and public experience with fast-action, multi-sensory images that communicate more than many word. In the battle over media influence, movies and television have been, and continue to be, perceived as more powerful than print media. In the early days of film, movie theaters were not permitted to show news reels of certain volatile stories - such as violent labour disputes between union members and industry owners - that newspapers were free to cover. Although a Supreme Court ruling in the 1950s included movies under the free speech and free press protections of the First and Fourteenth Amendments, even today, cigarette and liquor advertisements are banned from television but not from newspapers and magazines.

The television medium became central in the power struggle to influence mass media content. Although commercial interests dominated television broadcasting, special-interest groups such as the National Association for the Advancement of Coloured People (NAACP) began challenging stations that did not give balanced treatment to certain issues. In 1966, the U.S. court of appeals ordered the Federal Communications Commission (FCC) to include more public input in licensing hearings, thus giving women and minority organizations the ability to advocate their agendas. The struggle over media influence has included "government, private enterprise, advocacy groups, and, in more recent years, philanthropic foundations". In 1967, the Carnegie Commission proposed establishing the Corporation for Public Broadcasting. Foundations, and activists working in government and education, created the Public Broadcasting System (PBS) in an effort to shape a more intellectual culture.

The issue of commercialized media continues to be at the forefront of debates over mass media influence on culture. The evolution of communication technology has enabled fewer and fewer people to have greater and greater control over the distribution of information and entertainment. Both conservative and liberal scholars, educators, and activists are concerned with the mass media's ability to limit democratic discourse and propagandize through entertainment messages. Their perspectives inform potential solutions for mitigating the influence of mass media on American teen sexual culture.

Democratic Discourse

A specter now haunts the world: a global commercial media system dominated by a small number of superpowerful, mostly U.S.A.-based transnational media corporations. It is a system that works to advance the cause of the global market and promote commercial values, while denigrating journalism and culture not conducive to the immediate bottom-line or long-term corporate interests. It is a disaster for anything but the most superficial notion of democracy. Through recent mergers, corporations have restructured media information sources into powerful global entities. Nine giant firms control the global media system including much of the Internet that was seen by some activists as a way to offset the globalization of media monopoly.

Merging media conglomerates are gaining increasing control over information as large corporations buy up small companies that fit with other corporate holdings. Global media ownership takes power away from small, local news outlets and puts it in the hands of large corporations. Corporations that control mass media entertainment, news, and advertising are better able to manage information than many totalitarian governments. Corporate ownership has given mass media global reach that would be envied by anyone who wanted to limit free exchange of information in order to indoctrinate, propagandize, and control the thoughts of people in society. The successful propaganda of today's corporations goes unchallenged because media ownership "is based on a symbiotic relationship with a handful of media moguls like Disney, America on-Line/ Time Warner, News Corp., and Viacom-CBS". Corporations, with complete control over media news and information, have a considerable impact on free democracy. In an ideal democracy, all voices, not just those of the rich and powerful, should be heard.

Media moguls' monopolization of ideology, social culture, and the information that establishes these, interferes with democratic freedom of speech. American democracy depends on open debate and freedom of information that informs its "citizens who act to set the tone for the culture and the nation, through their votes, their opinions expressed in polls, their priorities expressed in how they spend money, and through their advocacy for or against issues". Mass media interferes with this process by determining what gets discussed, what gets reported, and what is meaningful. In government and society, democracy requires two-way discourse so that audiences are not just receivers but responders. Americans tend to spend more time with mass media in their homes which further diminishes democracy by limiting discourse in public and private spaces.

Media moguls control government through what one author calls "'corpocracy'-defacto government by mega corporations". In the United States, and in other countries around the world, people are often ignorant about media propaganda. Entertainment and news broadcasts are continually influencing a public that believes it is not being influenced. People rarely consider what is put in by the media and what is "screened out". One scholar compares "corporate moguls peddling cosmetics, pharmaceuticals, and automobiles" to "Hitler, Mussolini, Hirohito, and Stalin," saying that "people today do not realize they are being programmed any more than did the people of Germany, Italy, Japan, and, later the Soviet Union". Current mass media ownership allows mega-corporations to manipulate information to promote political and social agendas that enhance corporate bottom-lines.

Corporations are places of power where money and influence have instituted an unelected authority through which profiteers who control the global media grow richer and thus more powerful as they influence consumer buying. Mass media have fostered a shared consumer identity through which we accept rather than debate what is happening in our world. Media-nurtured consumer culture encourages people to identify with media images, and to buy products to fit their media-based self-identities. This encourages individuals to identify with symbols such as brands of clothing, genres of music, and hairstyles that can unite diverse perspectives under a presumption of shared ideology. Corporations, such as General Motors, may capitalize on American symbolism - baseball, hotdogs, apple-pie, etc. - by advertising automobile ownership through standardized social conceptions.

Symbolism not only stifles true social diversity, it helps stifle political diversity as well. Political symbols can create perceptions of unity that divert attention from the lack of information on truly diverse perspectives. Too often, the sides with wealth, power, and influence are dead-locked in bipartisan political conflict that excludes multi-faceted viewpoints. The general public is encouraged to buy into political symbolism. Those who do not choose one side or the other are excluded in a voiceless void that pretends there are no alternate solutions - possibly because the issues are too complex for non-experts to understand. Conflict without communication offers no hope of mediated solutions, only backroom deals that exclude the diverse voices of 'we the people' who theoretically participate in American democracy.

When Americans buy products that are manufactured in countries that do not have American labour and environmental restrictions, corporations are able to maximize profits rather than ensure human safety and dignity or to protect the environment. By buying into a culture of consumerism that supports corporate profit, Americans widen the void between prosperous and poor both in the United States and around the world. The impact of corporate-sponsored consumerism on global conditions of war, poverty, disease, and hunger is eclipsed by a corporate-run mass media that distracts attention from social and political issues and provides a corporate-biased view of information.

Mass media-fuelled consumerism continues to encourage economic growth, according to one researcher, while it depletes resources and basically throws away everything except consumerism. Americans relinquish their ability -and responsibility - to think independently by accepting, rather than challenging, mass media information. Another researcher notes that "[t]he merger between media culture and politics, which began in earnest with the birth of TV, is now nearly complete". Commercialism has become the dominant force in today's corporate-controlled mass media. Advertisements have moved into programming where characters are defined by their consumerism and endorse commercial products by using them in the show. For example, J-Crew clothing was promoted in the popular teen television program Dawson's Creek.

While the success of product placement in big-screen movies has given advertisers "enormous control" over movie content, it has offered even greater opportunities for corporations to cross-promote their own products. Now, corporate giants that own music, movie, and television media use entertainment to market their own music, videos, toys, and other products. The industry has built on this multipurpose-marketing so that entertainment becomes an endless line of tie-ins. According to one scholar, "the fashionable term for all of this vertical and lateral corporate integration is synergy, and synergy turns out to be just another word for monopoly".

Synergy is a monopoly in which only the big companies are able to participate. Mega-corporation synergy controls global media and information that impacts society.

The blurring of the line between entertainment and advertising not only increases the marketing potential of entertainment but also decreases the information and usefulness of entertainment as advertising begins to "appropriate the icons and formulae of media content". In other words, marketing diminishes the potential of entertainment and news to provide information and messages that may be "democratically valuable". Corporate control has also commercialized news programing. What was once called "the separation of church and state" in the media referred to the separation of news from the influence of ownership in an attempt to allow journalists to cover the news and to make journalistic decisions.

Corporate control influences what gets reported. For example, the substandard pay and working conditions for Chinese labourers who manufacture Disney merchandise are unlikely to be publicized in national news because Disney owns a major network. Corporations have control over the news, but present the appearance of separation between the corporate owners and the content of the information being distributed. News reports are now forced to be profitable so that journalist managers have been replaced with marketing professionals, and the boundaries between entertainment and news have virtually disappeared. News consultants, who have very secretive relationships with the news organizations that they serve, work behind the scenes to manage news content in order to attract viewers and build profits.

The consultants' marketing data, gives them enormous influence over what was once journalistic decision-making. International news is neglected because foreign bureaus are expensive and do not fit with the profit agendas of corporations. Although other mass media sources - print, radio, and cable television - provide varying levels of international news coverage, broadcast television networks are usually limited to the high-impact stories that concern a large number of Americans. Meanwhile, celebrity activity often obscures world news. For example, in 1977, entertainment news averaged 15% of total content on television evening news; by 1997, entertainment news averaged 43% of total content.

Mass media news increasingly focuses on celebrity gossip and viewer entertainment rather than information about the politics and technologies that are changing our world. Mass media virtually ignores stories about companies such as Monsanto that genetically alter crops and pump huge amounts of chemicals (drugs and pesticides) into food and water supplies. While incredible new advances in technology, science, and medicine offer prospects for a healthier future, they also present dangers of a Brave New World. Corporate-controlled media focus Americans' attention on entertainment rather than news and information about these critical issues.

In the new millennium, new media technology, including digitalized broadcast signals, cable television, and Internet access, have fragmented media audiences and further complicated media control issues. Mass media no longer entertains the masses. Unlike the early years of television, in which all Americans watched the same programs, new technologies have enabled the fragmentation of media. Audiences have been compartmentalized into consumer packages through programming for specific interests. Therefore, unlike earlier disputes over radio, movies, and television, when audiences had to share entertainment, audiences now can be isolated with their own preferred images of society.

Scholars claim that even the Internet, which was touted as the new media information source for the masses, is succumbing to corporate control. People who hoped that the Internet would be a "cyberspace for the new millennium" may be disappointed as companies such as America On Line (AOL), with a 42% market share of America's home Internet service, exercise control by eliminating offensive chat rooms and shutting off user accounts. "Current trends toward Internet portals and the consolidation of media ownership," according to one scholar, "demonstrate that the tendency to control information and literacy is always at work". The Internet has also become more and more about marketing as commercial forces are quickly turning search engines into shopping tools. While the public may be seeking information, what they're ending up with is more consumerism.

Mass media's political and social influence on global culture impacts access to information, focuses on consumerism, and entertains audiences with sex and violence. Teens, and other mass media consumers, are encouraged to buy into the media images, to adopt media-generated identities, and to purchased the accouterments of those identities. Through entertainment, as well as other direct mass media advertising and marketing tools, teens are encouraged to focus on sex and purchase products that will make them attractive and popular. Teens, and other entertainment consumers, are provided limited, corporate perspectives that are typically unchallenged in mass media news and entertainment programming.

Solutions to Mass Media Influence

Although many scholars and activists agree that mass media influence threatens democratic discourse, their various solutions tend to be politically polarized. Some assert that a 1969 Supreme Court ruling guaranteeing First Amendment rights should prevent corporate monopolies from controlling mass media dissemination of information to the American public. They call for government regulation, noting that the United States is the only major nation to permit completely privatized ownership of mass media - even though the media have been given the responsibility for public information. They point out that the FCC, which is responsible for licensing and regulation, has increasingly permitted the corporate monopolization of mass media, while legislative incumbents are pressured by media owners who can easily impact political campaigns.

Some activists encourage citizens to lobby for media legislation that will seize power from commercial corporate giants and restructure the mass media. Some advocate censorship, especially to protect children, while others argue that government censorship poses its own threat to free speech . Other solutions include: 1) FCC action promoting women and minority ownership of media; 2) low-powered, localized television and radio broadcasting; 3) community-access cable channels; 4) independent production and distribution of films; 5) internet "broadcasting" web sites; and 6) funding for Alternative Public Television (APT). While scholars and activists debate political solutions to thwart mass media influence, many of them share an interest in educational solutions that teach media literacy. Media literacy, according to supporters, can incorporate competing political and social ideologies in order to foster critically aware citizens who are capable of political and social action.

Media literacy can look at how media interacts with culture, society, and government to influence how audiences view the world, their society, and ultimately themselves. Both left-wing and right-wing ideologies see media literacy as a means for reestablishing democratic discourse among Americans who may be only marginally aware of mass media influence in their lives. Media literacy may also provide an educational solution for the problem of mass media influence on American teen sexual culture. Media literacy in K-12 education can encourage students to question and challenge information sources and consider how mass media messages may impact individuals and influence society. It can teach aural and visual literacy that not only help students read complex, embedded electronic messages, but also help them create alternatives to mass media images.

The United States lags behind other English-speaking nations that teach media literacy, according to advocates who encourage the development of educational responses to the proliferation of new communication technologies. Technology in the classroom can provide educational enrichment for students who are accustomed to learning and communicating through technology. Media literacy can focus on making students critical consumers and creators of multimedia messages and allow them to interact with information in "multimedia, and hypermedia learning experiences".

Media literacy in the United States is not a unified area of educational theory. Teachers' personal ideologies influence their approaches to media literacy and classroom education. Some educators believe that media education should challenge culture by teaching critical analysis as well as production, while others believe that students should be protected from media influences. A surge of government funding in the 1970s directed research and teaching efforts toward critical viewing skills, and further direction came from funding for media arts and video production. In the 1980s, movement toward teaching core subjects severely diminished support for media literacy. However, there was a resurgence of interest as national government agencies for drug control, education, and health recognized media literacy's potential to teach students to identify and resist "inappropriate messages" relating to marketing, personal image, behaviours, and the depiction of society.

By the mid 1990s, school standards began to reflect a new focus on communications skills and a growing interest in media literacy. For example, the State of Minnesota added media literacy standards to the public school core curriculum, and the Pennsylvania State Board of Education approved goals that required students to be able to communicate and persuade, as well as discern propaganda and create their own persuasive messages . In 1996, the IRA/NCTE English Language Arts Standards recognized the need for students to work with oral, written, and visual communication.

As state education departments, government agencies, and educators show increasing interest in media literacy, some advocates cite the practical problems of implementing K-12 media literacy education. These include time constraints of crowded curricula, inadequate teaching materials, and a lack of media literacy training in teacher preparation programs. These advocates claim that educators in the classroom, rather than teacher education programs, are building media literacy education. Some media literacy educators reject academic resources that offer archetypes with strict standards. These grassroots advocates encourage teachers to develop their own teaching resources as an alternative to academic (or corporate media) curricula that reinforce social norms and the top-down distribution of hierarchical knowledge.

According to these advocates, media literacy educators commonly "recognize that all media are constructed representations, that meaning is derived from the intersection of reader, text, and culture, and that messages have economic, political, social, and historical contexts". While some grassroots media literacy educators shun academic scholarship, others identify a need for academic research that informs practice and justifies media literacy education. Some academic scholars, who share the concerns of grassroots educators, argue that media literacy "must be conceived as political, social, and cultural practice" that engages postmodern theories while recognizing the hierarchy of educational practice. Educational reformers encourage a shift away from traditional top-down pedagogy toward a learning-centered approach for pre-service teachers to develop a deeper understanding, awareness, and critical attitude toward teaching practice that incorporates the knowledge and experience of students. This teaching practice, according to scholars, can transform the power structures in the classroom in order to access the knowledge of students who best understand the multimedia environment and their learning capabilities within it.

Postmodern perspectives may unite scholars with grassroots educators, but competing ideologies, politics, and research perspectives may pose an obstacle to the development of academic approaches to media literacy education. Although a broad range of academic disciplines contributes knowledge and research to media literacy theory, according to some media literacy advocates academics often "suffer from cultural myopia because of the limitations of academic specialization and their own special-interest groups". These advocates criticize the lack of interdisciplinary cooperation that results in individual disciplinary perspectives that target "narrowly defined academic discourse communities". English education, uniquely situated as the academic discipline responsible for language arts in the K-12 core curriculum, can provide a unified, multi-disciplinary program of study that expands traditional literacy skills to include communication in non-print media. English teacher education programs can centrally focus cross-disciplinary scholarly perspectives on the interconnectedness of mass communications, public discourse, power structures, and social cultures.

As communication becomes increasingly computerized and electronic, some English scholars are revising the focus on printed text and written composition. Some English educators suggest that using multimedia technology for teaching literary texts can give students a critical way of approaching sign systems and visual symbols. For example, hypermedia can be used to critically respond to literature using print, visuals, video, sound, and links to web sites. Other English educators advocate expanding the "deep reading" of print media to include the "deep viewing" of visual media. In some English programs, students are developing critical skills to deconstruct mass media messages and practical skills to construct their own persuasive, multimedia communications.

Although critical studies in English literature programs can contribute to media literacy education, rhetoric - often located in modern composition and rhetoric programs - provides proven analysis methods for both print and non-print literacy. Rhetorical scholarship, historically situated in educational practices as well as democratic discourse, has evolved along with communication technologies since the early days of oratory in ancient Greece and Rome. Rhetoric, according to Aristotle, is "the faculty of observing in any given case the available means of persuasion". According to Cicero, the power of oratory persuades people and establishes civil order. Both Aristotle and Cicero focus on persuasion through orators' words as well as aural and visual aspects of performances.

Rhetoric's roots in a primarily oral culture provide analysis tools for decoding embedded messages and symbols in modern, multi-sensory entertainment that is designed to persuade a non-interactive audience. Rhetoric not only evaluates the content of mass media messages, it looks at the intent of mass media message-makers by focusing on both the purpose and method of persuasion. Teaching rhetorical analysis techniques can mitigate the influence of modern mass media on culture and democratic discourse by creating critical awareness. Thus, rhetoric can impact teen sexual culture by helping students discern specific influences of entertainment content and general influences of mass media.

Rhetoric: An Interpretive Theory

Rhetoric is an interpretive theory that frames the message as an interested party's attempt to influence an audience. The sender's intention is understood to be manifested in the argument, the evidence, the order of argumentation, and the style of delivery. Formal elements are selected according to the sender's expectations in accordance with how the audience will approach the genre, the speaker, and topic. Rhetoric is often disparaged by non-academics who associate the term with the negative connotations of its current common use. However, rhetorical theory - by any name - belongs in education.

Rhetorical theory, according to Brummett, should not be tested by criticism to determine its usefulness, but should be viewed as a method of inquiry that helps build knowledge about persuasive devices. Brummett states that rhetorical theory should be seen less as a "store of scholarly knowledge possessed by the academic community," and more as a resource of "general knowledge" for non-scholars. He asserts that if scholars see students as the "primary audience of rhetorical theory and its criticisms, then rhetorical theory and criticism's ultimate goal and justification is pedagogical: to teach people how to experience their rhetorical environments more richly". Thus, rhetorical theory offers students multiple perspectives for interpreting new experiences. Brummett makes my argument for "restoring rhetoric to the foundations of liberal arts education". In other words, return rhetoric - in the academic sense of the word - to the scholarly training of student communicators.

The long history of rhetorical scholarship encompasses many theoretical perspectives. Current academic studies tend to separate rhetoric into three periods: ancient, medieval, and modern. Current academic scholarship in rhetoric, as in other disciplinary areas, includes a wide range of both research methods and political and social ideologies. For example, using feminist criticism to critique Hollywood movies and MTV videos, theorists, such as bell hooks and Sut Jhally, seek to empower students, and others, to resist the messages of dominant, white males in American society. Other scholars draw on a variety of theories ranging from Marxism to Dramatism.

Media literacy education can benefit from theories such as Walter R. Fisher's narrative paradigm in which public moral argument replaces the rational world paradigm. Fisher affirms the communications expertise that all humans have in any given society. Fisher's democratic approach asserts that everyone has social knowledge and reasoning to determine who is telling a story and which story to believe. Fisher suggests that people base their understanding of messages on a social hierarchy of values with love at the apex.

In this perspective, common people do not have to rely on specialists in order to determine the veracity of arguments. Stephen Toulmin also offers a perspective that moves away from formally structured argument and provides non-specialist methods to evaluate real-world persuasive messages. Although age-demographic statistics for current movies and television programs are not readily available, web sites and teen magazines provide insights into which media teens are watching. Teens, who often attend the same movie multiple times, make up the largest percentage of the movie-going audience in the United States. Television programs continue to be popular among teens, while new media technology including Internet web sites, games, and chat rooms are becoming increasingly attractive for those who have access to computer technology.

Rhetorical analysis, as a discovery tool, should assist students in evaluating media without making students feel that their favourite music or television entertainment is being attacked. Aristotle's approach to rhetorical analysis continues to be valid in modern multimedia environments. Aristotle's rhetorical theory focuses on the speaker's character (ethos), the listener's emotion (pathos), and the subject's logic (logos). Audiences continue to be influenced by perceptions of message sources, audience attributes, and appeals to logical reasoning. This perspective sees the audience in terms of message construction and intended persuasion.

Media managers look at audiences through ratings systems in order to "[r]econstitute them as institutionally effective audiences that have social meaning and economic value in the system". Aristotle's theory can help students evaluate persuasive messages that are targeted at them. The first rhetorical critique method, based on Aristotle's theory of persuasion, could be. assigned to early middle school students. The teacher would facilitate student definitions for ethos, logos, and pathos by using newsprint, an easel, and coloured markers, or a more high-tech, multimedia approach. Students might define ethos as ethics, morals, rules, "right and wrong," traditions, etc.

Logos might be called logic, common sense, "using your head," etc. And, pathos might translate to emotions such as love, anger, fear, joy, etc. Students would discuss their own experiences of ethos, logos, and pathos (ELP) appeals that come from mass media, home, school, and society. Teachers would then focus the discussion on ways that visual elements can clarify, reinforce, or argue against spoken words. Once students become familiar with ELP terms, and how visual and oral elements interact, they can practice their new knowledge in a rhetorical critique of a movie, either as an in-class exercise, a homework assignment, or an after-school activity.

Character ethos, in many cases, is visually established prior to dialogue. For example, in one scene, the head bad guy, a Euro-American, is joined on the elevator by two new characters. Within seconds, before any words are spoken, the viewer is cued that the new characters - a straight-backed, angularly thin, Asian-featured female, and a strongly-built, determined-looking, African-American male - are also bad guys. The visual rhetoric implies that a non-submissive, Asian female is somehow foreign, and a stern-faced, African-American male is somehow threatening. In a scene near the end of the film, both the Asian woman and the African American man are shown in a quick shot just before the good guys express their fear that the bad guys are going to kill them.

Visual stereotyping includes Francesca's character who sometimes appears ethnically exotic and other times appears completely Americanized. The visual elements, especially her clothing which shifts from vulnerable skirts to sporty athletic wear, support the oral elements as her character sometimes speaks with a strong Hispanic accent and other times speaks distinctly American English.

7

Depiction of Violence

The debate over media violence has eluded definitive answers for more than three decades. At first blush, the debate is dominated by one question-whether or not media violence actually causes real-life violence. But closer examination reveals a political battle. On the one hand, there are those who blame media violence for societal violence and want to censor violent content to protect children. On the other hand are those who see regulation as the slippery slope to censorship or a smokescreen hiding the root causes of violence in society.

One thing is certain: the issue of media violence is not going away. Increasingly the debate is focusing on the "culture of violence," and on the normalization of aggression and lack of empathy in society. This chapter describes how the depiction of violence is evolving in a number of media formats. It analyses how, and why, violence is used by the entertainment and information industries. It offers an overview of research findings, an outline of government responses to the issue, and a look at some of the key arguments in the debate. It also explores the role that media education can play in helping young people to put media violence into perspective.

Violence in Media

Between 2000 B.C. and 44 A.D., the ancient Egyptians entertained themselves with plays re-enacting the murder of their god Osiris -- and the spectacle, history tells us, led to a number of copycat killings. The ancient Romans were given to lethal spectator sports as well, and in 380 B.C. Saint Augustine lamented that his society was addicted to gladiator games and "drunk with the fascination of bloodshed." Violence has always played a role in entertainment. But there's a growing consensus that, in recent years, something about media violence has changed.

For one thing, there's more of it. Laval University professors Guy Paquette and Jacques de Guise studied six major Canadian television networks over a seven-year period, examining films, situation comedies, dramatic series, and children's programming (though not cartoons). The study found that between 1993 and 2001, incidents of physical violence increased by 378 per cent. TV shows in 2001 averaged 40 acts of violence per hour. Francophone viewers experienced the greatest increase. Although physical violence on the three anglophone networks in the study increased by 183 per cent, on their francophone counterparts it increased by 540 per cent. One network, TQS, accounted for just under half (49 per cent) of all the physical violence on the networks studied.

Paquette and de Guise also identified a disturbing increase in psychological violence, especially in the last two years. The study found that incidents of psychological violence remained relatively stable from 1993 to 1999, but increased 325 per cent from 1999 to 2001. Such incidents now occur more frequently than physical violence on both francophone and anglophone networks. Canadians are also heavily influenced by American programming. Paquette and de Guise found that over 80 per cent of the TV violence aired in Canada originates in the U.S. They speculate that francophone networks and stations may have a higher incidence of violence because they broadcast more movies, and this, in turn may be due to lower production budgets.

Canadian-made violence is most likely to appear on private networks, which broadcast three times as many violent acts as public networks do. Other research indicates that media violence has not just increased in quantity; it has also become much more graphic, much more sexual, and much more sadistic. Explicit pictures of slow-motion bullets exploding from people's chests, and dead bodies surrounded by pools of blood, are now commonplace fare. Millions of viewers worldwide, many of them children, watch female World Wrestling Entertainment wrestlers try to tear out each other's hair and rip off each other's clothing. And one of the top-selling video games in the world, Grand Theft Auto, is programmed so players can beat prostitutes to death with baseball bats after having sex with them.

Globalization of Media

On average, children in the 23 countries surveyed watch television three hours each day, and spend 50 per cent more time watching the small screen than they spend on any other activity outside of school. Concerns about media violence have grown as television and movies have acquired a global audience. When UNESCO surveyed children in 23 countries around the world in 1998, it discovered that 91 per cent of children had a television in their home -- and not just in the U.S., Canada and Europe, but also in the Arab states, Latin America, Asia and Africa. More than half (51 per cent) of boys living in war zones and high-crime areas chose action heroes as role models, ahead of any other images; and a remarkable 88 per cent of the children surveyed could identify the Arnold Schwarzenegger character from the film Terminator. UNESCO reported that the Terminator "seems to represent the characteristics that children think are necessary to cope with difficult situations."

Moral judgment

The notion of violence as a means of problem solving is reinforced by entertainment in which both villains and heroes resort to violence on a continual basis. The Center for Media and Public Affairs (CMPA), which has studied violence in television, movies and music videos for a decade, reports that nearly half of all violence is committed by the "good guys." Less than 10 per cent of the TV shows, movies and music videos that were analyzed contextualized the violence or explored its human consequences. The violence was simply presented as justifiable, natural and inevitable -- the most obvious way to solve the problem.

Parental guidance

Busy parents who want to protect their children from media violence have a difficult task before them. The CMPA found that violence appears on all major television networks and cable stations, making it impossible for channel surfers to avoid it. Nightly news coverage has become another concern. In spite of falling crime rates across North America, disturbing images of violent crime continue to dominate news broadcasting. As news shows compete with other media for audiences, many news producers have come to rely on the maxim: "If it bleeds, it leads." Violence and death, they say, keep the viewer numbers up. Good news doesn't.

As well, movie ratings are becoming less and less trustworthy in terms of giving parents real guidance on shows with unsuitable content. PG-13 movies tend to make more money than R-rated films, and as a result, the industry is experiencing a "ratings creep": shows that the Motion Picture Association of America would once have rated R are now being rated as PG-13, in order to increase box-office profits and rental sales. In movie theatres, there is some control over who watches what. But at home, there's little to stop children from watching a restricted movie on one of the many emerging specialty channels. Kids may also have access to adult video games at the local video store.

In December 2001, the U.S. Federal Trade Commission reported that retailers allowed 78 per cent of unaccompanied minors, ages 13 to 16, to purchase video games rated "mature." To make supervision even more problematic, American children often have their own entertainment equipment. According to the Annenberg Public Policy Center, 57 per cent of kids aged 8 to 16 have TVs in their bedrooms, and 39 per cent have gaming equipment. While many parents are concerned about the graphic violence and put-down humour in many kids' shows, there's a growing subculture of violence that parental radar often misses.

Music and music videos are pushing into new and increasingly violent territory. Violence in general, and sexual violence in particular, is also a staple of the video game industry. The current trend is for players to be the bad guys, acting out criminal fantasies and earning points for attacking and killing innocent bystanders. Although these games are rated M, for mature audiences, it's common knowledge that they are popular among pre-teens and teenaged boys.

The level of violence in the gaming habits of young people is disturbingly high. In MNet's 2001 study Young Canadians In A Wired World (which found that 32 per cent of kids 9 to 17 are playing video games "every day or almost every day"), 60 per cent cited action/combat as their favourite genre. Stephen Kline of Simon Fraser University reported similar findings in his 1998 study of over 600 B.C. teens. Twenty-five per cent of the teens he surveyed played between seven and 30 hours a week and when asked for their one favourite game, their choice was "overwhelmingly" in the action/adventure genre.

Virtual violence is also readily available on the World Wide Web. Children and young people can download violent lyrics (including lyrics that have been censored from retail versions of songs), and visit Web sites that feature violent images and video clips. Much of the violence is also sexual in nature. Many kids view these sites as the online equivalent of harmless horror movies. But their pervasive combination of violence and sexual imagery is disturbing. Gorezone's front-page disclaimer describes the images on its site as "sexually oriented and of an erotic nature" and then warns viewers that they also contain scenes of death, mutilation and dismemberment.

The presence of violence, degradation and cruelty in a range of media means that children are exposed to a continuum of violence, which ranges from the in-your-face attitude of shows like South Park to extreme depictions of misogyny and sadism. Young people generally take the lead when it comes to accessing new media but the MNet survey found that only 16 per cent of children say their parents know a great deal of what they do online. This is particularly problematic, given the results of a 1999 AOL survey which that found online activities are emerging as a central facet of family life; and that a majority of parents believe that being online is better for their children than watching television.

Business of media violence

Media entertainment is big business: popular culture products are now the United States' biggest export. In 2001, people around the world spent US$14 billion going to the movies. The U.S. domestic box office alone hit US$9 billion-a 75 per cent increase from 1991-and there are huge revenues from home video/DVD sales, rentals and spin-off merchandise. But even these profits are dwarfed by music, the largest global media sector. In 2000, sales reached US$37 billion, with music consumption high among young audiences everywhere. Video games are not far behind: global sales for 2002 were anticipated to be US$31 billion.

American media corporations earn at least half of their profits from foreign sales. And global markets are growing fast as standards of living are rising around the world. Sales of TVs, stereos, VCRs and satellite dishes are increasing, and in the last decade or two, new and expanding markets have emerged in countries that have abandoned state control of media and distribution. Today, U.S. films are shown in more than 150 countries worldwide, and the U.S. film industry provides most of the pre-recorded videos and DVDs sold throughout the world.

American television programs are broadcast in over 125 international markets, and MTV can be seen in more foreign households than American ones. This international success has a tremendous impact not just on the recipient countries, but also on the cultural environment of the U.S. To some extent, the tail is wagging the dog: more and more, the demands and tastes of foreign markets are influencing what popular products get made in the U.S.

Nowhere is this influence more evident than in the film industry. In the U.S. and Canada, movies rated "G" (General) and "PG" (Parental Guidance) consistently bring in more revenues than R-rated films. Yet the number of G and PG films has dropped in recent years, and the number of restricted films has risen. Two-thirds of Hollywood films in 2001 were rated "R." Action travels well. Action movies don't require complex plots or characters. They rely on fights, killings, special effects and explosions to hold their audiences. And, unlike comedy or drama-which depend on good stories, sharp humour, and credible characters, all of which are often culture-specific-action films require little in the way of good writing and acting. They're simple, and they're universally understood. To top it off, the largely non-verbal nature of the kind of films that journalist Sharon Waxman refers to as "short-on-dialogue, high-on-testosterone" makes their dubbing or translation relatively inexpensive.

There are, of course, exceptions to the rule. The film Titanic made almost US$2 billion in worldwide sales as of 2001-making it the biggest-grossing movie of all time. The British film The Full Monty was an international hit; and My Big Fat Greek Wedding debunked all the profit formulas in 2002. But such offbeat successes are hard to predict. A flick such as Die Hard or Terminator (or better yet, a sequel to such a film) is much more of a sure thing. Most film budgets today average US$75-100 million, so Hollywood studios don't like to take chances. All this means enormous pressures on the American movie industry to abandon complexity in favour of action films. The effect is a kind of "dumbing-down" of the industry in general.

Foreign investors are much less likely to invest in films focusing on serious social themes or women's issues, or ones that feature minority casts. Such films, however brilliant, are not where the big money is. Worldwide appeal determines casting and script decisions-and the overwhelming demand is for white actors and action. Success breeds success, and the sheer ubiquity of these productions and all their spin-off products and businesses around the world is in turn fueling an ever-growing demand for U.S. popular culture products. Foreign market pressures are driving the $1.9 billion Canadian film and television industry as well: international sales are essential for a country with such a small domestic market. And so, as the Writers' Guild of Canada points out, "distributors are now the gatekeepers of Canadian television."

According to the Guild, the pressures of foreign markets are resulting in more non-Canadian writers, and television series that look less and less Canadian. It's hard to compete with the giant next door. Because American studios export so widely, they can sell an hour's worth of TV entertainment to Canadian broadcasters at a cost well below what it would cost Canada to produce its own. (It's been said that two minutes of original television production can buy an hour of American drama). And getting a film shown in Canadian theatres can be a challenge when most theatres are owned by large multinational corporations.

In the last decade, social analysts have also noted a steady increase in violent and anti-social music lyrics and images. Once relegated to the fringes, "rage" music, filled with profanity and hate, has become a cash cow for the mainstream music industry. The world's largest music company, Universal Music Group, is putting the might of its international marketing machine behind artists like Eminem, Dr. Dre and Limp Bizkit-all known for their bleak anthems of violence and hatred, often aimed at women, gays and lesbians. This kind of violence reached mainstream status in 2001, when the U.S. Grammy awards nominated Eminem for four awards. He won three, and his 2002 CD, The Eminem Show made US$3.63 million in its first month of sales.

Rap music, too, has been co-opted by the major corporations. The Recording Industry Association of America says that rap/hip-hop, which sprang out of the East Coast music scene 25 years ago, replaced pop music in 2001 as the third most popular music genre. Gansta Rap artists are now being accused of destroying the soul of original rap and hip hop movements with their violent lyrics and lifestyles.

Marketing violence to youngsters

No one knows better than the communications industries that children and young people represent a huge market, due to both their own spending power and their influence on family spending decisions. In September 2000, a Federal Trade Commission (FTC) report revealed what many suspected: U.S. media corporations were routinely ignoring their own rating restrictions and actively marketing violent entertainment to children and teens. In fact, the study showed that 80 per cent of R-rated movies, 70 per cent of restricted video games, and 100 per cent of music with "explicit content" warning labels were being marketed to kids under 17.

The report revealed a number of standard (though illicit) practices for marketing adult media products to kids. These included advertising in publications for adolescents, such as YM, Teen and Marvel comics; screening trailers for restricted movies on TV at times when kids are likely to be watching; and recruiting teens and children (sometimes as young as nine) to evaluate story concepts, commercials, trailers and rough cuts-even for R-rated movies. The study also revealed that the film and videogame industries often target children as young as four with toy tie-ins for adult-rated movies and games.

Follow-up reports from the FTC indicate that the film and gaming industries have improved their practices somewhat. However, ads for R-rated movies continue to appear on television shows popular with kids (TV is considered the most important medium for drawing an audience to a film), and the video game industry still advertises games rated M (Mature) in magazines with young readers. The music industry has done little to clean up its act. All five major record labels continue to advertise albums with explicit or violent content on television programs and in magazines that have substantial followings of kids under the age of seventeen.

Whether or not exposure to media violence causes increased levels of aggression and violence in young people is the perennial question of media effects research. Exposure to media violence causes children to behave more aggressively and affects them as adults years later. The scientific evidence simply does not show that watching violence either produces violence in people, or desensitizes them to it.

Andrea Martinez at the University of Ottawa conducted a comprehensive review of the scientific literature for the Canadian Radio-television and Telecommunications Commission (CRTC) in 1994. She concluded that the lack of consensus about media effects reflects three "grey areas" or constraints contained in the research itself. First, media violence is notoriously hard to define and measure. Some experts who track violence in television programming, such as George Gerbner of Temple

University, define violence as the act (or threat) of injuring or killing someone, independent of the method used or the surrounding context.

Accordingly, Gerber includes cartoon violence in his data-set. But others, such as University of Laval professors Guy Paquette and Jacques de Guise, specifically exclude cartoon violence from their research because of its comical and unrealistic presentation. Second, researchers disagree over the type of relationship the data supports. Some argue that exposure to media violence causes aggression. Others say that the two are associated, but that there is no causal connection. (That both, for instance, may be caused by some third factor.) And others say the data supports the conclusion that there is no relationship between the two at all.

Third, even those who agree that there is a connection between media violence and aggression disagree about how the one effects the other. Mechanism is a psychological one, rooted in the ways we learn. For example, Huesmann argues that children develop "cognitive scripts" that guide their own behaviour by imitating the actions of media heroes. As they watch violent shows, children learn to internalize scripts that use violence as an appropriate method of problem-solving. Other researchers argue that it is the physiological effects of media violence that cause aggressive behaviour. Exposure to violent imagery is linked to increased heart rate, faster respiration and higher blood pressure. Some think that this simulated "fight-or-flight" response predisposes people to act aggressively in the real world.

Still others focus on the ways in which media violence primes or cues pre-existing aggressive thoughts and feelings. They argue that an individual's desire to strike out is justified by media images in which both the hero and the villain use violence to seek revenge, often without consequences. In her final report to the CRTC, Martinez concluded that most studies support "a positive, though weak, relation between exposure to television violence and aggressive behaviour." Although that relationship cannot be "confirmed systematically," she agrees with Dutch researcher Tom Van der Voot who argues that it would be illogical to conclude that "a phenomenon does not exist simply because it is found at times not to occur, or only to occur under certain circumstances."

The lack of consensus about the relationship between media violence and real-world aggression has not impeded ongoing research. Here's a sampling of conclusions drawn to date, from the various research strands:

Media violence debates

The issue of media violence just doesn't go away. The debate raged when the Reagan administration deregulated children's television in the United States, and was revisited after the Montreal massacre on December 6, 1989. And the rash of high school shootings in North America and Europe at the end of the century has fuelled the debate anew.

Many pundits argue that media violence is at least partly to blame for the school shootings in Littleton, Colorado, Taber, Alberta and Erfurt, Germany. Hollywood films have desensitized kids to the consequences of violence, and video games have taught them how to handle a gun. But others, like psychiatrist Serge Tisseron, maintain, "just because a film has a murder scene doesn't mean people are going to commit the act... That overstates the power of the image and under-estimates the role of parents."

It is important to recognize that the discussion is not a purely scientific one. Social scientists have been unable to establish clearly that media violence causes real-life aggression. As early as 1985, Anthony Smith noted that the demand for "evidence" was driven more by the intensity of the debate than the desire to find definitive answers: "Social science has gotten itself into something of a scrape in the matter of television, especially in the area of violence; none of the various sides of the argument about violence will permit social science to depart the field."

On the other hand, many social scientists have concluded that there is a weak correlation between watching media violence and real life aggression-enough to convince organizations like the Canadian Pediatric Society and the American Medical Association that media violence is a public health issue. After all, governments don't wait for scientific certainty before they act to protect the public from smoking or drinking; all that's required is proof of a risk. If there is evidence that an activity or substance will increase the probability of negative effects, then the state is justified in intervening.

However, others maintain that the crusade against media violence is a form of censorship that, if successful, would seriously hamper artistic expression. Media violence is qualitatively different from real violence: it is a natural signifier of conflict and difference, and without representations of conflict, art of the past and present would be seriously impoverished. Many commentators, from artists to film makers to historians, agree. Comic-book creator Gerard Jones contends that violent video games, movies, music and comic books enable people to pull themselves out of emotional traps, "integrating the scariest, most fervently denied fragments of their psyches into fuller sense of selfhood through fantasies of superhuman combat and destruction." Pullitzer-Prize-winning author Richard Rhodes says that video game violence enables young people to safely challenge their feelings of powerlessness.

Psychologist Melanie Moore concludes:

> Fear, greed, power-hunger, rage: these are aspects of our selves that we try not to experience in our lives but often want, even need, to experience vicariously through stories of others. Children need violent entertainment in order to explore the inescapable feelings that they've been taught to deny, and to reintegrate those feelings into a more whole, more complex, more resilient selfhood.

The American Booksellers Foundation for Free Expression lists a number of reasons to protect media violence as a form of free expression:

— censorship won't solve the root causes of violence in society

— deciding what is "acceptable" content is necessarily a subjective exercise

— many of the plays, books and films banned in the past are considered classics today

— it's up to individuals and not governments to decide what's appropriate for themselves and their children

Center for Media and Public Affairs (CMPA) noted in its 1999 study of entertainment violence, media violence can be compelling social commentary. Many media critics, like George Gerbner and Joanne Cantor, agree that censorship is not the answer. However, they question whose rights are protected when governments give, in Gerbner's words, a "virtual commercial monopoly over the public's airwaves," in effect delivering our "cultural environment to a marketing operation."

Parents used to tell children scary stories face-to-face, so they could moderate the content and teach life lessons: Children today, in contrast, grow up in a cultural environment that is designed to the specifications of a marketing strategy. Shari Graydon, past president of Canada's Media Watch, and Québec activist René Caron remind us that the air waves are a public utility, and those who control their access and distribution must do so in ways that represent the best interests of all Canadians. Caron states, "violence has been used by the industry to capture the attention of boys, to captivate them and manipulate them." Although this strategy may be profitable, "from a social viewpoint, from a moral viewpoint, this approach has had abominable repercussions."

Uncivil society

The repercussions aren't limited to a potential increase in aggressive behaviour. Many commentators worry that media violence has become embedded in the cultural environment; that, in some sense, it's part of the "psychic air" that children and young people constantly breathe. That environment of violence, profanity, crudeness, and meanness may erode civility in society by demeaning and displacing positive social values.

Todd Gitlin argues that media violence is a red herring that allows politicians to divert attention away from very real social problems. He writes, "There is little political will for a war on poverty, guns, or family breakdown... we are offered instead a crusade against media violence. This is largely a feel-good exercise, a moral panic substituting for practicality... It appeals to an American propensity that sociologist Philip Slater called the Toilet Assumption: once the appearance of a social problem is swept out of sight, so is the problem. And the crusade costs nothing."

Rather than focusing on violent content, Gitlin argues we should be condemning "trash on the grounds that it is stupid, wasteful, morally bankrupt: that it coarsens taste, that it shrivels the capacity to feel and know the whole of human experience."

Inequitable society

Gerbner warns that the search for a link between media violence and real life aggression is in itself a symptom of the problem itself. For Gerbner, media violence demonstrates power: "It shows one's place in the 'pecking order' that runs society." For example, Gerbner's decades-long study of television violence indicates that villains are typically portrayed as poor, young, male members of visible minorities, and victims are overwhelmingly female. He argues that by making the world look like a dangerous place, especially for white people, the majority will be more willing to give the authorities greater power to enforce the status quo.

This is an argument that Michael Moore used in the award-winning movie, Bowling for Columbine. Journalist Thierry Jobin writes, "Moore denounces the way in which the government and the media foster a feeling of insecurity, pushing Americans to barricade themselves in their homes, a loaded 44 Magnum under their pillows." Gerbner worries that this sense of insecurity and powerlessness will be used to justify a weakening of democratic values.

Opponents of regulation argue that it's up to the viewer to decide what to watch. If you don't like television violence, they say, then turn off the TV. The popularity of a TV show depends less on content and more on scheduling. As Gerbner points out, "... violence as such is not highly rated. That means it coasts on viewer inertia, not selection. Unlike other media use, viewing is a ritual; people watch by the clock and not by the program."

Joanne Cantor criticizes the media industry for saying it's up to parents, not the industry, to decide what their children watch: "They make harmful products, which come into our homes automatically through television, they market them to children too young to use them safely, and they try to keep parents in the dark about their effects." Cantor argues parents need tools to help them decide what is healthy and unhealthy for their kids. One such tool is the V-chip, which enables parents to program their televisions with pre-set industry ratings to screen out certain shows. Keith Spicer, former chair of the Canadian Radio-television and Telecommunications Commission, calls the V-chip a "sexy, telegenic little gizmo that fulfills the fantasy of a magic wand."

The industry has been quick to endorse V-chip technology but critics argue that its real function is to protect the industry from parents, not the other way around. Gerbner states, "It's like major polluters saying, 'We shall continue business as usual, but don't worry, we'll also sell you gas masks to 'protect your children' and have a 'free choice!'... Programming needs to be diversified, not just 'rated.' A better government regulation is antitrust, which could create a level playing field, admitting new entries and a greater diversity of ownership, employment, and representation. That would reduce violence to its legitimate role and frequency." Todd Gitlin agrees with Gerbner that the real issue is broadcaster irresponsibility-though he does endorse the V-chip because, "parents deserve all the technology they can get."

Researchers like David Buckingham in the U.K. and Henry Jenkins in the U.S. argue that rather than focusing on what media do to people, we should focus on what people do with media. Media images "are not simple chemical agents like carcinogens that produce predictable results upon those who consume them. They are complex bundles of often contradictory meanings that can yield an enormous range of different responses from the people who consume them."

From this perspective, people don't just passively absorb messages transmitted through the media; they choose which media to consume and are actively involved in determining what the meaning of the messages will be. And that process doesn't occur in a social vacuum. Personal experiences affect what we watch and how we make sense of it. Our class position, our religious upbringing, our level of education, our family setting, and our peer groups all have a role to play in how we understand violent content.

Responsibilities of public

Media violence has been taken up as a public policy issue by a number of Western countries. Central to the debate has been the challenge of accommodating what may appear to be opposing principles-the protection of children from unsuitable media content and upholding the right to freedom of expression. In the U.S., where television began as a commercial enterprise, the First Amendment, ensuring free speech and freedom of the press, has been used forcefully to argue against any government intervention in the operation of media organizations.

The Canadian Constitution also guarantees freedom of expression, but it embodies a greater acceptance that reasonable limits can be placed on individual rights for the greater good of society. In Canada, the United Kingdom, Australia and many European countries, television followed on the heels of state-owned radio and began with the premise that any enterprise using public airwaves had a social responsibility. This premise from the 50s may seem somewhat archaic in today's competitive media environment, but in Canada it provided the foundation for a public policy framework to address media violence.

For example Canada has long been the largest importer of American television programming. This is due to its geographical proximity to the U.S., as well as an inability to produce profitable programming for a small domestic market. Violence in this programming had become a public policy issue by the 70s, but it was the deregulation of children's programming in the U.S. and the emergence of the VCR during the 80s that led to a substantial increase in public concern about the issue. Children's TV programming, especially cartoons, suddenly became less benign, and children and young teens had access to adult fare that had previously been denied to them in theatres.

In the early 90s, the federal broadcast regulator, the Canadian Radio-television and Telecommunications Commission (CRTC), began consultations on the issues relating to television violence with the broadcasting, cable and program production industries, as well as public health professionals, educators, policy-makers and consumer groups. At the same time, following several tragic "flashpoints," a petition against media violence, signed by 1.3 million Canadians, was presented to the Prime Minister.

The Code's provisions included:

— a prohibition on airing programs that are gratuitously violent and that promote or glamorize violent acts

— a "watershed hour" of 9:00 p.m. before which only violence suitable for adults could be aired

— a promise to develop a program classification system

— a commitment to sensitivity about violence against vulnerable groups, such as women and minorities

— a statement that violence would not be shown as a preferred way of solving problems, or as the central theme of children's programming and that children's programming would not invite dangerous imitation

All privately-owned conventional television stations and networks were obliged to follow this code, and it led to the creation of similar codes by specialty and pay-TV services. The CAB also established the Canadian Broadcast Standards Council (CBSC), an industry self-regulatory body mandated to respond to complaints from the public about violence and other matters. If a complaint is dealt with satisfactorily through the self-regulatory process, it is not included on the CRTC's public record that is reviewed at licence renewal time for the station/network involved. If not resolved, complaints are brought to the federal regulator.

In late 1993, after a two-day meeting hosted by the CRTC, representatives of Canadian parent and teacher organizations recommended the formation of an online clearinghouse for resources on media education and information on media issues. This resulted in the formation of the Media Awareness Network under the aegis of the National Film Board of Canada. MNet incorporated as an independent not-for-profit organization in 1996. In June

1994, the V-chip entered the picture as a technological tool that parents could use to control children's exposure to televised violence. This invention was tested in the field, but not immediately put into operation, since the program classification system on which it depended was not in place.

Canadian broadcasters raised concern at this time that American stations available in Canada over-the-air, via cable or by satellite did not have to adhere to any violence guidelines. This led the CRTC to conduct a series of national and regional public consultations on Violence in Television Programming, that resulted in establishing deadlines for launching a V-chip-based classification system and ensuring that foreign signals offered by Canadian distributors were encoded with a classification system.

In spring 1997, the industry group AGVOT launched a classification system, using on-screen, age-related icons similar to those employed in the U.S. In March 2000, broadcasters began to encode Canadian programs so that the classification system could be used in conjunction with V-chip technology. At the same time, private broadcasters and cable companies launched a Web site to provide information on the classification system, the V-chip and other related matters. These initiatives-the V-chip, a classification system, industry codes and a public education initiative-remain in place today. All programs (excluding sports, news, talk shows and music videos) display an age-appropriate rating. Most Canadian-bought TVs are equipped with a V-chip (though less than 10 per cent of households use it). The CBSC reviews and adjudicates complaints from the public and adherence to the voluntary industry codes remains a condition of CRTC licensing.

In Canada, film and video classification is a provincial matter. The classification boards were established in the early 1900s as tools for film censorship but the responsibility has shifted over the years from censoring films to rating them. Most boards still retain the ability to censor and ban movies through their theatre legislation; few exercise this power except in the case of adult sex videos and even these cases are rare. Films coming from the U.S. have generally been self-censored already by producers to avoid the MPAA N-17 rating (a rating that prevents anyone under 17 being admitted without an adult).

When a film is released on video, it is rated by the national Canadian Rating System for Home Videos. Ratings are produced by averaging the film classifications assigned by the seven provincial boards. All provinces, except Quebec, now require the Canadian Home Video ratings stickers to be displayed on rental video jackets. The system is voluntary, but video stores are encouraged to display posters explaining the classifications to customers. Though video rental stores are not supposed to rent adult videos to children, there is no legislation to prevent them from doing so.

The entertainment communications environment has changed considerably since the establishment of codes, ratings and filtering devices to protect children from unnecessary and excessive violence on television. The Internet and video games are competing seriously with TV for young people's leisure time, and violence in these media has grown unchecked. Music videos continue to "push the envelope" on a number of issues and, with more theatrical movies on TV, the amount of violence after 9:00 p.m. has grown. Large multi-theatre entertainment complexes make it easy for children and young teens to sneak into R-rated films and many stores are lax about renting videos and videogames with adult ratings to under-aged clients:

The convergence of media platforms and the availability of wireless (and hand-held) communications technologies are challenging former protection strategies such as "watershed hours" and "putting the TV in a well-trafficked area of the home." Furthermore, the CRTC, in its 1999 Report on New Media, announced that it would not regulate new media activities on the Internet (including Web sites, video games and online radio and television programming) under the Broadcasting Act.

It seems clear that in a globalized, increasingly unregulated world, the protection of children is going to rely increasingly on the vigilance of media-aware parents, public pressure from consumers and professional groups, and the responsiveness of a responsible media sector.

Education about media

Media education is not going to stop the World Wrestling copycat behaviour of six-year-olds in the playground. It's also unlikely to influence a teen's choice of a video for Saturday-night viewing. But what media education can do is give young people the tools to respond thoughtfully and critically to media content. It can help kids to put media violence into perspective, and perhaps diffuse some of its power. A critical engagement with the media inspires young people to question how violence is portrayed in films or video games-and even to ask why it's there in the first place.

Is violence essential to the plot, or is it factored in for thrills and excitement? Does the violence have realistic consequences, or does it show people smashing through plate glass windows with barely a scratch? And is the psychological trauma of violence and injury shown, or does the story just proceed without skipping a beat? Violence used to be the territory of the "bad guy" but there's been a major shift in the last few decades to violence as the hero's prerogative. Do positive motives justify violent action?

A search for patterns in the portrayal of media violence helps young people to understand media entertainment for what it is-fiction. Crime plays a far greater role in movies than it does in our society. In Canada, the average policeman draws his gun less than once a year. Research has shown that frequent watchers of cop shows, thrillers and the nightly news may come to see the world as a meaner and scarier place than it really is.

One of the primary lessons of media education is that media productions are not "windows on reality," whatever their producers might like us to believe. They're deliberate constructions, the result of a series of choices. This includes the news. Is The World Today really that? Kids need to understand the relationship between how many people watch a TV program (the ratings) and the choices producers make about the news lineup. Most people are familiar with the "If it bleeds it leads" notion, but what about natural disasters and Third World crises where thousands of children can lose families and limbs in Sierra Leone one week, and are never heard of again? And what about the phenomenon of "compassion fatigue": an inability to keep feeling what we would normally feel in the face of human tragedy?

Of course, violence is a time-honoured element in stories told through the ages about what it means to live in a society and relate to other people. Media education helps us examine today's media versions of these stories, probe whether the presentation of violence is different than it's been in the past, and ask: Who benefits from this endless menu of violence, and how? It's an eye opener for young people to realize that the main reason for the proliferation of media violence is money. Films chock-a-block with action and violence are easier to sell abroad because they "translate" with less difficulty and jump over cultural barriers. Comedy and serious drama require intelligent scripting and cultural reference points. People may laugh over different things in Moose Jaw and Dar-es-Salaam but violence and action are understood by all in a global market.

It's also a revelation to young people when they realize that no one sees the same media production. How we respond to a film, a song, a video game or TV series is coloured by our own personal package of attitudes, values and experiences-including past exposure to media violence. If kids are growing up in a media-saturated culture-and they are-media education can help them articulate their attitudes and feelings towards violence, in real life as well as on the screen. It can also teach young people that they have a voice and a role to play as active media consumers who can talk to the entertainment industry and present their opinions in public forums. The Internet has opened up important avenues for reaching producers and sharing views.

8

Mass Media and Factual Information

The power of the news media to set a nation's agenda, to focus public attention on a few key public issues, is an immense and well-documented influence. Not only do people acquire factual information about public affairs from the news media, readers and viewers also learn how much importance to attach to a topic on the basis of the emphasis placed on it in the news. Newspapers provide a host of cues about the salience of the topics in the daily news - lead story on page one, other front page display, large headlines, etc.

Television news also offers numerous cues about salience - the opening story on the newscast, length of time devoted to the story, etc. These cues repeated day after day effectively communicate the importance of each topic. In other words, the news media can set the agenda for the public's attention to that small group of issues around which public opinion forms. What we know about the world is largely based on what the media decide to tell us.

More specifically, the result of this mediated view of the world is that the priorities of the media strongly influence the priorities of the public. Elements prominent on the media agenda become prominent in the public mind.

Social scientists examining this agenda-setting influence of the news media on the public usually have focused on public issues. The agenda of a news organization is found in its pattern of coverage on public issues over some period of time, a week, a month, an entire year. Over this period of time, whatever it might be, a few issues are emphasized, some receive light coverage, and many are seldom or never mentioned. It should be noted that the use of term "agenda" here is purely descriptive. There is no pejorative implication that a news organization "has an agenda" that it relentlessly pursues as a premeditated goal.

The media agenda presented to the public results from countless dayto-day decisions by many different journalists and their supervisors about the news of the moment. The public agenda - the focus of public attention - is commonly assessed by public opinion polls that ask some variation of the long-standing Gallup Poll question, "What is the most important problem facing this country (U.S) today?". Comparisons of the media agenda in the weeks preceding these opinion polls measuring the public agenda yield significant evidence of the agenda-setting role of the news media. When Chapel Hill, North Carolina, voters were asked to name the most important issues of the day - in the very first empirical study of this agenda-setting influence - their responses closely reflected the pattern of news coverage during the previous month in the mix of newspapers, network television news, and news magazines available to them.

Since that initial study during the 1968 U.S. presidential election, more than 300 hundred published studies worldwide have documented this influence of the news media. It should be noted that this evidence encompasses a wide variety of research designs, including numerous panel studies, time-series analyzes, and controlled laboratory experiments. To summarize the extent of this influence - and to facilitate comparisons from one research setting to another - social scientists frequently calculate the correlation between the ranking of issues on the media agenda and the ranking accorded those same issues on the subsequent public agenda. This quantitative measure provides a substantial degree of precision for the comparisons, much as a thermometer's precise numbers are better than simply saying it seems cooler today than it was yesterday.

The vast majority of comparisons between how issues are ranked on the media agenda and how the public ranks the importance of these same issues yield correlations of +.50 or better. That reflects a substantial degree of influence. The original study of the agenda-setting influence of the news media, which was conducted in Chapel Hill, examined a month during that 1968 U.S. presidential election. Subsequent studies have examined much longer periods of time - for example, a yearlong, nine-wave panel study during the 1976 U.S. presidential election - and found similar evidence of strong agenda-setting effects among the public. A look at the entire decade of the 1960s found a substantial correlation (+.78) between the patterns of coverage in news magazines and the trends in public opinion reflected by responses to the Gallup Poll's question about the most important problem facing the country.

Agenda-setting effects also have been found at the local level, and the evidence for both national and local effects is found in a wide variety of settings around the world. In Spain, unemployment and urban congestion were the major concerns of Pamplona, Spain, residents in the spring of 1995. Agenda-setting at the community level also occurred in a 1986 Japanese mayoral election. Voters in Machida City, a municipality of 320,000 residents in the Tokyo metropolitan area, regarded welfare policies, urban facilities, and local taxes as the three most important issues in the election. Comparison of the public agenda, which had seven issues in all, with the coverage across a three-week period of the four major newspapers serving Machida City yielded a modest, but positive, correlation of +.39.

In Argentina, agenda-setting effects were found in the 1997 legislative elections in the Buenos Aires metropolitan area. Corruption was prominent on both the public and media agendas throughout the fall, always ranking first or second. But in September there was only modest overall agreement (+.43) between the public agenda and the combined issue agenda of five major Buenos Aires newspapers. However, as election day approached in October, the correspondence between the agendas soared to +.80, an increase that suggests considerable learning from the news media in the closing weeks of the election campaign.

Returning to the national level, in the U.K. during the final decade of the 20th century there was significant correspondence (+.54) between public concern about international issues and the pattern of international coverage in The Times. In sum, the news media have a substantial influence on the content of the public agenda, and the phrase "setting the agenda" has become commonplace in discussions of journalism and public opinion.

Influence of Pictures

The agenda-setting influence of the news media is not limited to this initial step of focusing public attention on a particular topic. The media also influence the next step in the communication process, our understanding and perspective on the topics in the news. If you think about the agenda in abstract terms, the potential for a broader view of media influence on public opinion becomes very clear. In the abstract, the items that define the agenda are objects. For all the agendas, the objects are public issues, but they could be other items or topics, such as the agenda of political candidates during an election. The objects are the things on which the attention of the media and the public are focused.

In turn, each of these objects has numerous attributes, those characteristics and traits that describe the object. For each object there also is an agenda of attributes because when the media and the public think and talk about an object, some attributes are emphasized, others are given less attention, and many receive no attention at all. This agenda of attributes is another aspect of the agenda-setting role of the news media. 'The pictures in our heads', the agenda of issues or other objects presented by the news media influence what the pictures in our heads are about. The agenda of attributes presented for each of these issues, public figures, or other objects literally influences the pictures themselves that we hold in mind. Images held by the public of political candidates and other public figures are the most obvious examples of attribute agenda-setting by the news media.

During the 1996 general election in Spain, the descriptions by voters in Navarra of the three major party leaders showed considerable correspondence with the media's presentation of these men. For the local newspapers, the median match with the local voters' descriptions was +.70; for the national newspapers, +.81; for national television, +.54. Similar matches between the imagery of the news media and the images in the public mind have been found in U.S. national elections. Comparison of New York Democrats' descriptions of the contenders for their party's presidential nomination in 1976 with the agenda of attributes presented in Newsweek's early January sketches of these 11 men found significant evidence of media influence. Especially compelling in this evidence is that the correspondence between the news agenda of attributes and the voter agenda of attributes increased from +.64 in mid-February to +.83 in late March.

Voters not only learned the media's agenda, but with some additional exposure over the weeks of the primaries they learned it even better. Turning to a very different political and cultural setting, the voters' images of the three candidates for mayor of Taipei were compared with the descriptions of these men by the local newspapers and TV stations. The agenda of attributes included 12 categories representing a wide variety of personal and political attributes. Comparisons of the voters' images with the agenda of attributes in the China Times and United Daily News ranged from +.59 to +.75. The median value of these six comparisons (3 candidates x 2 newspapers) was +.68.

None of the comparisons with TV news were significant, no doubt because the voters were well aware that all three television stations at that time were under the direct domination of the government and long-ruling KMT political party. This is a specific evidence in support of the general observation that the appearance of agenda-setting effects requires the existence of reasonably free and open media and political systems. There also are examples of attribute agenda-setting for public issues. The aspects of issues selected for attention by the media influence the public's perception of these issues.

Nationally, during the 2000 presidential election in the U.S., the correspondence between the news media's presentation of social welfare and the way in which U.S. voters talked about this issue was +.60. For a very different set of issues, the environment, the results are very similar. For global environmental problems, there was a strong level of correspondence (+.78) between the presentation of this issue in Japanese newspapers and the way that Tokyo residents thought about eight aspects of this issue.

For an environmental situation in the U.S., there was a similarly strong level of correspondence (+.71) between the pictures in people's minds and local newspaper coverage on six aspects of a project to develop a large man-made lake in central Indiana. Which aspects of an issue are covered in the news - and the relative emphasis on these various aspects of an issue-makes a considerable difference in how people view that issue. From the pattern of the total news coverage, the public learns what journalists consider the important issues are and who the prominent public figures of the day are.

From the details of this coverage - the agenda of attributes presented by the news media — the public forms its images and perspective about these issues and public figures. Influencing the focus of public attention is a powerful role, but, arguably, influencing the agenda of attributes for an issue or political figure is the epitome of political power. Determining the way that an issue is framed - setting the ground rules for deliberation, if you will - can significantly influence the ultimate outcome.

Public and media

Although the influence of the media agenda can be substantial, it alone does not determine the public agenda.

Information and cues about object and attribute salience provided by the news media are far from the only determinants of the public agenda. This substantial influence of the news media has no way overturned or nullified the basic assumption of democracy that the people at large have sufficient wisdom to determine the course of their nation, their state, and their local communities. In particular, the people are quite able to determine the basic relevance - to themselves and to the larger public arena - of the topics and attributes advanced by the news media. The media set the agenda only when citizens perceive their news stories as relevant.

The spectacular failure in the U.S. of the intensive news coverage on the Clinton- Lewinsky scandal to set the public agenda and sway public opinion, an effort that failed despite gargantuan and persistent coverage frequently described as "All Monica, all the time," speaks in a loud voice about the limits of media influence. Overwhelmingly, the U.S. public rejected the relevance of that scandal as the basis of their opinion about the president's success or failure in governance. The presence - or absence - of agenda-setting effects by the news media can be explained by a basic psychological trait, our need for orientation. Innate within each one of us is the need to understand the environment around us.

Whenever we find ourselves in a new situation, there is an uncomfortable psychological feeling until we explore and mentally grasp at least the outlines of that setting. Recall, for example, your initial feeling upon visiting a foreign city. This innate need for orientation also exists in the civic arena, especially in those elections where citizens are faced with unfamiliar candidates or referendum questions on which they are less than fully knowledgeable.

In all these situations, and many more, people experience a need for orientation.

Because it is a psychological trait, the degree of need for orientation varies greatly from one individual to another. For some individuals in any situation, there is a high need for orientation. For other individuals, there is little or no need for orientation at all. They just aren't interested. Need for orientation is defined by two components: relevance and uncertainty. Relevance is the initial defining condition that determines the level of need for orientation for each individual. If a topic is perceived as irrelevant - or very low in relevance - then the need for orientation is low. Individuals in this situation pay little or no attention to news media reports and, at most, demonstrate weak agenda-setting effects.

For individuals among whom the relevance of a topic is high, their degree of uncertainty about the topic determines the level of need for orientation. If this uncertainty is low, that is, they feel that they basically understand the topic, then the need for orientation is moderate. These individuals - for whom a situation has high relevance and low uncertainty - will monitor the media for new developments and perhaps occasionally dip into a bit of additional background information. But they are not likely to be avid consumers of news reports about the topic. Agenda-setting effects among this group are moderate.

Among individuals for whom both the relevance and their uncertainty about a situation are high, need for orientation is high. These individuals typically are avid consumers of the news, and strong agenda-setting effects typically are found among these individuals. Table 1 illustrates two patterns that vary according to individuals' levels of need for orientation: attention to the news and agenda-setting effects. Both frequent use of the news media to follow an election and the agenda-setting effects of the news media on the perceived importance of the issues steadily increase with the level of need for orientation among members of the public.

Table 1. Need for Orientation Effects

	Level of Need for Orientation		
	Low	Moderate	High
Frequent users of newspapers, TV and news magazines for political information	54%	63%	74%
Agenda-setting effect of TV (Issue agenda)	+.05	+.41	+.55
Agenda-setting effect of newspapers (Issue agenda)	+.29	+.59	+.68

When the news media do provide information that citizens find relevant and useful in coming to a decision about how to cast their ballots, there is a substantial audience - and there is substantial media influence on the priorities that citizens assign to the issues of the day.

Consequences of agenda-setting

Attitudes and behavior are usually governed by cognitions - what a person knows, thinks, believes. Hence, the agenda-setting function of the mass media implies a potentially massive influence whose full dimensions and consequences have yet to be investigated and appreciated. To begin at the beginning, the salience of objects in the mass media is linked to the formation of opinions by the audience. With the increasing salience of public figures in the news, for example, more people move away from a neutral position and form an opinion about these persons. An examination of US presidential candidates in all five elections between 1980 and 1996 found exceedingly strong correlations between the pattern of media emphasis, which varied widely across these elections, and the number of citizens who expressed ambivalent opinions about the candidates by checking the midpoint of various rating scales.

Twenty of the 24 comparisons between media salience and opinions about a candidate as measured in the National Election Study were significant with a median value of -.90. Note that these correlations are negative because high salience for a candidate in the media was associated with a low number of people selecting the neutral mid-point on the rating scales. Analogous links have been found between issue salience and people's attitudes. In the German state of Baden-Wurttemberg, the personal salience of two major issues, the reunification of East and West Germany and East German migrants, was strongly linked to both the strength and direction of personal opinions.

For the strength of opinion on both issues, personal salience was a far stronger predictor than media exposure or demographic characteristics. For the direction of opinion, personal salience was a slightly stronger predictor than age for German reunification and only slightly weaker predictor than education (and equal to the use of television) for East German migrants.

Priming public opinion

By far the best documented consequence of object and issue salience is the priming of perspectives that subsequently guide the public's opinions about public figures. By calling attention to some matters while ignoring others, television news [as well as the other news media] influences the standards by which governments, presidents, policies, and candidates for public office are judged. The psychological basis of priming is the selective attention of the public. People do not, indeed, can not, pay attention to everything.

Moreover, in making judgments - whether in casting a ballot on election day or simply in responding to a pollster's question - people use simple rules of thumb and intuitive shortcuts. Rather than engaging in a comprehensive analysis based on their total store of information, citizens routinely draw upon those bits of information that are particularly salient at the time judgment must be rendered. In other words, citizens rely upon the agenda of salient objects and attributes in their minds, the agenda that is shaped to a considerable degree by the mass media.

An extensive series of agenda-setting experiments conducted by Shanto Iyengar and Donald Kinder produced significant evidence of a priming effect by television news on people's opinions about the president's overall performance in office. Among subjects exposed to extensive news coverage on one or more of five different issues - defense, inflation, arms control, civil rights, and unemployment-their ratings of presidential performance on the issue or issues receiving heavy news coverage influenced their overall opinion about the president's performance more than among persons not exposed to this news coverage. This influence existed whether or not the news story implied a substantial degree of presidential responsibility for the issue.

In subsequent experiments where the degree of presidential responsibility for an issue was explicitly manipulated, the impact of problem performance ratings on opinions about the president's overall performance was greater when the news stories emphasized presidential responsibility. Turning to a very different setting, public opinion about Hong Kong's last British governor was strongly influenced by news coverage on his proposals to broaden public participation in the election of the Legislative Council.

Tracked in 52 consecutive weekly polls from the fall of 1992 when the governor made his initial policy speech, public opinion about his overall performance was significantly primed by the pattern of news coverage on his reform proposals in Hong Kong's three leading newspapers. Both the distinction and link between traditional agenda-setting effects and priming as a consequence of these effects is illustrated by American public opinion regarding the Persian Gulf War.

Extensive television coverage resulted in the high salience of the war on the public agenda as the most important problem facing the country, a traditional firstlevel agenda-setting effect. Analyses of public opinion about President Bush from 1988 to 1991 further indicated a shift in the basis of his popularity from economics to foreign policy, a priming effect. And demonstrating the effects of attribute agenda-setting on opinions, members of the public who reported higher levels of exposure to television news, which emphasized military options in its framing of the war, favored a military rather than a diplomatic solution in the Persian Gulf.

This priming effect also occurs for political parties. Among German voters, political party preference during 1986 was influenced by the television news agenda. Preference for the Christian Democrats was substantially influenced by news coverage of two issues, the energy supply and East German situation. Preference for the SPD was influenced by three issues, East-West relations, environmental protection, and pensions. Similar patterns were observed in the weekly opinion polls for other political parties. Although the overall pattern is one in which issues on the television news agenda resonated in unique ways with political partisanship, the general finding is that salient issues on the media agenda were strongly linked with shifts in political partisanship during the year.

Mass communication effects can result from the sheer volume of exposure. First level agenda-setting effects demonstrate that phenomenon. But as both attribute agenda-setting and priming demonstrate, closer attention to the specific content of mass media messages — including the tone of those messages - provides a more detailed understanding of the pictures in our heads and of subsequent attitudes and opinions grounded in those pictures. In Germany, the tone of the news about Helmut Kohl in news magazines and major newspapers influenced public opinion between 1975 and 1984 about his political performance, first, as leader of the opposition and, later, as chancellor.

Shifting patterns of positive and negative tone in the media, summed across six attributes of Kohl, prompted significant shifts in his level of approval among the German public. The median correlation between the affective tone of six news media's attribute agendas and subsequent public opinion with a lag time of six months was +.48. In the US, a day-by-day observation of the final three months in the 1992 and 1996 presidential elections found that the tone of television news coverage about key campaign events influenced voters' preference for the candidates. Favorable coverage of Republican campaign events on four national television networks increased support for the Republican candidate.

Conversely, favorable coverage of Democrat campaign events decreased support for the Republican candidate. The strength of these media effects on voters' opinions was similar in the two years. Effects of tone are not limited to attitudes and opinions about political leaders. Negative newspaper headlines about the economy influence the public's perceptions about the health of the economy. In turn, these opinions become self-fulfilling prophecies as people adjust their behavior to fit their beliefs. Comparisons of economic headlines in the New York Times, monthly measures of consumer sentiment about the health of the economy, and major monthly statistical indicators of the actual economy from 1980 through 1993 found a series of significant effects.

Influence of media on behavior

The salience of issues and other topics on the media agenda also influences observable behavior. Extensive news coverage of crime and violence, including a murder and rapes, on the University of Pennsylvania campus a few years ago contributed to a significant drop in applications by potential first-year students, according to the university's dean of admissions. This decline occurred predominantly among women.

Moreover, other comparable universities experienced an increase in applications during the same period. Another example of media influence on the behavior of young adults is Harvard University's successful use of entertainment television programming to spread the idea of "the designated driver," that member of a party group who abstains from drinking in order to safely drive his or her friends home afterward.

A 1988 Indiana Poll brought together all these aspects of agenda-setting and its consequences. Replicating a familiar pattern, the salience among the public of a major issue of that time, the US federal budget deficit, was significantly correlated with the frequency of exposure to both newspapers and television news. In turn, issue salience in conjunction with use of both newspapers and television news predicted public opinion about a possible solution to the problem as well as what people knew about the issue.

Further, issue salience in conjunction with use of a single medium, television news, predicted the strength of people's opinions while issue salience in combination with newspaper reading predicted actual behavior, such as writing a letter or attending a meeting. Here in a single setting is evidence of significant relationships between media exposure and issue salience and of subsequent effects by both on knowledge, opinions and observable behavior.

9

Media and Consumerism

Ever since mass media became mass media, companies have naturally used this means of communications to let a large number of people know about their products. There is nothing wrong with that, as it allows innovative ideas and concepts to be shared with others. However, as the years have progressed, the sophistication of advertising methods and techniques has advanced, enticing and shaping and even creating consumerism and needs where there has been none before, or turning luxuries into necessities.

FREE MEDIA CHANNELS

Various public and free media such as the numerous channels available in America and other nations are naturally subsidized with advertising to help pay the costs. However, as corporate competition has increased, so too has the need for returns on massive expenditures on advertising. Industries spending from millions to billions to win our hearts and influence our choices towards their products and ideas. The sheer amounts of money this brings to media companies is significant and for many cases forms then main form of support for the media company. Hence if something is reported that the advertiser doesn't like, the media company risks losing much needed revenue to stay alive.

Mainstreaming Media

Additionally, as Noam Chomsky points out in his article, *What Makes Mainstream Media Mainstream*, for a company such as the New York Times, it too has to sell products to its customers. For the New York Times and other such companies, Chomsky points out that the product is the audience, and the customers are the corporate advertisers.

This at first thought doesn't seem to make sense. It is not, as we would normally think, and it should be that the product is the newspaper, and the customers are the audience/readers. Sure, readers buy the paper, but as he further points out, readers fit a demography and it is this that is valuable information that can be used by advertisers. Hence, to the advertisers, the product that the New York Times and such companies bring to them, is the audience itself and it is the advertisers that bring the money to the media companies, not the audience.

Ben Bagdikian, a prominent media critic, and author of the well-acclaimed book The Media Monopoly, provides more detail and examples. Bagdikian describes in detail the pressure on media companies to change content (to "dumb down") and to shape content based on the demographics of the audiences. Slowly then, the content of media isn't as important as the type of person being targeted by the ads. He also shows that the notion of "giving the audience what they want" is also a bit misleading because, if anything, it is more about targeting those readers that can afford the products that are advertised and so it is almost like giving the advertisers what they want!

The "dumbing down" of the content also acts to promote a "buying mood". Hence, as Bagdikian summarizes, "programming is carefully noncontroversial, light, and nonpolitical". As he traces briefly the history of advertising in magazines he also hints that this has happened for a long time: "The influence of advertising on magazines reached a point where editors began selecting articles not only on the basis of their expected interest for readers but for their influence on advertisements. Serious articles were not always the best support for ads. An article that put the reader in an analytical frame of mind did not encourage the reader to take seriously an ad that depended on fantasy or promoted a trivial product. An article on genuine social suffering might interrupt the "buying" mood on which most ads for luxuries depend. The next step, seen often in mid-twentieth century magazines, was commissioning articles solely to attract readers who were good prospects to buy products advertised in the magazine. After that came the magazine phenomenon of the 1970s—creating magazines for an identifiable special audience and selling them to particular advertisers."

Sometimes, news stories or editorials are often subtle product advertisements, even with a rise of new terms in critical circles, such as "advertorials". In other cases, due to large ownership, a news company will advertise another program belonging to the parent network and highlight it as a news story, as recent issues of "reality TV" programs in America, such as the Survivor series, have shown. Such use of news time to promote entertainment has come under criticism of late. Richard Robbins also captures this well:

"Protected by the free speech provision of the First Amendment, corporations marshal huge public relations efforts on behalf of their agendas. In the United States the 170,000 public relations employees whose job it is to manipulate news, public opinion and public policy in the interests of their clients outnumber news reporters by 40,000. A study in 1990 discovered that almost 40 percent of the news content of a typical U.S. newspaper originates as public relations press releases, story memos, and suggestions. The Columbia Journalism Review reported that more than half the news stories in the Wall Street Journal are based solely on corporate press releases (cited in Korten 1995:146. United States corporations spend almost half as much on advertising as the state spends on education."

On April 7, 2002, UK's BBC aired a documentary called "Century of the Self" looking back at the rise of consumerism in the 20th century. In discussing the role of the media, it was pointed out how journalism also changed as big business started to gain more influence. Many, in order to get stories that would attract readers, would have to agree to editorial content being dictated by business, such as placement of specific advertising in the pictures, placing certain sentences and paragraphs, and mentioning key products related to the story, etc.

Some sophisticated techniques, such as short films where the aim is to sell a product but to cleverly do the advertising in a subtle way. These mini films can be very entertaining and exciting, but also promote a product behind the main theme. While it could be argued that there is nothing wrong with this, it is just a more sophisticated way to sell products, more forthcoming and explicit mention that this is a commercial would be good for more people to be aware of what they are watching.

Also, the enormous sums of money that can back up this sort of entertainment versus others, can in the long run further affect the type and diversity of the content we receive. Bagdikian also goes on to show that mass advertising also "introduced a new factor in selling: It began to prevent competition" and that it would "negate the classical theory of supply and demand" that was described by Adam Smith. And this isn't just an observation limited to Bagdikian. Robert McChesney, for example also observes similar things:

As globalization becomes ever more prominent, the role of media and advertising and consumerism also increases. Ideal for the large multinationals that can take best advantage of globalization include the even larger "market" to which products can be sold. However, diverse cultures could sometimes be an obstacle to easy selling. Ideally then, attitudes and consumption habits need to be similar for best effect. As a result many media companies promote and project a more aligned culture that will cross these boundaries but also allow easier consumption of their products.

The United Nations Development Programme's 1998 Human Development Report summarizes this quite well: "Globalization is integrating not just trade, investment and financial markets. It is also integrating consumer markets. ... [Economically,] there is fierce competition to sell to consumers worldwide, with increasingly aggressive advertising. On the social side local and national boundaries are breaking down in the setting of social standards and aspirations in consumption.

Market research identifies "global elites" and "global middle classes" who follow the same consumption styles, showing preferences for "global brands". There are the "global teens" - some 270 million 15- to 18-year-olds in 40 countries - inhabiting a "global space", a single pop-culture world, soaking up the same videos and music and providing a huge market for designer running shoes, t-shirts and jeans. An average American, it is estimated, sees 150,000 advertisements on television in his or her lifetime. And advertising is increasing worldwide, faster than population or incomes. Global advertising spending, by the most conservative reckoning, is now $435 billion.

Also worth quoting at some length is part of a paper looking at democracy and transnational media, and a part on the "promotion of consumerism at all costs": The leading transnational media giants are often American or at least Western corporations. To expand markets they must continue to look for new regions for expansion. Southeast Asia, for example, may be one of the last major regions to be affected by international satellites. It really was not until the 1990s, for example, that Southeast Asia saw Western television enter on a massive scale.

Advances in technology plus market liberalization were reasons. Asia, of course, is the largest worldwide market (2.8 billion) and has one-third of the world's television sets. While Asia has been known to foster a distinct culture and linguistic heritage, this specialty is now in jeopardy. MTV, Western news and movie channels, and other Western media influences spreading across Asia. The cultural heritage of these countries is being threatened by trans border data flow, media images moving across national borders thanks to new electronic forms of media delivery. People are told they need products they never "realized" they required. They are told via media that Western styles and habits may be better or more desirable than their own traditions and customs. Young people in particular now grow up with stronger ties to New York and Los Angeles than their own capitals and families.

Then there is the danger that comes when making money is more important than quality of information flow. China's 1.2 billion people are a very desirable audience. Consider what happened when News Corporation purchased STAR TV in 1993. A controversial program on the Chinese government on BBC Work Television News lead to PRC official complaints. Murdock simply pulled the plug. Note that he also was an investor in the Beijing People's Daily. Similar pressures caused him to pressure Harper Collins of London to cancel a book contract with a former ambassador to China because it too was critical of the regime.

The problem goes beyond economic concentrations. Because the product of media industries is cultural programming, the concern centers on the very fabric of life. As stated earlier, the movement is toward grabbing attention and creating a desire for things that people never knew was needed. It also is about using the media to homogenize culture. It involves the world's children, even in the most communication-savvy communities where children below the age of ten are targeted with clever media campaigns. Yet these children are incapable of cognitively understanding what media does. Hence we have animated television programs as those developed several years ago, He-Man and She Ra, where the programs primarily were introduced to market massive lines of toys for the Christmas season. MTV is another example. Here we have entertainment programming which doubles as a continuous commercial for music CDs, clothing lines, talk shows involving music personalities, and a variety of other marketing ploys.

Marketing Strategies

People under the age of twenty-the "Echo Generation," as they're often called-make up a major portion of world's population. Not only is this generation strong in numbers, it also exerts enormous economic influence within the family-a fact not lost on the marketing and advertising industries. Once an ignored demographic for advertisers, today's young people have become the most marketed-to generation in history, thanks to their spending power and their future clout as adult consumers.

The amount of advertising and marketing North Americans are exposed to daily has exploded over the past decade; studies show, that on average 3,000 ads per day. At the gas pumps, in the movie theatre, in a washroom stall, during sporting events-advertising is impossible to avoid. Even outer space isn't safe from commercialization: the Russian space program launched a rocket bearing a 30-foot Pizza Hut logo, and some companies have investigated placing ads in space that will be visible from earth.

The challenge of the future may be finding public and private spaces that are free of advertising. Marketers are pressed to find even more innovative and aggressive ways to cut through the "ad clutter" or "ad fatigue" of modern life.

Ambient advertising

Ambient advertising refers to intrusive ads in public places. With the cost of traditional media advertising skyrocketing and a glut of ads fighting for consumers' attention, marketers are aggressively seeking out new advertising vehicles. Cars, bicycles, taxis and buses have become moving commercials. Ambient ads appear on store floors, at gas pumps, in washrooms stalls, on elevator walls, park benches, telephones, fruit and even pressed into the sand on beaches.

Even some members of the industry itself are critical of this trend to slap ads on everything. Bob Garfield, columnist for the ad industry magazine Advertising Age, calls this plethora of commercial messages "environment pollutants." Others worry that this deluge of advertising will create a backlash with consumers.

Stealth- endorsers

Marketers are moving away from the traditional use of celebrities as product hucksters, since a cynical public no longer believes that celebrities actually use the products they endorse in commercials. The trend now is to brand celebrities with specific merchandise by having them use or wear products in public appearances or promote them in media interviews-without making it clear that the celebrities are paid spokespeople.

Naming rights

Corporations are turning public spaces into commodities by purchasing naming rights to arenas, theatres, parks, schools, museums and even subway systems. Cash-strapped municipalities see naming rights as a way to raise much-needed revenues without raising taxes.

Targeted advertising

Targeted ads are a form of Internet marketing. Using sophisticated data collecting technologies, Web sites can combine a user's personal information with surfing preferences to create ads that are specifically tailored for that user.

Cross-merchandizing

A wave of media mergers over the past decade has produced a handful of powerful conglomerates that now own all the major film studios, TV networks, radio and television stations, cable channels, Internet, book and magazine publishing and music companies. These giant conglomerates use their various media holdings to promote products and artists through massive cross-promotional campaigns. For example, when the world's largest entertainment conglomerate AOL Time Warner was preparing the release of the film Harry Potter and the Sorcerer's Stone, it enlisted all its various media divisions-cable systems, speciality channels, TV networks, magazines and Internet companies-to help mass-market the movie and the spin-off merchandise.

Commenting on the phenomenally successful cross-promotional approach used to market the film (Harry Potter smashed all previous opening records, grossing $90 million in its first weekend) AOL Time Warner executive Richard Parsons explained: "This drove synergy both ways. Not only did we use our promotional and advertising platforms to help create awareness, we used the film to drive traffic to those vehicles."

Product placement

The future of product placement as a successful advertising tool was assured when the 1982 film ET featured Reese's Pieces in a pivotal scene-causing sales of the candy to jump 65 per cent. Since that time, product placement in movies, on TV, and increasingly in video games, has become a commonplace marketing technique. With the advent of technologies such as TiVo, which allow consumers to edit out TV commercials, product placement is taking on an even greater importance. TV producers are looking for new ways to integrate advertising and content. Basing an entire show around a product is one technique; and giving viewers the capability of immediately purchasing products featured on the program is another. In the near future, Interactive TV will allow users to order a pair of pants that your favourite TV star is wearing, merely by clicking on them.

Digital advertising

Digital advertising goes one step further than product placement by using computer technology to add products to scenes that were never there to begin with. This practice is common in sporting events coverage, where ads are digitally inserted onto the billboards, sideboards and playing surfaces in arenas and stadiums. While digital ads are mainly used in sports coverage, virtual advertising is starting to break into the entertainment world as producers digitally insert products into TV scenes after the scenes are shot. The technology also allows product names to be altered in scenes, creating the potential for new advertising revenues when series are sold into syndication.

Kids represent an important demographic to marketers because they have their own purchasing power, they influence their parents' buying decisions and they're the adult consumers of the future. Industry spending on advertising to children has exploded in the past decade, increasing from a mere $100 million in 1990 to more than $2 billion in 2000. Parents today are willing to buy more for their kids because trends such as smaller family size, dual incomes and postponing children until later in life mean that families have more disposable income. As well, guilt can play a role in spending decisions as time-stressed parents substitute material goods for time spent with their kids.

Today's kids have more autonomy and decision-making power within the family than in previous generations, so it follows that kids are vocal about what they want their parents to buy. "Pester power" refers to children's ability to nag their parents into purchasing items they may not otherwise buy. Marketing to children is all about creating pester power, because advertisers know what a powerful force it can be. According to the 2001 marketing industry book Kidfluence, pestering or nagging can be divided into two categories-"persistence" and "importance." Persistence nagging (a plea, that is repeated over and over again) is not as effective as the more sophisticated "importance nagging." This latter method appeals to parents' desire to provide the best for their children, and plays on any guilt they may have about not having enough time for their kids.

Effective Marketing

To effectively market to children, advertisers need to know what makes kids tick. With the help of well-paid researchers and psychologists, advertisers now have access to in-depth knowledge about children's developmental, emotional and social needs at different ages. Using research that analyzes children's behaviour, fantasy lives, art work, even their dreams, companies are able to craft sophisticated marketing strategies to reach young people.

The issue of using child psychologists to help marketers target kids gained widespread public attention in 1999, when a group of U.S. mental health professionals issued a public letter to the American Psychological

Association (APA) urging them to declare the practice unethical. The APA is currently studying the issue.

Marketers plant the seeds of brand recognition in very young children, in the hopes that the seeds will grow into lifetime relationships. According to the Center for a New American Dream, babies as young as six months of age can form mental images of corporate logos and mascots. Brand loyalties can be established as early as age two, and by the time children head off to school most can recognize hundreds of brand logos. "Brand marketing must begin with children. Even if a child does not buy the product and will not for many years... the marketing must begin in childhood."

While fast food, toy and clothing companies have been cultivating brand recognition in children for years, adult-oriented businesses such as banks and automakers are now getting in on the act. Magazines such as Time, Sports Illustrated and People have all launched kid and teen editions-which boast ads for adult related products such as minivans, hotels and airlines.

Street marketing

The challenge for marketers is to cut through the intense advertising clutter in young people's lives. Many companies are using "buzz marketing"-a new twist on the tried-and-true "word of mouth" method. The idea is to find the coolest kids in a community and have them use or wear your product in order to create a buzz around it. Buzz, or "street marketing," as it's also called, can help a company to successfully connect with the savvy and elusive teen market by using trendsetters to give their products "cool" status. Buzz marketing is particularly well-suited to the Internet, where young "Net promoters" use newsgroups, chat rooms and blogs to spread the word about music, clothes and other products among unsuspecting users.

Commercialization in Education

School used to be a place where children were protected from the advertising and consumer messages that permeated their world-but not any more. Budget shortfalls are forcing school boards to allow corporations access to students in exchange for badly needed cash, computers and educational materials. Corporations realize the power of the school environment for promoting their name and products. A school setting delivers a captive youth audience and implies the endorsement of teachers and the educational system. Marketers are eagerly exploiting this medium in a number of ways, including:

— *Sponsored educational materials*: for example, a Kraft "healthy eating" kit to teach about Canada's Food Guide; or forestry company Canfor's primary lesson plans that make its business focus seem like environmental management rather than logging.

— Supplying schools with technology in exchange for high company visibility.

— Exclusive deals with fast food or soft drink companies to offer their products in a school or district.

— Advertising posted in classrooms, school buses, on computers, etc. in exchange for funds.

— *Contests and incentive programs*: for example, the Pizza Hut reading incentives program in which children receive certificates for free pizza if they achieve a monthly reading goal; or Campbell's Labels for

Education project, in which Campbell provides educational resources for schools in exchange for soup labels collected by students.

— *Sponsoring school events*: The Canadian company ShowBiz brings moveable video dance parties into schools to showcase various sponsors' products.

INTERNET: A MEDIUM FOR MARKETERS

The Internet is an extremely desirable medium for marketers wanting to target children:

— It's part of youth culture. This generation of young people is growing up with the Internet as a daily and routine part of their lives.

— Parents generally do not understand the extent to which kids are being marketed to online.

— Kids are often online alone, without parental supervision.

— Unlike broadcasting media, which have codes regarding advertising to kids, the Internet is unregulated.

— Sophisticated technologies make it easy to collect information from young people for marketing research, and to target individual children with personalized advertising.

— By creating engaging, interactive environments based on products and brand names, companies can build brand loyalties from an early age.

Children are often aware of and want to see entertainment meant for older audiences because it is actively marketed to them. In a report released in 2000, the U.S. Federal Trade

Commission (FTC) revealed how the movie, music and video games industries routinely market violent entertainment to young children. The FTC studied 44 films rated "Restricted," and discovered that 80 per cent were targeted to children under 17. Marketing plans included TV commercials run during hours when young viewers were most likely to be watching. One studio's plan for a violent R-rated film stated, "Our goal was to find the elusive teen target audience, and make sure that everyone between the ages of 12 and 18 was exposed to the film."

Music containing "explicit-content" labels were targeted at young people through extensive advertising in the most popular teen venues on television, and radio, in print, and online. Of the video game companies investigated for the report, 70 per cent regularly marketed Mature rated games to children. Marketing plans included placing advertising in media that would reach a substantial percentage of children under 17. The FTC report also highlighted the fact that toys based on characters from mature entertainment are often marketed to young children. Mature and Teen rated video games are advertised in youth magazines; and toys based on Restricted movies and M-rated video games are marketed to children as young as four.

Developmental concerns

Parents of young children have an important role to play in protecting their kids from invasive marketing, and in educating them about advertising from an early age. Young children have difficulty distinguishing between advertising and reality in ads, and ads can distort their view of the world. Research has shown that children between the ages of two and five cannot differentiate between regular TV programming and commercials. Young children are especially vulnerable to misleading advertising and don't begin to understand that advertisements are not always true until they're eight.

According to the Canadian Toy Testing Council the biggest area of concern with toy ads in Canada is exaggeration. Young children often think a toy actually can do a lot more than it can because of the way toys are portrayed in advertisements. These concerns have led some jurisdictions to ban all advertising to children. Québec has banned print and broadcast advertising aimed at kids under thirteen. Sweden has banned advertisements aimed at children under 12 and it is lobbying European Union members to adopt similar policies.

Advertising at its best is making people feel that without their product, you're a loser. Kids are very sensitive to that. Parents should be concerned about the effect excessive materialism can have on the development of their children's self image and values. Children's identities shouldn't be defined by their consumer habits; yet that is the main way they see themselves reflected in the media-as consumers, and advertisers are targeting younger and younger children with this message. The marketing of merchandise based on the popular pre-school TV programs Barney and Teletubbies marked the beginning of identifying toddlers as a consumer market.

Junk food advertising

A healthy society raises children to be responsible citizens rather than just consumers. According to the Canadian Paediatric Society, most food advertising on children's TV shows is for fast foods, soft drinks, candy and presweetened cereals-while commercials for healthy food make up only 4 per cent of those shown.

Fast food chains spend more than 3 billion dollars a year on advertising, much of it aimed at children. To directly target children, the fast food industry uses more than traditional commercials. Restaurants offer incentives such as playgrounds, contests, clubs, games, and free toys and other merchandise related to movies, TV shows and even sports leagues. A 2002 U.S. study showed that fast-food commercials during kids programming on Saturday mornings are pitching bigger and bigger portions, a trend that researchers link to an the alarming rise of obesity among young people.

Marketing toys

Marketing young children toys that are based on restricted movies and Mature rated video games is a common industry practice. A report in 2000 by the U.S. Federal Trade Commission exposed how the media industries actively target young children with violent entertainment meant for adults. Among their findings was the fact that action toys, based on characters from video games rated Teen and Mature, were labelled suitable for children (sometimes as young as 4 or 5 years old).

The packaging for one action figure recommended for kids four years old and up, invites them to "join in the blood bath" by playing the Nintendo version of the game-even though it's M-rated (for ages 17 and up). A company which produces toys based on the World Wrestling Federation encourages children four and up to use their play sets to "bash and dump opponents senseless with an array of street fighting accessories."

Marketers have discovered something about children that parents have long known-they love to collect things. Kids' collections used to consist of marbles, stamps or coins. But now, thanks to our consumer culture, kids amass huge collection of store-bought items such as Beanie Babies, Barbies or Pokémon cards and figures. The marketing strategy behind the Pokémon was simple and lucrative-create 150 Pokémon characters, then launch a marketing campaign called "Gotta Catch 'Em All," to encourage children to collect all 150 of the cheaply made, over priced figures.Because most collecting crazes are short-lived fads, the sheen quickly fades on the current collection and kids move on to the next big trend-leaving behind boxes of discarded toys.

Special Issues for Tweens and Teens

One of the most important recent developments in advertising to kids has been the defining of a "tween" market (ages 8 to 12). No longer little children, and not yet teens, tweens are starting to develop their sense of identity and are anxious to cultivate a sophisticated self-image. And marketers are discovering there's lots of money to be made by treating tweens like teenagers. The marketing industry is forcing tweens to grow up quickly. Industry research reveals that children 11 and older don't consider themselves children anymore. The Toy Manufacturers of America have changed their target market from birth to 14, tó birth to ten years of age.

A 2000 report from the Federal Trade Commission in the U.S. revealed how Hollywood routinely recruits tweens (some as young as nine) to evaluate its story concepts, commercials, theatrical trailers and rough cuts for R-rated movies. By treating pre-adolescents as independent, mature consumers, marketers have been very successful in removing the gatekeepers (parents) from the picture-leaving tweens vulnerable to potentially unhealthy messages about body image, sexuality, relationships and violence.

Body image and advertising

It's difficult for teens to develop healthy attitudes towards sexuality and body image when much of the advertising aimed at them is filled with images of impossibly thin, fit, beautiful and highly sexualized young people. The underlying marketing message is that there is a link between physical beauty and sex appeal-and popularity success, and happiness. Fashion marketers such as Calvin Klein, Abercrombie & Fitch and Guess use provocative marketing campaigns featuring young models. These ads are selling more than clothing to teens-they're also selling adult sexuality.

Studies show that while teens received most of their information about sex from the media: magazines, TV, the Web, radio and movies, the majority say their parents shape their sexual decisions most, so it's important that parents talk to their kids about healthy sexuality, and about exploitive media images. Media images can contribute to feelings of body-hatred and self-loathing that can fuel eating problems. While body image has long been considered a female issue, an increasing number of boys now also suffer from eating disorders. Studies have also found that boys, like girls, may turn to smoking to help them lose weight.

Tobacco and alcohol

Advertising has always sold anxiety, and it certainly sells anxiety to the young. It's always telling them they're losers unless they're cool. Tobacco and alcohol companies have long targeted young people, hoping to develop brand loyalties that will last a lifetime. It's crucial for the tobacco industry to continually cultivate new and younger smokers to replace the thousands who quit each year-and those who die of tobacco-related diseases.

The tobacco industry targets youth by:

— linking smoking in ads with being "cool" and independent and with taking risks (particularly physical risks)

— placing ads in magazines with high adolescent readerships, such as Rolling Stone, Maxim or People

— having movie stars, who are popular with young people, smoke in films

— sponsoring rock concerts and sporting events

— placing advertising near high schools: on billboards, in bus shelters and in variety stores.

The alcohol and beer industries were quick to recognize the value of the Internet as an effective tool for reaching young people. The Web offers marketers a medium that is a huge part of youth culture-with the added bonus that it's unregulated, with very little parental supervision.

In 1999, the U.S. Center for Media Education found that 62 per cent of beer and alcohol Web sites displayed what they call "youth-oriented features"-that is, activities that appeal to the adolescent and pre-adolescent set. The alcohol and beer industries also target youth by:

— running ads during TV shows with a high number of young views, such as The Simpsons, South Park or sporting events

— placing ads in magazines with high adolescent readerships, such as Rolling Stone, Maxim or People

— sponsoring rock concerts and sporting events

— creating and extensively marketing "alcopops"-sweetened, lightly carbonated drinks that don't taste like alcohol

What parents can do

— Educate your kids about advertising and how marketers target young people.

— Help kids understand that the main goal of advertising is to make them buy things-often things they don't need, and didn't even know they wanted until they've seen the ad.

— Explain that advertising is big business, one of the largest businesses in the world.

— Using the Advertising Strategies handout (right sidebar), talk about the techniques marketers use to target kids.

— Using the Rules For Advertising To Kids (right sidebar), discuss what advertisers are not allowed to do when making ads for kids. Examine commercials and print ads to see if they follow the rules.

— Using the Talking to Kids About Advertising tip sheet (right sidebar), start to integrate media literacy questions into the conversations you have with your kids about advertising.

Challenge your children's definition of "cool" Ask them the following questions:

— Do you ever feel bad about yourself for not owning something?

— Have you ever felt that people might like you more if you owned a certain item?

— Has an ad made you feel that you would like yourself more, or that others would like you more, if you owned the product the ad is selling?

— Do you ever worry about your looks? Have you ever felt that people would like you more if your face, body, skin or hair looked different?

— Has an ad ever made you feel that you would like yourself more, or others would like you more, if you changed your appearance with the product the ad was selling?

For marketers, kids represent a lucrative demographic with enormous amounts of disposable income and tremendous purchasing power. The surfing habits of young people make them an ideal target group. In its 1999 study The Net-Powered Generation, Forrester Research found that young Internet users:

— Stay online for longer periods than adults

— Are more likely to access the Internet from different locations

— Participate in a wider range of online activities

— Are more likely to adapt quickly to new technology, and embrace its changes

Strategies of online marketers

In a Wired World, 99 per cent of kids have gone online, and 79 per cent have Internet access at home. Among Canadian kids ages 9-17, the most popular online activities include:

— Playing and downloading music

— Sending and receiving email messages

— Surfing for fun

— Playing and downloading games

Each of these activities presents opportunities to marketers, who seek to develop relationships with young people at the earliest possible age. A few online marketing strategies used to bombard kids with brand-related messages include:

— Words and images that make a Web site feel like a "place" or a "world"

— Friendly cartoon "spokes-characters" that encourage kids to identify with products and companies.

— Interactive games and activities such as colouring pages, crossword puzzles and word searches featuring brand products and characters

— Clubs that kids can join, and contests they can enter to win prizes

— Banner ads linking visitors to other commercial Web sites

— Brand-related "e-cards" that kids can send to friends and family

Similar marketing strategies are used to build relationships with older kids.

— Present themselves as being part of a teen subculture-no adults allowed!

— Use celebrities as spokespersons

— Feature bold graphics and attitude-laden content

— Build online communities through chat and email

— Feature the latest music, sports and celebrity gossip, as well as sophomoric humour and party talk
— Offer quizzes, contests and brand-related games

Even sites that promote products for adults use strategies like these to draw in children and teens. Alcohol sites are the chief offenders; but some gambling sites also use kid-friendly tactics to win the loyalty of the next generation of consumers. Surveys show that most young people view the Internet as a communication and socialization tool. As a result, companies offer young people "virtual communities" or forums where they can interact and talk with like-minded people. These communities can take the form of simple chat rooms, or more elaborate "palaces" where visitors can use avatars (pictures or cartoons) to assume visual identities when they interact.

Marketers value these "virtual communities" for a number of reasons:

— They attract a specific target audience.
— They bring visitors back again and again.
— They provide a place to promote and sell products, collect demographic and product-use information, and interact one-on-one with consumers. Marketers can also lace chat-room discussion with subtle promotions, or "plant" personalities to enliven talk or encourage visitors to disclose personal information.

Marketers also see great opportunities in online game playing. Researchers say that when they play electronic games or surf the Net, they enter a "flow state" that makes us receptive to the images and messages we encounter. Traditional commercials don't work online-they interrupt that flow state. Games, on the other hand, are an ideal vehicle for keeping kids in the marketing loop. With their seamlessly integrated product promotions, "advergames" keep kids happily engaged with products and brands for hours at a time.

Online spending

Creating engaging online communities builds brand recognition, loyalty and trust, but the ultimate goal is to get young people to spend money online. This accounts for the increasing presence of Web sites that aggressively promote online spending. In A Wired World found that only 15 per cent of Canadian teens have actually made online purchases. To encourage online spending, some of these "teen com" sites permit teens to earn points that can be redeemed as discounts. Others provide alternatives to credit cards for Web purchases by teens, usually by allowing their parents to create debit accounts.

No Canadian guidelines specifically address electronic marketing to children. Instead, responsible kids' sites adhere to the Canadian Marketing Association's "Special Considerations in Marketing to Children" and, to a lesser extent, Advertising Standards Canada's "Broadcast Code for Advertising to Children." In the United States, many sites for kids voluntarily adhere to the Children's Advertising Review Unit's guidelines for online marketing to children. These guidelines require companies to let kids know when they're being advertised to. However, this can be a fuzzy area. A site may identify a banner ad as an "advertisement"- but not the online games and activities where kids interact with brand characters.

Culture of Commercialism

Over the years, the sophistication of marketing has

increased a great deal. The messages that encourage us to buy are designed by creative, talented people. Modern scientific knowledge of human psychology and of how the brain processes visual information is used in developing ads. An array of technical equipment and resources is also used. Ads talk to our conscious, rational mind and to our subconscious fears and desires.

Of course, no one would advocate a ban on marketing. Ads provide information that can be helpful to us as consumers. Ads increase our understanding of the product choices available to us. And in an economy based on free enterprise, ads play a vital role for the business community. Ads are a valid part of modern life.

Some people are concerned about all the advertising we're exposed to. The information is not presented as an objective argument on the pros and cons of commercialism. Following are the effects of advertising and commercialism:

1. Commercialism distorts our culture by turning every event into a reason to consume. Anthropologists say that holidays reflect a culture's values. In America, every holiday is a sales event.

2. Advertising projects false images. For example, some ads imply that you're not cool unless you drive an expensive car, that smoking means you're an independent spirit, or that to be mature means drinking alcohol.

3. Commercialism contributes to environmental problems by encouraging wasteful use of natural resources. Over-packaging, disposable goods, and buying things we don't really need all contribute to unnecessary use of limited resources. The manufacture and disposal of the things we buy cause other environmental

problems, including habitat loss and increased air and water pollution. Billboards cause visual pollution.

4. Advertising perpetuates stereotypes. Examples include stereotypes related to race (African-Americans as musicians and athletes), gender (women as sex objects, men as business people), and class (middle-class whites as the social norm).

5. Advertisers influence the content of publications and broadcasts. Government censorship of the media is illegal. Yet it is well documented that newspapers and other media are censored by advertisers. For example, a beer producer may pressure a magazine in which it buys ad space not to print articles on the dangers of drinking.

6. Corporate sponsorship of civic, environmental, or other non-profit groups may influence those groups. For example, tobacco industry contributions may discourage an organization from joining anti-smoking campaigns.

7. Commercialism has influenced our political process. Many politicians try to attract votes with an image created by advertising and media coverage. In the past, candidates tried to attract votes by their stand on the issues.

8. The public's perception of a company's activities and priorities can be distorted by image advertising. For example, ads can portray major polluters as environmentally conscious companies that give to worthy causes.

9. Advertising costs us money. Businesses pass many of their advertising costs on to us. Also, the price of a product increases when ads successfully cultivate the

idea that a certain product can give us status or a cool image.

10. Ads cost us more in taxes, too. Advertising is a fully tax-deductible business expense. Because of this, state and federal treasuries receive billions of dollars less in business taxes each year. Tax rates for citizens must make up for this, so individual taxpayers indirectly subsidize advertising.
11. Ads can be misleading. They emphasize the benefits of products and services and ignore the drawbacks.
12. Ads encourage a brand-name mentality, or buying on the basis of the maker rather than quality or price.
13. Advertising fosters dissatisfaction, envy, and insecurity. It can make us feel unattractive, uncool, and unhappy with what we do or don't have.
14. Our commercialized society places a strong emphasis on appearance, encouraging us to care about our own and others' appearances rather than about characters, talents, and personalities.
15. Constant exposure to ads may encourage materialism and selfishness. This may make people less inclined to help others. Statistics show that giving to charitable causes has decreased in recent years. Similarly, there has been a decline in public support for government programs to aid the least fortunate members of our society.
16. Corporate sponsorship may influence content and undermine the objectivity of exhibits at science and art museums. For example, is an exhibit sponsored by a company that makes insecticides likely to examine human/insect relationships in a fair and balanced way?

17. Ads take a lot of our time. The average person spends almost an hour a day reading, watching, or listening to ads through TV, radio, theaters, videotapes, newspapers, magazines, mail, or telephone. By the time the average American is seventy-five years old, advertising will have taken four years of his or her life.

18. Paid product placements influence the content of movies, TV shows, books, and board games. This compromises artistic integrity.

19. Advertising promotes alcohol and tobacco use, which kill half a million Americans annually. Problems related to alcohol hurt more people's lives and cost society more money than all illegal drugs combined.

20. Marketers compile detailed electronic portraits of shoppers. Companies sell mailing lists for everything from foreign car ownership to sexual preference. These computer databases present a staggering potential for abuse.

21. Commercialism has spread into almost every aspect of life. Being unable to escape it is annoying to many.

22. Advertising aimed at young children intrudes on the parent-child relationship, can undermine parental authority, and can create friction in the home.

23. Commercialism may erode values - such as sharing, co-operation, and frugality - fostered by families, religious institutions, and schools.

24. Commercial foods and the ads for them tend to encourage unhealthy eating habits.

25. Commercialization of school materials and equipment may undermine objective, unbiased education.

26. Heavy promotion of shopping and buying distracts us from other activities such as reading, thinking, and playing. All the ads we're exposed to make it easy to forget how many different kinds of activities we enjoy.

27. Our commercialized culture encourages people to spend money that they don't really have. The number of Americans with financial problems has increased steadily in recent years.

28. Advertising implies that there's an easy solution to everything, from being healthy to having friends.

29. Many ads imply, even if they don't say outright, that happiness is something we can buy. When we act as though this is true, our personal horizons and ability to find fulfilment in life are limited.

30. Commercialism does not just promote specific products. It promotes consumption as a way of life.

Cumulative effect of commercialism

Commercialism has clear parallels with industrial pollution. Just as modest amounts of waste can be absorbed by the natural environment, so modest amounts of commercialism can be assimilated by our cultural environment. Large amounts, however, can totally overwhelm either environment, and such is the case today. In some cases, such as air pollution from coal-burning furnaces, the problems were obvious but were either ignored or justified on the basis of short-term economic gain. In other cases, such as toxic chemicals that pollute the air and water, the dangers were not even recognized.

Again as with pollution several decades ago, the consequences of excessive commercialism remain unexamined and unproven. The fact is that, despite the dominance of commercialism in our culture, social scientists have barely begun to explore its nature and its consequences. Moreover, government regulatory programs are inadequate to contain commercialism. Agencies that focus on deceptive advertising have such small budgets - totalling only about one thousandth as much as what is spent on advertising - that only the most blatantly dishonest advertising can be stopped. Other forms of commercialism go completely unexamined.

OWNERSHIP

Some nations can influence and control their media greatly. In addition, powerful corporations are becoming major influences on mainstream media. In some places major multinational corporations own media stations and outlets. Moreover, even as numbers of media outlets increase, the ownership is becoming ever more concentrated as mega mergers take hold. At the same time, vertical integration gives the big players even more avenues to cross-sell and cross-market their products for even more amazing profits. An effect of this though is a reduction in diversity and depth of content that the public can get, while increasing the political and economic power of corporations and advertisers. An informed population is crucial element to a functioning democracy.

In some places major multinational corporations own media stations and outlets. Often, many media institutes survive on the advertising fees, which can lead to the media outlet to be influenced by various corporate interests. News coverage and other media content can therefore be adversely affected. For example, stories end up biased or omitted so as not to offend their advertisers or owners.

While corporate media per se may not be a bad thing, it is when there is a concentration of ownership that there is a risk of increased economic and political influence that can be somewhat unaccountable, which is of concern.

The deregulation of media ownership, the privatization of television in lucrative European and Asian markets, and new communications technologies have made it possible for media giants to establish powerful distribution and production networks within and among nations. In short order, the global media market has come to be dominated by the same eight transnational corporations, or TNCs, that rule US media: General Electric, AT&T/Liberty Media, Disney, Time Warner, Sony, News Corporation, Viacom and Seagram, plus Bertelsmann, the Germany-based conglomerate. At the same time, a number of new firms and different political and social factors enter the picture as one turns to the global system, and the struggle for domination continues among the nine giants and their closest competitors. But as in the United States, at a global level this is a highly concentrated industry; the largest media corporation in the world in terms of annual revenues, Time Warner, is some fifty times larger in terms of annual sales than the world's fiftieth-largest media firm.

A few global corporations are horizontally integrated; that is, they control a significant slice of specific media sectors, like book publishing, which has undergone extensive consolidation in the late nineties. "We have never seen this kind of concentration before," says an attorney who specializes in publishing deals. But even more striking has been the rapid vertical integration of the global media market, with the same firms gaining ownership of content and the means to distribute it. What distinguishes the dominant firms is their ability to exploit the "synergy" among the companies they own. Nearly all the major Hollywood studios are owned by one of these conglomerates, which in turn control the cable channels and TV networks that air the movies.

The major media companies have moved aggressively to become global players. Even Time Warner and Disney, which still get most of their revenues in the United States, project non-US sales to yield a majority of their revenues within a decade. The point is to capitalize on the potential for growth abroad--and not get outflanked by competitors--since the US market is well developed and only permits incremental expansion. As Viacom CEO Sumner Redstone has put it, "Companies are focusing on those markets promising the best return, which means overseas."

Prior to the eighties and nineties, media systems were typified by domestically owned radio, television and newspaper industries. Newspaper publishing remains a largely national phenomenon, but the face of television has changed almost beyond recognition. Neoliberal free-market policies have opened up ownership of stations as well as cable and digital satellite TV systems to private and transnational interests, producing scores of new channels operated by the media TNCs that dominate cable ownership in the United States. The channels in turn generate new revenue streams for the TNCs: The major Hollywood studios, for example, expect to generate $11 billion from global TV rights to their film libraries in 2002, up from $7 billion in 1998.

While media conglomerates press for policies to facilitate their domination of markets throughout the world, strong traditions of protection for domestic media and cultural industries persist. Nations ranging from Norway, Denmark and Spain to Mexico, South Africa and South

Korea keep their small domestic film production industries alive with government subsidies. In the summer of 1998 culture ministers from twenty nations, including Brazil, Mexico, Sweden, Italy and Ivory Coast, met in Ottawa to discuss how they could "build some ground rules" to protect their cultural fare from "the Hollywood juggernaut." Their main recommendation was to keep culture out of the control of the World Trade Organization.

A similar 1998 gathering, sponsored by the United Nations in Stockholm, recommended that culture be granted special exemptions in global trade deals. Nevertheless, the trend is clearly in the direction of opening markets. Proponents of neoliberalism in every country argue that cultural trade barriers and regulations harm consumers, and that subsidies inhibit the ability of nations to develop their own competitive media firms. There are often strong commercial-media lobbies within nations that perceive they have more to gain by opening up their borders than by maintaining trade barriers. In 1998, for example, when the British government proposed a voluntary levy on film theater revenues (mostly Hollywood films) to benefit the British commercial film industry, British broadcasters, not wishing to antagonize the firms who supply their programming, lobbied against the measure until it died.

Focusing on democracy-enhancing principles and the institutions needed for it such as the media and journalism, the concern that arises is that there are very few media owners in the mainstream that reach out to the masses. As a result, there is the risk of reduced diversity of issues and perspectives and of political influence and interests from a few affecting the many. Most citizens get their views and understandings of the world around them from the mainstream media. It is therefore critical to understand some of these underlying issues.

Many of the large media company owners are entertainment companies and have vertical integration (i.e. own operations and businesses) across various industries and verticals, such as distribution networks, toys and clothing manufacture and/or retailing etc. That means that while this is good for their business, the diversity of opinions and issues we can see being discussed by them will be less well covered. (One cannot expect Disney, for example, to talk too much about sweatshop labor when it is accused of being involved in such things itself.)

Vertical Integration was once looked upon with alarm by government. It was understood that corporations which have control of a total process, from raw material to fabrication to sales, also have few motives for genuine innovation and the power to seize out anyone else who tries to compete. This situation distorts the economy with monopolistic control over prices. Today, government has become sympathetic to dominant vertical corporations that have merged into ever larger total systems. These corporations, including those in the media, have remained largely unrestrained.

Vertical integration is also a part of a business strategy that serves to enhance market power, by allowing cross-promotion and cross-selling. On such television channels or newspapers/magazines owned by such large corporations, you are understandably not going to read much criticism about those companies. Furthermore, you are not likely to see much deep criticism about economic, political or other policies that go against the interest of that parent company. So, while it is understandable why a company would aim for such cross selling and integration, the threat to diversity and real competition is real. For smaller companies without such an arsenal of distribution and cross-selling possibilities, the competition is very difficult, and they face either going out of business, or being bought out, or if lucky, the dictum of "if you can't beat them, join them" (or try to emulate them!) rings true.

Interlocking directorates is also another issue. Interlocking is where a director of one company may sit on a board of another company. As pointed out by U.S. media watchdog, Fairness an Accuracy In Reporting (FAIR) for example, Media corporations share members of the board of directors with a variety of other large corporations, including banks, investment companies, oil companies, health care and pharmaceutical companies and technology companies. Ben H Bagdikian, in his book, *The Media Monopoly*, details some of the impacts of this interlocking. In these cases where directors from numerous large corporations sit on each others boards and own or sit on boards of large media companies, he points out that conflicts of interest can be numerous.

The deeper social loss of giantism in the media is not in its unfair advantage in profits and power; this is real and it is serious. But the gravest loss is in the self-serving censorship of political and social ideas, in news, magazine articles, books, broadcasting, and movies. Some intervention by owners is direct and blunt. But most of the screening is subtle, some not even occurring at a conscious level, as when subordinates learn by habit to conform to owners' ideas. But subtle or not, the ultimate result is distorted reality and impoverished ideas.

Corporations have multimillion-dollar budgets to dissect and attack news reports they dislike. But with each passing year they have yet another power: They are not only hostile to independent journalists. They are their employers. In this respect, as the mainstream media is more corporate owned, the same market pressures that affect those companies, affect the media as well and hence, the media itself is largely driven by the forces of the market. In the US, for example, it is very noticeable how competitive the media companies are between themselves. While competition can be a healthy aspect of news reporting and media in general, pushing for better quality, the oligopoly and concentrated control of media companies has meant that the competition has reduced itself to attracting viewers through sensationalism etc rather than quality, detailed reporting etc.

Many stations report news on the very same stories at the exact same time and have commercial breaks at the same time! The sensationalism they compete for is what they hope will drive audiences to their channel. This type of competition affects the ability to provide quality news and affects the depth and even reputation of professional journalism. As an example of influence, Disney's size and popularity provides a good example. Disney is well regarded for providing wholesome family entertainment, with numerous films, cartoons/animation movies and so on. However, with the increasing size, owning the ABC news station, and enormous vertical integration, there have been increasing criticisms of Disney as well, ranging from the subtle cultural and even racial, gender and class bias depicted in their cartoons and movies, to their ability to naturally (directly or indirectly) influence major news stories via their ABC ownership.

That is not to say that Disney is necessarily sexist, racist and so on by intent. It is possible that the drive for profits is more important and leads to less criticism, because from a business perspective, they have been very successful and implemented the most "appropriate" strategies to expand and grow.

Concentration of ownership is where the problem largely lies

— If the number of outlets is growing and the number of owners declining, then each owner controls even more formidable communications power.

— It isn't necessarily the corporate ownership that is problematic.

For example, in U.K. the Independent Television Network (ITN), and Channel 4 are highly regarded for their quality documentaries and ITN's evening news program was said to challenge the BBC's news programming for quality (until ITN seemed to succumb to pressure to use that prime time for movies instead of news). In some respects, even large media companies can be potentially beneficial. But when big media is owned by big business, there is less criticism of big business or related political issues in big government.

Corporate-Owned Media

Large, corporate-owned media are "free" trade proponents. As a consequence, the coverage of alternative views and critique has been either avoided, or almost ignored, because the same international system (given the label of "free trade") benefits the large media companies and their owners that are also global. Diverse views are therefore not expressed and not available for most people.

An almost ironic situation for example is how "free market" capitalism is said to be supported and promoted by the mainstream when the concentration in media ownership itself, as well as in other industries, is anything but free market capitalism. It is more akin to the older mercantile or monopoly capitalism that Adam Smith exposed and so decried.

Adam Smith, often regarded as the father of modern capitalism, wrote the influential famous book, *The Wealth of Nations* in 1776. This book exposed the mercantile and monopoly capitalism of the preceeding centuries as unjust and unfair, and proposed a free market system. He himself was very critical of the influences of concentrated ownership (which is also a way to reduce competition) and large corporations as interfering with free market capitalism (although many who do exert influence don't mind doing so in his name, and calling it "free market"!) Smith is worth quoting at length:

> Merchants and master manufacturers are ... the two classes of people who commonly employ the largest capitals, and who by their wealth draw to themselves the greatest share of the public consideration. As during their whole lives they are engaged in plans and projects, they have frequently more acuteness of understanding than the greater part of country gentlemen. As their thoughts, however, are commonly exercised rather about the interest of their own particular branch of business, than about that of the society, their judgment, even when given with the greatest candour (which it has not been upon every occasion) is much more to be depended upon with regard to the former of those two objects than with regard to the latter.
>
> Their superiority over the country gentleman is not so much in their knowledge of the public interest, as in their having a better knowledge of their own interest than he has of his. It is by this superior knowledge of their own interest that they have frequently imposed upon his generosity, and persuaded him to give up both his own interest and that of the public, from a very simple but honest conviction that their interest, and not his, was the interest of the public. The interest of the dealers, however, in any particular branch of

trade or manufactures, is always in some respects different from, and even opposite to, that of the public. To widen the market and to narrow the competition, is always the interest of the dealers.

To widen the market may frequently be agreeable enough to the interest of the public; but to narrow the competition must always be against it, and can serve only to enable the dealers, by raising their profits above what they naturally would be, to levy, for their own benefit, an absurd tax upon the rest of their fellow-citizens. The proposal of any new law or regulation of commerce which comes from this order ought always to be listened to with great precaution, and ought never to be adopted till after having been long and carefully examined, not only with the most scrupulous, but with the most suspicious attention. It comes from an order of men whose interest is never exactly the same with that of the public, who have generally an interest to deceive and even to oppress the public, and who accordingly have, upon many occasions, both deceived and oppressed it.

As Adam Smith warns, only after great precaution, careful, scrupulous and "suspicious attention" should commerce-related policies from corporate interests be accepted. Yet, the mainstream media itself is owned by various multinational companies (primarily in the entertainment industries, but from other industries as well).

— These multinationals in the area of the media as a result have worked to "widen the market and narrow the competition" as described ealier in the ownership section.

— Being a carrier of information to the general public, the importance of a mainstream media free from such political influences is important.

This concentration of ownership brings with it political and economic agendas that are less accountable.

— Furthermore, the interests of the multinationals in their own, and related industries, will naturally be reflected in the mainstream media.

— Even a warning from over 200 years ago by Adam Smith has been ignored!

Hence, this makes it even more difficult these days for the general public to apply great precaution, careful, scrupulous and "suspicious attention" to the claims from monied interests. Instead we see continued support at national and international level for those aspects of political, economic and trade agreements that benefit the interests of the concentrated owners. Furthermore, politicians and businesses have continued to label the system that they promote as being "free trade" or "free market" etc.

At the beginning of 2000, keen to avoid the embarrassment of Seattle, the world economic powerhouses (corporate leaders and major governments) met again at Davos, Switzerland at the World Economic Forum. Here, as well as reiterating the positive benefits of free trade, the mainstream media were actually urged to be the message carriers of the virtues of free trade and the New World Order. That should perhaps start to ring alarm bells. This surely sounds like the mainstream media are being asked to push forth a certain propaganda, rather than remain (or, more accurately, become!) objective and allow alternative views to be voiced, fairly.

Former US president Bill Clinton, indicated similar things himself. He stressed how open, or free, rules-based trading was the only possible way forward and that the media would have to be responsible for selling that message to the public to gain their support for this New World Order. But no-one questioned him (or Bush) about the reality it actually is;

— Who is free? (And what is free -- it is mainly capital, which has had the increasing ability to move around unchecked. It is part of the reason that volatile capital flows have led to economic collapse in some countries during the global financial crisis towards the end of the 1990s.)

— What are the actual rules (are the rules themselves actually fair or not)?

— Who can get away with not having to abide by the rules? (Typically it is the multinational corporations and more powerful western governments -- after all, who would be able to force them to abide by the rules?)

— And, ultimately, who benefits, and who doesn't?

These are the types of points that the protestors are typically trying to make. Yet, the media helps to generally avoid voicing such hard-hitting criticisms that are close to home. If these questions are allowed to be tackled and answered from a diverse set of perspectives, it may help result in increased public debate. This may help pressurize fairer rules, practices and accountability on to corporations which they would then need to abide by. This in turn would increase the possibility for globalization to become a positive force compared to how it is seen today by so many.

While national control of the media can give rise to censorship, propaganda and other forms of control, as with America and elsewhere, too much corporate ownership can also have numerous negative effects. Towards the end of the 1990s, even the mainstream media's reporting on the global financial crisis can warrant criticism. Their phrases used, their angles portrayed, the influences of western corporations etc. all resulted in coverage that tended to implicitly, sometimes explicitly, blame others. It came over as though excuses and other explanations had to be provided so as not to let us imagine that some of the root causes would ever come from the home-grown "prescriptions."

The current form of corporate globalization has been criticized for increasing the vast inequalities around the world, including in the richest nations in the world. J.W. Smith offers a warning, "Looking only at their bottom line, and listening to their own rhetoric, the managers of capital are unaware they are moving society back towards the wealth discrepencies of the early Industrial Revolution; this return to quasi-aristocratic privileges is a recipie for eventual contraction of commerce and destruction of their own wealth along with that of labor."

While Smith wrote the above in 1994, it is applicable today as well, with the recent wave of news about "corporate crime" and fascination of some CEOs and other executives as some major American companies have faced bankruptcy or have collapsed. Yet, the media, while offering an outpouring of news and analysis have by and large concentrated on individual characters and looked for scapegoats. The impacts of the underlying system itself has been less discussed and when it has, often been described as basically ok, but just affected by a few "bad apples".

Access to Information and Economics

While it sometimes appears as though trade and economic issues are boring and not of interest for most people in a society, it is in fact one of the most important. Economic decisions affect not only businesses, but individuals. Most wars throughout history have had economic and trade resources at their core. Legislation, or removal of some, can have an impact on factors such as working conditions, job security and wage stability. Access to information, then, plays an important part of enabling a society to know more about its nation's trade and economic policies.

Most agree that one part of allowing access to information is to ensure governments make their information available to their public in the first place. This is also enshrined in the UN's Declaration of Human Rights. However, while there is some progress being made in increasing the transparency of some governments, it is often just rhetoric. In addition, it is just one aspect of society. In the increasingly globalized world where some transnational corporations wield a lot of political power as well, there are legitimate questions about whether private corporations should also be held accountable to the public via access to their information.

International institutions like the World Bank recognize the importance of the media in development issues. As a result they are attempting to address this more. However, they wish to directly influence journalists to promote their ideas and perspectives of markets and globalization etc, whereas critics, including Frank Vogl, former World Bank Director of Information and Public Affairs suggest that the Bank instead supports NGOs and independent foundations to carry out education for journalists. This way, the Bank is not seen as unfairly influencing important issues. Additionally, by supporting a myriad of NGOs and others, they may provide a better forum, or potential, to provide more balanced critique and support, based on issues at hand, rather than ideological influences and perspectives, which would be the effect if the World Bank was to directly influence journalists.

10

Women Portrayals

We all know the stereotypes-the femme fatale, the supermom, the sex kitten, the nasty corporate climber. Whatever the role, television, film and popular magazines are full of images of women and girls who are typically white, desperately thin, and made up to the hilt-even after slaying a gang of vampires or dressing down a Greek legion. Many would agree that some strides have been made in how the media portray women in film, television and magazines, and that the last 20 years has also seen a growth in the presence and influence of women in media behind the scenes. Nevertheless, female stereotypes continue to thrive in the media we consume every day.

In this chapter we can see the issues around the media's portrayal of women and girls-from effects on body image and self-identity to ramifications in sports and politics. It looks at the economic interests behind the objectification and eroticization of females by the media as well as efforts to counter negative stereotyping. And it provides the latest articles and studies that explore the ways in which media both limit and empower women and girls in society.

Beauty and Body Image

Images of female bodies are everywhere. Women-and their body parts-sell everything from food to cars. Popular film and television actresses are becoming younger, taller and thinner. Some have even been known to faint on the set from lack of food. Women's magazines are full of articles urging that if they can just lose those last twenty pounds, they'll have it all-the perfect marriage, loving children, great sex, and a rewarding career. Why are standards of beauty being imposed on women, the majority of whom are naturally larger and more mature than any of the models? The roots, some analysts say, are economic.

By presenting an ideal difficult to achieve and maintain, the cosmetic and diet product industries are assured of growth and profits. And it's no accident that youth is increasingly promoted, along with thinness, as an essential criterion of beauty. If not all women need to lose weight, for sure they're all aging. And, according to the industry, age is a disaster that needs to be dealt with. The stakes are huge. On the one hand, women who are insecure about their bodies are more likely to buy beauty products, new clothes, and diet aids. It is estimated that the diet industry alone is worth $100 billion (U.S.) a year. On the other hand, research indicates that exposure to images of thin, young, air-brushed female bodies is linked to depression, loss of self-esteem and the development of unhealthy eating habits in women and girls.

One out of every four college-aged women uses unhealthy methods of weight control-including fasting, skipping meals, excessive exercise, laxative abuse, and self-induced vomiting. And the Canadian Fitness and Lifestyle Research Institute warns that weight control measures are being taken by girls as young as nine. American statistics are similar. In 2003, Teen magazine reported that 35 per cent of girls 6 to 12 years old have been on at least one diet, and that 50 to 70 per cent of normal weight girls believe they are overweight. Media activist Jean Kilbourne concludes that, "Women are sold to the diet industry by the magazines we read and the television programs we watch, almost all of which make us feel anxious about our weight."

Perhaps most disturbing is the fact that media images of female beauty are unattainable for all but a very small number of women. Researchers generating a computer model of a woman with Barbie-doll proportions, for example, found that her back would be too weak to support the weight of her upper body, and her body would be too narrow to contain more than half a liver and a few centimeters of bowel. A real woman built that way would suffer from chronic diarrhea and eventually die from malnutrition. Still, the number of real life women and girls who seek a similarly underweight body is epidemic, and they can suffer equally devastating health consequences.

Researchers report that women's magazines have ten and one-half times more ads and articles promoting weight loss than men's magazines do, and over three-quarters of the covers of women's magazines include at least one message about how to change a woman's bodily appearance-by diet, exercise or cosmetic surgery. Television and movies reinforce the importance of a thin body as a measure of a woman's worth. Over three-quarters of the female characters in TV situation comedies are underweight, and only one in twenty are above average in size. Heavier actresses tend to receive negative comments from male characters about their bodies ("How about wearing a sack?"), and 80 per cent of these negative comments are followed by canned audience laughter.

There have been efforts in the magazine industry to buck the trend. For several years the Quebec magazine Coup de Pouce has consistently included full-sized women in their fashion pages and Châtelaine has pledged not to touch up photos and not to include models less than 25 years of age. However, advertising rules the marketplace and in advertising thin is "in." Twenty years ago, the average model weighed 8 per cent less than the average woman-but today's models weigh 23 per cent less. Advertisers believe that thin models sell products. When the Australian magazine New Woman recently included a picture of a heavy-set model on its cover, it received a truckload of letters from grateful readers praising the move. But its advertisers complained and the magazine returned to featuring bone-thin models. Advertising Age International concluded that the incident "made clear the influence wielded by advertisers who remain convinced that only thin models spur the sales of beauty products."

Self-improvement

The barrage of messages about thinness, dieting and beauty tells "ordinary" women that they are always in need of adjustment-and that the female body is an object to be perfected. Jean Kilbourne argues that the overwhelming presence of media images of painfully thin women means that real women's bodies have become invisible in the mass media. The real tragedy, Kilbourne concludes, is that many women internalize these stereotypes, and judge themselves by the beauty industry's standards. Women learn to compare themselves to other women, and to compete with them for male attention. This focus on beauty and desirability "effectively destroys any awareness and action that might help to change that climate."

Women become a sexual object

The pressure put on women through ads, television, film and new media to be sexually attractive-and sexually active-is profound. The National Eating Disorders Association reports that one out of four TV commercials send some kind of "attractiveness message," telling viewers what is and is not attractive. Children Now reports that 38 per cent of the female characters in video games are scantily clad, 23 per cent baring breasts or cleavage, 31 per cent exposing thighs, another 31 per cent exposing stomachs or midriffs, and 15 per cent baring their behinds.

Provocative images of women's partly clothed or naked bodies are especially prevalent in advertising. Shari Graydon, former president of Canada's MediaWatch, argues that women's bodies are sexualized in ads in order to grab the viewer's attention. Women become sexual objects when their bodies and their sexuality are linked to products that are bought and sold.

Women's sexuality is no longer a taboo subject, many researchers question whether or not the blatant sexualization of women's bodies in the media is liberating. The biggest problem with women's magazines is "how much we lie about sex." Those "lies" continue to perpetuate the idea that women's sexuality is subservient to men's pleasure. The presence of misinformation and media stereotypes is disturbing, given research that indicates young people often turn to media for information about sex and sexuality. In 2003, David Buckingham and Sara Bragg reported that two-thirds of young people turn to media when they want to learn about sex - the same percentage of kids who ask their mothers for information and advice.

Many researchers argue that the over-representation of thin women in mass media reinforces the conclusion that "physically attractive" and "sexually desirable" mean "thin." Amy Malkin's study of magazine covers reveals that messages about weight loss are often placed next to messages about men and relationships. The fascination with finding out what men really want also tends to keep female characters in film and television busy. Professor Nancy Signorielli reports that men are more likely than women to be shown "on the job" in movies and television shows. Female characters, on the other hand, are more likely to be seen dating, or talking about romance.

Sex and violence

That romance often has a darker side. As Graydon notes, the media infantilize women, portraying them as child-like, innocent and vulnerable. Being vulnerable is often closely linked to being a potential victim of violence. Kilbourne argues that ads like the Fetish scent ad (right) imply "women don't really mean 'no' when they say it, that women are only teasing when they resist men's advances." The ad's copy reads: "Apply generously to your neck so he can smell the scent as you shake your head 'no.'" The obvious implication here is, "he'll understand that you don't really mean it and he can respond to the scent like any other animal."

Kilbourne notes that sex in the media is often condemned "from a puritanical perspective-there's too much of it, it's too blatant, it will encourage kids to be promiscuous, etc." But, she concludes, sex in the media "has far more to do with trivializing sex than with promoting it. The problem is not that it is sinful but that it is synthetic and cynical. We are offered a pseudo-sexuality that makes it far more difficult to discover our own unique and authentic sexuality."

Women in News and Politics

Although there has been a steady increase in the number of women professionals over the past 20 years, most mainstream press coverage continues to rely on men as experts in the fields of business, politics and economics. Women in the news are more likely to be featured in stories about accidents, natural disasters, or domestic violence than in stories about their professional abilities or expertise.

Women in politics are similarly sidelined. Canadian journalist Jenn Goddu studied newspaper and magazine coverage of three women's lobby groups over a 15-year period. She discovered that journalists tend to focus on the domestic aspects of the politically active woman's life (such as "details about the high heels stashed in her bag, her habit of napping in the early evening, and her lack of concern about whether or not she is considered ladylike") rather than her position on the issues. Quebec political analyst Denis Monière uncovered similar patterns. In 1998, Monière analysed 83 late evening newscasts on three national networks-the Canadian Broadcasting Corporation, Radio-Canada (the French-language public broadcaster) and TVA. He observed that women's views were solicited mainly in the framework of "average citizens" and rarely as experts, and that political or economic success stories were overwhelmingly masculine.

Monière also noted that the number of female politicians interviewed was disproportionate to their number in Parliament or in the Quebec National Assembly; nor, he noted, was this deficiency in any way compensated for by the depth and quality of coverage. Inadequate women's coverage seems to be a worldwide phenomenon. In 2000 the Association of Women Journalists (Association des femmes journalistes - AFJ) studied news coverage of women and women's issues in 70 countries. It reported that only 18 per cent of stories quote women, and that the number of women-related stories came to barely 10 per cent of total news coverage.

News talk shows are equally problematic. The White House Project reports that only 9 per cent of the guests on Sunday morning news shows such as Meet the Press and Face the Nation are women, and even then they only speak 10 per cent of the time-leaving 90 per cent of the discussion to the male guests. Project president Marie Wilson warns that the lack of representation for women will have profound consequences on whether or not women are perceived as competent leaders, because "authority is not recognized by these shows. It is created by these shows."

Politically active women are often disparaged and stereotyped by the media. When Hillary Clinton was still first lady, she was referred to as a "witch" or "witchlike" at least 50 times in the press. Rivers writes, "male political figures may be called mean and nasty names, but those words don't usually reflect superstition and dread. Did the press ever call Presidents Carter, Reagan, Bush, or Clinton warlocks?"

Women athletes

Women athletes are also given short shrift in the media. Margaret Carlisle Duncan and Michael Messner studied sports coverage on three network affiliates in Los Angeles. They report that only nine per cent of airtime was devoted to women's sports, in contrast to the 88 per cent devoted to male athletes. Female athletes fared even worse on ESPN's national sports show Sports Center, where they occupied just over two per cent of airtime. And, according to the Canadian Association for the Advancement of Women,

Sports and Physical Activity, women athletes receive just three per cent of sports coverage in major Canadian dailies.

Commentators (97 per cent of whom are men) use different language when they talk about female athletes. Where men are described as "big," "strong," "brilliant," "gutsy" and "aggressive," women are more often referred to as "weary," "fatigued," "frustrated," "panicked," "vulnerable" and "choking." Commentators are also twice as likely to call men by their last names only, and three times as likely to call women by their first names only. The Prix Déméritas (Brickbat Prize) for sexist reporting was awarded by Quebec's Gazette des femmes to the journalists who covered the 2000 International Women's Tennis Cup. The Gazette noted in particular the journalists' keen interest in any of the athletes' poses that could be seen as suggestive, as well as the excessive attention accorded Anna Kournikova-for her beauty rather than her game.

Media images of women in sports are also very different from the familiar pictures of male athletes in action. Female athletes are increasingly photographed in what Professor Pat Griffin calls "hyper-sexualized poses." Griffin notes, "When it was once enough to feminize women athletes, now it is necessary to sexualize them for men. Instead of hearing, 'I am woman, hear me roar,' we are hearing 'I am hetero-sexy, watch me strip.'"

When well-respected news-show host Greta Van Susteren moved from CNN to Fox in early 2002, she not only had a makeover; she surgically altered her face to appear younger and more "beautiful." When her new show, On the Record, premiered, her hair was perfectly coiffed and she sat behind a table so viewers could see her short skirt and legs. Robin Gerber notes that, "Before her surgery, Van Susteren had been an increasingly visible beacon projecting the hope that women had made progress. You believed that she had made it in television because she was so darn smart, clearly the best legal analyst on the air." However, her surgery symbolizes what many analysts have argued for decades: that the way a woman looks is far more important than what she has to say. Gerber concludes that Van Susteren "has become a painful reminder of women's inequality... Being smart, smarter, smartest isn't enough. By trying to become just another pretty face, Van Susteren instead became another cultural casualty."

Media and girls

The statistics are startling. The average North American girl will watch 5,000 hours of television, including 80,000 ads, before she starts kindergarten. In the United States, Saturday morning cartoons alone come with 33 commercials per hour. Commercials aimed at kids spend 55 per cent of their time showing boys building, fixing toys, or fighting. They show girls, on the other hand, spending 77 per cent of their time laughing, talking, or observing others. And while boys in commercials are shown out of the house 85 per cent of the time, more than half of the commercials featuring girls place them in the home.

The mass media, especially children's television, provide more positive role models for girls than ever before. Kids shows such as Timothy Goes to School, Canadian Geographic for Kids, and The Magic School Bus feature strong female characters who interact with their male counterparts on an equal footing. There are strong role models for teens as well. A Children Now study of the media favoured by teenage girls discovered that a similar proportion of male and female characters on TV and in the movies rely on themselves to achieve their goals and solve their own problems. (The one discrepancy was in the movies, where 49 per cent of male characters solve their own problems, compared to only 35 per cent of their female counterparts.)

Television shows like Buffy, the Vampire Slayer and computer games such as Tomb Raider and Perfect Dark, star girls who are physically assertive and in control. And of course, Lisa has been acknowledged as the brains of the Simpson family since the start. However, the messages media send to young girls are mixed. On the small screen, male characters continue to outnumber females by a ratio of 2 or 3 to 1, and 90 per cent of the actors starring in American children's programming are male.

Magazines are the only medium where girls are over-represented. However,almost 70 per cent of the editorial content in teen mags focuses on beauty and fashion, and only 12 per cent talks about school or careers. Research indicates that these mixed messages make it difficult for girls to negotiate the transition to adulthood. In its 1998 study Focus on Youth, the Canadian Council on Social Development reports that while the number of boys who say they "have confidence in themselves" remains relatively stable through adolescence, the numbers for girls drop steadily from 72 per cent in Grade Six students to only 55 per cent in Grade Ten.

Children Now points out that girls are surrounded by images of female beauty that are unrealistic and unattainable. And yet two out of three girls who participated in their national media survey said they "wanted to look like a character on TV." One out of three said they had "changed something about their appearance to resemble that character." In 2002, researchers at Flinders University in South Australia studied 400 teenagers regarding how they relate to advertising. They found that girls who watched TV commercials featuring underweight models lost self-confidence and became more dissatisfied with their own bodies. Girls who spent the most time and effort on their appearance suffered the greatest loss in confidence.

The pressures on girls are exacerbated by the media's increasing tendency to portray very young girls in sexual ways. Over the past decade, the fashion industry has begun to use younger and younger models, and now commonly presents 12- and 13-year-old girls as if they were women. Camera angles (where the model is often looking up, presumably at a taller man), averted eyes, wounded facial expressions, and vulnerable poses mimic the visual images common in pornographic media.

The most cursory examination of media confirms that young girls are being bombarded with images of sexuality, often dominated by stereotypical portrayals of women and girls as powerless, passive victims. As these girls become teenagers, many choose to tune out, but others maintain a hungry appetite for these messages. As Shawn Doherty and Nadine Joseph note, those who continue to consume media images are strongly influenced "by stereotypical images of uniformly beautiful, obsessively thin and scantily dressed objects of male desire. And studies show that girls who are frequent viewers have the most negative opinion of their gender."

Economics of Gender Stereotyping

Women working for their side are up against a conspiracy of the money-hungry, whose job is to pull in the big bucks- and often the grosser the movie, the bigger the gross. No one would deny that the mass media is big business.

According to the American Motion Picture Association, Hollywood films alone pulled in $9 billion in 2001, and that doesn't include the renting and selling of videos and DVDs. However, media executives argue that the economics of the industry make it impossible to avoid stereotypes of women.

Many commentators argue that media content is driven by advertising. All advertisers are chasing the elusive 18- to 34-year-old male market. Little wonder that the starring role in two-thirds of TV situation comedies is played by a young man. Advertisers claim they can be far less aggressive about chasing female viewers because women are less picky about what they watch. Advertisers' lack of interest in women is complicated by the fact that shows with women in leading roles don't perform as well in syndication as shows starring male actors. Since networks make most of their money on re-runs, prime-time programming tends to be "male-skewed." In addition, as Nancy Hass argues, "shows that don't focus on men have to feature the sort of women that guys might watch."

Movie studios use the same economic arguments to explain the abundance of female stereotypes on the big screen. Movies featuring sex and violence are big international sellers. Why? Sex and action films do not rely on clever, intricate, culture-based scripts or convincing acting. Sex and action films therefore "translate" easily across cultures. Since at least 60 per cent of the movie industry's profits come from the international market, studios continue to pump out the same old stereotypes.

Screenwriter Robin Swicord says, "It is very hard to get movies made that are genuinely feminist, or even portray women in a fair way. I genuinely believe there is a big domestic audience for this kind of movie, but if there is only a domestic audience, it won't get made." Overseas audiences still want sex and violence. That's what sells outside the U.S. The whole world may have to change before the picture for women in Hollywood gets brighter.

Women working in the media have made some inroads. In 2001, the International Federation of Journalists reported that around the world, 38 per cent of all working journalists are women. Studies conducted by Canadian researchers Gertrude Robinson and Armande Saint-Jean have found that 28 per cent of newspaper editors are female. And according to San Diego State University communications professor Martha Lauzen, 24 per cent of American television producers, writers, and directors are women.

In 2002, the Canadian Newspaper Association reported that 43 per cent of Canadian newspaper employees are women. However, they account for only eight per cent of editors-in-chief and twelve per cent of publishers. Women employed in the sector tend to work in "pink-collar ghettos"; they make up 70 per cent of the advertising department, and 80 per cent of the accounting and finance staff. In addition to being un-represented in positions of authority, Monière thinks women are also under-utilized in covering the subjects considered most important-politics, economy and social trends. And when it comes to the evening news, women are almost invisible.

A study carried out in France in 2000 by the Association of Women Journalists (Association des femmes journalistes-AFJ) pointed out that French television devotes five to nine per cent more news coverage to women than do the other media-clearly the result of more women journalists working in television than in the radio and newspaper industries. The same study showed that women journalists select six per cent more stories on women than men journalists.

However, men continue to occupy approximately 75 per cent of the positions of power in the mass media. And the prospects become much bleaker for women as they climb the corporate ladder. Lauzen's annual studies of the film industry reveal that women account for only 17 per cent of the creative talent behind the highest grossing Hollywood pictures-16 per cent of executive producers, 11 per cent of producers, and 2 per cent of cinematographers. Robinson and Saint-Jean report that in the newspaper industry, only 5 per cent of managing editors and editors-in-chief are women.

The 2001 study conducted by the Annenberg Public Policy Center at the University of Pennsylvania is equally damning. The Center reports that only 13 per cent of the top executives of American media, telecommunications and e-companies are female. And that 13 per cent is not concentrated at the top: women constitute only 9 per cent of the boards of directors for these companies, and they hold only 3 per cent of the most powerful positions.

Women in Decision-Making

Studies show that a difference can be made when women hold positions of power. In 2000, women editors and journalists took over the newsroom for one day at a newspaper in Wichita Falls, Texas. For the day's top story a choice had to be made between a crime-stopper's story about a peeping tom and an item about local women fighting for equal rights. When the women opted for the latter story, a heated argument erupted. Journalist Laurence Pantin reports that "the women finally won, but only because they held the key positions on that day. All other times, the peeping tom and stories like it would have prevailed."

As women continue to struggle for equality in the media, Lauzen's research shows that the biggest difference is made by the women who actually work in the industry. Behind the scenes, they can have a definite impact on the ways women are portrayed on the screen and in print. Lauzen concludes, "When women have more powerful roles in the making of a movie or TV show, we know that we also get more powerful female characters on-screen, women who are more real and more multi-dimensional."

Ideas of what women should look like and how they should act change over time. The size 12 sex goddess of the 1950s who spent her on-screen time breathlessly trying to marry a millionaire may have yielded to the trials and tribulations of the neurotic, ultra-thin professional woman. But not much has really changed-both Ally McBeal and the 1950s sex goddess are consumed by their search for a man.

Many media activists argue that producers should be called to account, and that images of women should be forced to be more realistic. Teen magazines are also getting a makeover. Women's networks and alternative magazines that purport to break with stereotypes have been met with ambivalence and disappointment by many commentators. Women's networks like Oxygen and Lifetime TV have been criticized for equally mixed messages.

11

Media: The Critical Path of Democracy

Many countries have signed the United Nations Universal Declaration of Human Rights, Article 19 (about freedom of expression, opinion and information) has not been made a reality. A free and impartial media is a key pillar to a functioning democracy to help spread informed views and opinions. Yet developed and developing countries alike are plagued with various problems in the media in numerous ways. International news coverage is declining which is an increasing concern at a time when the world is attempting to globalize. In many countries, journalists face threats of censorship, beatings and even death for reporting issues that may be controversial or not in the interests of power holders. The mainstream media of the developed and freer, nations pose an often unmentioned or poorly analyzed problem: the lack of objective reporting that is not influenced and, to a growing degree, controlled by elites with concentrated ownership to advance their interests.

A Critical Aspect of a Functioning Democracy

A critical aspect of a functioning democracy is of being well informed in order to be able to participate in that democracy. One of the most important ways that most people are informed is through their mainstream media. Yet the world over, we know that the media is far from perfect. Many countries have signed the Universal Declaration of Human Rights but freedom of opinion, expression and information (Article 19) has hardly been a reality.

Some journalists in certain developing counties are subject to torture, incarceration, beatings, or even death, just for reporting something that those with power want suppressed. Even in the developed and freer nations, news and information is subject to partiality and unbalanced coverage or just plain omissions of the major issues. While September 11, 2001 terrorist attacks in the United States had increased some world news reporting for a while, in general, for many years coverage of international news has been declining. In November 1998, U.N. Secretary General, Koffi Annan also highlighted this decline.

Accurate media representation of world issues is crucial. Whenever media reports are censored or biased, the people's basic rights are systematically undermined. In these situations, violations and unaccountability often go unnoticed and suppressed viewpoints become commonplace. Most people get their view of the world from mainstream media. It is, therefore, important that mainstream media be objective and present accurate and diverse representations of what goes on around the world.

Press Freedom

Some have commented in the past that various freedoms and democratic principles etc come after a nation has been able to increase its prosperity. But, as Reporters Sans

Frontiers commented for 2002, "Costa Rica and Benin are examples of how growth of a free press does not just depend on a country's material prosperity." You can find more information from their web site which also includes information and details of all country rankings.

Of course, press freedom is just one amongst many, many variables that would indicate a healthy democracy, but it is one of a number of variables to indicate a healthy and diverse media, which itself is an integral component to a functioning democracy. But even with a fairly free press, problems of political and other influences can still be a big factor in the quality of the media. And this impacts the media in industrialized countries, as well as in poorer countries. For example, Reporters Sans Frontiers also reports that after the September 11 atrocity, the media in the U.S. was torn by "the pull of patriotism and self-censorship" such that the diversity of media coverage was affected and therefore "cast [a] doubt on the objectivity of the American press."

Even one of the most famous media personalities in American news, Dan Rather of CBS, has admitted that there has been a lot of self-censorship and that the U.S. media in general has been cowed by patriotic fever. There are many aspects of media reporting in the wake of the war on terror that are discussed below:

— War, Propaganda and the Military.

— War On Terror and Media, includes a number of articles from various authors on different aspects of the media.

— Media in the United States, looks at some aspects of U.S. media in more depth.

Impact of Globalization

In a world of increasing globalization, the media has many potentials. It has the possibility of spreading information to places where in the past it has been difficult to get diverse views. It has the potential to contribute to democratic processes and influences especially on countries and regimes that are not democratic. On the negative side though, it also has the ability to push the ideas and cultures of more dominant interest.

The phenomenon of "cultural imperialism" raises concerns in many countries where people fear that their culture gets diluted or given a back seat to the demands of large media and corporate interests in the name of globalization, where products and imagery, mainly from the west, make it into the televisions and homes of people. The fear of many people is that if people around the world are molded into model consumers, following a western standard, then it is easier for large companies to sell their products and know their buyer's habits etc, while eroding local cultures and traditions. There is often extensive debate as to how likely this will be, whether local cultures and traditions will exert their influence on local forms of globalization, or if there will be more extremist backlash. In different parts of the world, many of these and other reactions are already seen.

A documentary by the Open University in UK, aired on the BBC2 channel, October 29, 2003. The documentary, titled Images over India looked at the positive and negative consequences that globalization of media had in India on various parts of society. Amongst many things, the documentary noted the following:

—India is one of the world's largest markets for satellite tv, with some 300 million viewers.

—The Indian economy opened up in the 1990s after decades of being closed. (Pressure came from western and international institutions such as the IMF, World Bank, etc.)

—This led to an explosion in global consumer goods

—There was also an explosion in Indian television

While globalization of television has been going on since the 1980s (with the likes of CNN, MTV, Sky, Star TV, etc), in India, demand from urban middle classes came around 1991 for the likes of CNN for coverage of international events such as the first Gulf War.

— Star TV (a Hong Kong based company, owned by Rupert Murdoch's News Corp and present in many, many Asian countries) found it easy to penetrate in India. This was because of many reasons, including that

— The existing broadcast was based on an old system

— The existing broadcast was state-owned primarily a vehicle for news, education, and social issues, such as how to deal with various health issues, etc. Entertainment was usually films of religious stories.

— While such things were very useful for the rural poor, the growing urban middle class wanted more entertainment, western soaps, etc.

— While televisions used to be rare, they were now becoming widespread.

— Initially Star TV only catered to the small minority of people that spoke English, showing western soaps, serials, hollywood movies. Hindi's first commercial channel, Zee TV introduced programs in the natural language, Hindi. Zee TV's launch heralded private television. Zee was and is primarily focused on entertainment. Just 5 years after the launch of Star TV, there are a dozen satellites broadcasting over 50 channels, in English, Hindi, and some 16 regional languages.

— India is the second largest tv market in the world, after the United States.

— These new networks offer many programs. However, India has seen a number of trends including:

— An increase in programming and hours, especially more music, films, talk shows, game shows, soaps, etc.

— But there has also been an increase in the number of repeats, of music channels, etc, which has made the changes appear shallow, according to an Indian media activist interviewed on the documentary.

— The film industry, known as bollywood, is the largest feature film producer in the world, larger than Hollywood, with some 300 feature films a year.

— While there has been a long tradition of cinema movies in India, satellite tv has meant more foreign films being broadcast. Local industries have seen the effects too, for example, by being forced to innovate, to improve effects of their own films, or increase violence, etc. Those television channels that have localized the most are succeeding in the tough competition.

Advertisers are also seeing a large audience as potential consumers of their products:

— The audience targeted by cable and satellite companies are the same as those desired by multinational companies at the forefront of globalization:

— Large middle class segment (some 700 million people -- one of the largest middle class segments in the world)

— Imagery generally is geared towards them

— A positive impact of companies such as Zee TV was that it allowed advertisers in India to advertise their products, thus helping India's industries and the country's economy as it began to liberalize. It also created competition for the state-owned broadcaster potentially contributing to a better situation for consumers.

— One thing Star TV has able to deliver to advertisers is highly focused programs, reaching targeted groups of people. Delivering a mass market is key for advertisers.

However, with all the advertising and so forth, "some wastage is inevitable."

— There is an increase in "flamboyant corruption" that didn't used to be there before in the same way. This has been attributed to some of the new imagery seen in the media.

— It seemed as though the message was now about how to show or flaunt your money, which was opposite to what it was in the past.

— Yet, the documentary noted, many in India do not see the wealth of many people there as being legitimate.

— A lot is seen as coming through corruption and criminal connections

— Such conspicuous consumption was not looked at so well by such people

— For women too, the results have included a loss of what little security they may have had in their lives. This has been because

— There has been an increase in violence on them by their husbands

— Their little savings for say their daughter's education is now being used by husbands to buy things they see on tv.

— Furthermore, a lot of programming doesn't relate for many Indian audiences

— Fragile lives and more sensitive issues are not really portrayed

— Only a small minority would relate to the characters on soaps and films, yet these are the dominant representations found on television.

— While satellite and cable are reaching far out in India, including rural communities, rural people are finding no space for their concerns in these commercial media, or even the new government channels.

— While more people are being exposed for the first time to messages from different cultures, the concern raised was that it might be happening so quickly as to introduce social problems including those mentioned above.

From the economic sense, the documentary also showed an interesting observation.

— That is, the notion of the "average" Indian person was getting more real.

— In the past, the "average" Indian person didn't exist, because of the immense diversity of cultures and customs.

— Now, with the introduction and dominance of a few large companies there is a significant proportion of Indians who fall into this category, close to this average.

While this is good for globalization companies, who do better from conformity than diversity, the overall picture for Indians is a mixed one to say the least.

Media in Industrialized Countries

The mainstream media of the developed and freer, nations pose an often unmentioned or poorly analyzed problem: the lack of objective reporting that is not influenced and, to a growing degree, controlled by elites to advance their interests. According to former journalist and World Bank Director of Information and Public Affairs from 1981 to 1990, Frank Vogl "we have more TV channels than ever before, but they do little to bring us the fair, objective, tough reporting that we need to strengthen our society."

There is a growing awareness or realization of a problem that can be best summed up as a narrow range of discourse. That is, within presupposed views, there is much debate, but outside that range, there is less. As a result, it is often possible that many diverse views can be denied a public voice. As an example, a range of studies by the Scotland-based Glasgow University Media Group undertaken with other NGO's such as Save the Children, the Overseas Development Institute (ODI), and the Department For International Development, shows how the limited nature of media coverage of the developing world and the focus on disaster and conflict produces negative attitudes and a very partial understanding amongst audiences of the wider world. As the report mentions, "There is also a strong current in contemporary research which suggests that media are engaged in the mass production of social ignorance. This is well expressed in the title of Danny Schechter's The More You Watch The Less You Know." Their report also found the following:

1. That the decision made by broadcasters (on commercial criteria) about what viewers would desire to watch have in the long run produced very negative responses in TV audiences towards the developing world.

2. That audiences are misinformed about the developing world because of the low level of explanations and context which is given in television reporting and because some explanations which are present are partial and informed by what might be termed "post-colonial beliefs."

3. That a change in the quality of explanation which is given can radically alter both attitudes to the developing world and the level of audience interest in the subject.

British media has long been regarded as having good and wide coverage of international affairs, compared to other comparatively developed nations. However, this picture is changing, as with most nations. A number of organizations in Britain have formed a research organization called Third World & Environment Broadcasting Project (3WE). Amongst other things, it produces reports on the state of the media, monitoring the quantity of international programming on the UK's mainstream TV channels. It has found a trend of declining coverage of international issues and an increase in entertainment—a "dumbing down":

— 3WE's recent report for 2001, called Losing Reality, suggested that "The international documentary is virtually dead" in Britain.

— Instead it had found that "programme categories - such as politics, history, development, environment and human rights - were replaced by entertainment genres - reality TV, travel challenges, and holiday programmes."

— In addition, when foreign places were covered, British media often "showed British people experience foreign locations, as in 'Reality TV', travel challenges, holiday magazine programmes and docu-soaps;"

— They noted that in an era of globalization where it is even more important to understand the wider world as we affect it, and it affects us. (In Britain for example, the percentage of people that get their information about the developing world from the mainstream is some 85 percent.)

— The tragic events of September 11, 2001, were thought to lead to an increase in world issues coverage, but we found that this was hardly the case. And even while some of the mainstream channels were providing quality documentaries, there weren't many of them, and such programming was actually decreasing.

Probably every conflict is fought on at least two grounds: the battlefield and the minds of the people via propaganda. The "good guys" and the "bad guys" can often both be guilty of misleading their people with distortions, exaggerations, subjectivity, inaccuracy and even fabrications, in order to receive support and a sense of legitimacy. Propaganda can serve to rally people behind a cause, but often at the cost of exaggerating, misrepresenting, or even lying about the issues in order to gain that support.

While the issue of propaganda often is discussed in the context of militarism, war and war-mongering, it is around us in all aspects of life. As the various examples below will show, common tactics in propaganda often used by either side include:

— Using selective stories that come over as wide-covering and objective.

— Partial facts, or historical context

— Reinforcing reasons and motivations to act due to threats on the security of the individual.

— Narrow sources of "experts" to provide insights in to the situation. (For example, the mainstream media typically interview retired military personnel for many conflict-related issues, or treat official government sources as fact, rather than just one perspective that needs to be verified and researched).

— Demonizing the "enemy" who does not fit the picture of what is "right".

— Using a narrow range of discourse, whereby judgements are often made while the boundary of discourse itself, or the framework within which the opinions are formed, are often not discussed. The narrow focus then helps to serve the interests of the propagandists.

At times of war, or build up for war, messages of extremeties and hate, combined with emotions of honor and righteousnes interplay to provide powerful propaganda for a cause. Many say that it is inevitable in war that people will die. Yet, in many cases, war itself is not inevitable, and propaganda is often employed to go closer to war, if that is the preferred foreign policy option. Indeed, once war starts, civilian casualties are unfortunately almost a guaranteed certainty.

Those who promote the negative image of the "enemy" may often reinforce it with rhetoric about the righteousness of themselves; the attempt is to muster up support and nurture the belief that what is to be done is in the positive and beneficial interest of everyone. Often, the principles used to demonize the other, is not used to judge the self, leading to accusations of double standards and hypocrisy.

In preparing for or justifying war, additional techniques are often employed, knowingly or unknowingly. Ottosen identifies several key stages of a military campaign to "soften up" public opinion through the media in preparation for an armed intervention. These are:

— *The Preliminary Stage* - during which the country concerned comes to the news, portrayed as a cause for "mounting concern" because of poverty/dictatorship/anarchy;

— *The Justification Stage* - during which big news is produced to lend urgency to the case for armed intervention to bring about a rapid restitution of "normality";

— *The Implementation Stage* - when pooling and censorship provide control of coverage;

— *The Aftermath* - during which normality is portrayed as returning to the region, before it once again drops down the news agenda.

Following are the four stages in preparing a nation for war:

1. *The crisis*: The reporting of a crisis which negotiations appear unable to resolve. Politicians, while calling for diplomacy, warn of military retaliation. The media reports this as "We're on the brink of war", or "War is inevitable", etc.

2. *The demonisation of the enemy's leader*: Comparing the leader with Hitler is a good start because of the instant images that Hitler's name provokes.

3. *The demonisation of the enemy as individuals*: For example, to suggest the enemy is insane.

4. *Atrocities*: Even making up stories to whip up and strengthen emotional reactions.

One difficulty is that the media have little or no memory. War correspondents have short working lives and there is no tradition or means for passing on their knowledge and experience. The military, on the other hand, is an institution and goes on forever. The military learned a lot from Vietnam and these days plans its media strategy with as much attention as its military strategy.

Miren Guiterrez, editor-in-chief of Inter Press Service notes a number of elements of propaganda taking the more recent wars into account, the War on terror and the Iraq crisis. Summing up his short but detailed report, he includes the following as propaganda strategies:

— Incompleteness

— Inaccuracy

— Driving the agenda

— Milking the story

— Exploiting that we want to believe the best of ourselves

— Perception Management (in particular by using PR firms)

— Reinforcing existing attitudes

— Simple, repetitious and emotional phrases (e.g. war on terror, axis of evil, weapons of mass destruction, shock and awe, war of liberation, etc)

Military Control of Information

Military control of information during war time is also a major contributing factor to propaganda, especially when the media go along with it without question. The military recognizes the values of media and information control very well. The military often manipulates the mainstream media, by restricting or managing what information is presented and hence what the public are told. For them it is paramount to control the media. This can involve all manner of activities, from organizing media sessions and daily press briefings, or through providing managed access to war zones, to even planting stories. This has happened throughout the 20th century. Over time then, the way that the media covers conflicts degrades in quality, critique and objectiveness.

"Information is the currency of victory" an August 1996 U.S. Army field manual. From a military's perspective, information warfare is another front on which a battle must be fought. However, as well as needing to deceive adversaries, in order to maintain public support, information to their own public must no doubt be managed as well. That makse sense from a military perspective. Sometimes the public can be willing to scacrifice detailed knowledge. But that can also lead to unaccountability and when information that is presented has been managed such, propaganda is often the result.

For reporters covering this war [on terrorism], the challenge is not just in getting unfettered and uncensored access to U.S. troops and the battlefield - a long and mostly losing struggle in the past - but in discerning between information and disinformation. That is made all the more difficult by a 24-hour news cycle, advanced technology, and the military's growing fondness for a discipline it calls

"Information Operations." IO, as it is known, groups together information functions ranging from public affairs to military deception and psychological operations, or PSYOP. What this means is that people whose job traditionally has been to talk to the media and divulge truthfully what they are able to tell now work hand-in-glove with those whose job it is to support battlefield operations with information, not all of which may be truthful.

Danny Schechter, describes Information Operations more bluntly as being "a way of obscuring and sanitizing that negative-sounding term 'propaganda' so that our 'information warriors' can do their thing with a minimum of public attention as they seek to engineer friendly write ups and cumulative impact." This, he points out, can be accomplished via several strategies:

— Overloading the Media

— This can be done by providing too much information!

During the short invasion of Iraq in 2003, journalists were "embedded" with various Coalition forces. This was an idea born from the public relations industry, and provided media outlets a detailed and fascinating view for their audiences. For the military, however, it provided a means to control what large audiences would see, to some extent. Independent journalists would be looked upon more suspiciously.

In a way, embedded journalists were unwittingly (sometimes knowingly) making a decision to be biased in their reporting, in favor of the Coalition troops. If an embedded journalist was to report unfavorably on coalition forces they were accompanying they would not get any cooperation. In U.K., the History Channel broadcasted a documentary on August 21, 2004, titled War Spin:

Correspondent. This documentary looked at Coalition media management for the Iraq war and noted numerous things including the following:

— Embedded journalists allowed the military to maximize imagery while providing minimal insight into the real issues;

— Central Command (where all those military press briefings were held) was the main center from which to:

— Filter, manage and drip-feed journalists with what they wanted to provide;

— Gloss over set-backs, while dwelling on successes;

— Limit the facts and context;

— Even feed lies to journalists;

— Use spin in various ways, such as making it seems as though reports are coming from troops on the ground, which Central Command can then confirm, so as to appear real;

— Carefully plan the range of topics that could be discussed with reporters, and what to avoid.

In summary then, the documentary concluded and implied that the media had successfully been designated a mostly controllable role by the military, which would no doubt improve in the future. For more about the issues of embedded journalism during the Iraq invasion, various propaganda techniques employed, and more, see this web site's Iraq media section.

With military conflicts then, reporting raises an interesting dilemma for some; one the one hand, the military wish to present various aspects that would support a campaign, while on the other hand, a journalist is supposed to be critical and not necessarily fall in line. Shortly after the end of the American Civil War, journalist F. Colburn Adams wrote, "The future historian of the late war will have [a] very difficult task to perform... sifting the truth from falsehood as it appears in official records."

Similar to the oft-repeated axiom that truth is the first casualty of war, Adams' observation succinctly summarizes the nub of the conflict between the military and the news media. The military's mission is to fight, and to win, whatever conflict may present itself-preferably on the battlefield but certainly in public opinion and the history books. The journalist, on the other hand, is a skeptic if not a cynic and aims to seek, find and report the truth—a mission both parties often view as incompatible with successful warfare, which depends on secrecy and deception as much as superior strategy, tactics, weaponry and manpower.

Often, especially when covering conflicts, the media organizations are subject to various constraints by governments, military, corporate pressure, economic interests, etc. Sometimes, however, the media are more than willing to go along with what could be described as self-censorship, as highlighted vividly in the following:

We live in a dirty and dangerous world. There are some things the general public does not need to know about and shouldn't. Democracy flourishes when the government can take legitimate steps to keep its secrets and when the press can decide whether to print what it knows.

Other times, the sources of information are limited. For example, "Information warfare" of a military or government might be targeted at "enemy" nations and groups, but often affects their own populations:

In [many cases], the U.S. and other western news media depend on the military for information.... And when the information that military officers provide to the public is part of a process that generates propaganda and places a high value on deceit, deception and denial, then truth is indeed likely to be high on the casualty list.

The history of warfare suggests this is not a false antithesis. Governments, understandably, put a priority on nurturing the morale of the armed forces and the people, intimidating an enemy with the force of the national will They have few scruples about whether they are being fair and just as their propaganda demonizes an alien leader or even a whole population. The enemy is doing the same to them. That is the emotion wars generate, inviting a competitive ecstasy of hate. There is a duel in vicious stereotypes in propaganda posters, illustrations and headlines; populations would be astounded if they could see how they and their leaders are portrayed by the other side.

Propaganda in totalitarian regimes is easy to recognize for its blatant and crude methods. In democratic societies, propaganda exists, as most of the above atests to. But, it is harder to see. As a result, it is important to keep such elements of propaganda in mind when we see coverage of conflicts or even other issues in the media, regardless of the media organization and their apparent reputation.

In many democracies, people hold dear the freedom of speech that they are supposed to have. Yet, "propaganda is to democracy what violence is to totalitarianism," notes Noam Chomsky. Public accountability of major insitutions and of the government must be constantly maintained to avoid propaganda. In 1921, the famous American journalist

Walter Lippmann said that the art of democracy requires what he called the "manufacture of consent." This phrase is an Orwellian euphemism for thought control. The idea is that in a state such as the U.S. where the government can't control the people by force, it had better control what they think.

Power must be held accountable. The mainstream media is a pillar of a functioning democracy, and one of its roles therefore, is to hold power accountable. Propaganda seems to work because of a number of reasons, including:

— People wish to believe the best about themselves and their country;

— Fear-mongering, especially about the threat to cherished values such as freedom and justice;

— Presenting fears and claims that appear logical and factual.

— Managing thoughts by narrowing ranges of debate, thus minimizing widely discussed thoughts that deviate from the main agendas;

In democracies, people like to believe that they and their countries are generally good, for if it was any other way then it brings into moral question all they know and hold dear. The histories of some nations may have involved overcoming adversaries for legitimate reasons (e.g. the American war to gain its independence and freedom from the British Empire was one based on strong moral grounds of freedom from imperial rule).

Such important history is often recounted and remembered as part of the collective culture of the country and those same values are projected into modern times. Propaganda sometimes works by creating the fear of losing such cherished values. All propaganda must be so popular and on such an intellectual level, that even the most stupid of those towards whom it is directed will understand it.... Through clever and constant application of propaganda, people can be made to see paradise as hell, and also the other way around, to consider the most wretched sort of life as paradise.

Bibliography

Altheide, David.1985. *Media power*. Beverly Hills: Sage.

______________. 1996. *Qualitative Media Analysis*. Beverly Hills: Sage.

Armes, Roy. 1988. *On video*. NY: Routledge.

Barak, Greg . (ed.) 1994. *Media, process, and the social construction of crime: Studies in newsmaking criminology*. NY: Garland Press.

Berman, Ronald. 1987. *How television sees its audience*. Newbury Park, CA: Sage Publications.

Best, Joel. 1989. *Images of issues: Typifying contemporary social problems*. NY: Aldine de Gruyter.

Biskind, Peter. 1983. *Seeing is believing: How Hollywood taught us to stop worrying and love the Fifties*. NY: Pantheon.

Campbell, Christopher. 1995. *Race, myth, and the news*. Beverly Hills: Sage.

Campbell, Richard. (1991). *60 Minutes and the news*. Chicago: University of Illinois Press.

Carey, James (ed.). 1988. *Media, myths, and narratives*. Beverly Hills: Sage.

Cohen, Stanley and Jock Young (eds.). 1973. *The manufacture of news*. London: Constable.

Corner, John (ed.). 1986. *Documentary and mass media*. Baltimore: Edward Arnold.

Davies, R. Philip and Brian Neve (eds.). 1981. *Cinema, politics, and society in America*. NY: St. Martin's Press.

Denzin, Norman. 1995. *The Cinematic Society: The Voyeur's Gaze.* Sage

Dines, Gail & Jean M. Humez. (eds.). 1994. *Gender, race, and class in media.* Beverly Hills: Sage.

Ericson, Richard, Patricia Baranek, and Janet Chan. 1991. *Representing order: crime, law and justice in the news media.* Toronto: Open University Press.

Fishman, Mark. 1980. *Manufacturing the news.* Austin: University of Texas Press.

Fiske, John. 1987. *Television culture.* New York: Methuen.

Fowles, Jib. 1996. *Advertising and popular culture.* Beverly Hills: Sage.

Fox, James and Ira Levin. 1993. *How to Work with the Media. Survival Skills for Scholars, Volume* 2. Newbury Park, CA: Sage.

Gitlin, Todd. (ed.). 1986. *Watching television.* New York: Pantheon.

Graber, Doris. 1980. *Crime news and the public.* New York: Praeger.

Himmelstein, Hal. 1984. *Television myth and the American mind.* New York: Praeger.

Hise, James Van. *Calling Tracy: Six decades of Dick Tracy.*

Howitt, Dennis. 1982. *Mass media and social problems.* New York: Permagon Press.

Kaniss, Phyllis. 1991. *Making local news.* Chicago: University of Chicago Press.

Kracauer, Sigfried. 1960. *The theory of film.* New York: Oxford University Press.

Manoff, Robert Karl, and Schudson, Michael. (eds.). 1986. *Reading the news.* New York: Pantheon.

McManus, John. 1994. *Market-driven Journalism.* Newbury Park: Sage.

Meyrowitz, J. 1985. *No sense of place: The impact of electronic media on social behavior.* NY: Oxford University Press.

Sanders, Barry 1994. *A is for Ox: Violence, Electronic Media and the Silencing of the Written Word.* NY: Pantheon.

Schudson, Michael. 1978. *Discovering the news: A social history of American newspapers*. New York: Basic Books.

Selnow, Gary and Richard Gilbert. 1993. *The Impact of Society on Television.* NY: Greenwood Press.

Silver, Alain, and Ward, Elizabeth. (eds.). 1978. *Film noir: An encyclopedic reference to the American style*. New York: The Overlook Press.

Sparks, Richard. 1992. *Television and the Drama of Crime.* Buckingham: Open University Press.

Stein, Benjamin. 1979. *The view from Sunset Boulevard: America as brought to you by the people who make television*. New York: Basic Books.

Stoller, Robert. 1991. *Porn: Myths for the twentieth century*. New Haven: Yale University Press.

Strasburger, Victor. 1995. *Adolescents and the media.* Beverly Hills: Sage.

Surette, Ray. (ed.). 1984. *Justice and the media.* Springfield, IL: Charles C. Thomas Publishing.

_______________. 1989. *Media and the criminal justice system.* Springfield, IL: Charles C. Thomas Publishing.

Sussman Peter and Dannie Martin. 1993. *Committing Journalism: The Prison Writings of Red Hog*. NY: W. W. Norton.

Thaler, Paul. 1994. *The Watchful Eye: American Justice in the Age of the Television Trial.* NY: Greenwood Press.

Tuchman, Gaye. 1978. *Making news.* NY: Free Press.

Index